W9-AUG-450

Dreamers of a New Day

Dreamers of a New Day

Women Who Invented the Twentieth Century

SHEILA ROWBOTHAM

VERSO

London • New York

First published by Verso 2010
© Sheila Rowbotham 2010

All rights reserved

The moral rights of the author have been asserted

1 3 5 7 9 10 8 6 4 2

Verso
UK: 6 Meard Street, London W1F 0EG
US: 20 Jay Street, Suite 1010, Brooklyn, NY 11201
www.versobooks.com

Verso is the imprint of New Left Books

ISBN-13: 978-1-84467-613-2

British Library Cataloguing in Publication Data
A catalogue record for this book is available from the British Library

Library of Congress Cataloging-in-Publication Data
A catalog record for this book is available from the Library of Congress

Typeset in Bembo by Hewer Text UK Ltd, Edinburgh
Printed in the US by Maple Vail

Contents

List of Illustrations

Introduction

In 1902, an American suffragist and novelist, Winifred Harper Cooley, dreamed of a twenty-first century without oil trusts, sweatshops or slums. This future was revealed by a 'radiant' woman 'in flowing, graceful robes', who explained that in a hundred years' time, no one would be tramping the streets without a home, or be unemployed. By then the world's labour would be shared equally, so that each individual only worked five hours a day.[1] A few years later in Britain, a Crewe clothing worker turned socialist and feminist, Ada Nield Chew, declared, 'Most difficulties are caused by our age-long habit of looking upon what is, and what has been, as utterly desirable.'[2]

This capacity for optimistic imagining was characteristic among reformers and radicals in both America and Britain during the late nineteenth and early twentieth centuries. Running parallel with campaigns for women's suffrage and involving both feminists and anti-feminists, a diffuse but resilient attempt to alter daily life and culture was underway. From the 1880s, thought interacted with action in a whirl of speculation, proposals, policies and utopian visions. Exploratory and adventurous aspirations were expressed not only in books and articles, but through movements, organizations, local groups and projects. Women, along with men, were swept up by the impetus for changing everyday life. The conviction that social circumstances could be altered and that ways of living, as well as looking, might be transformed, contributed to the 'can-do' ethos which was particularly potent in the USA.

The ferment was encouraged by startling technological developments, paradigm-changing discoveries in science and iconoclastic forms of art. These, along with an unprecedented level of global trade and investment, new ways of organizing production and consumption, changes in communications and the growing ascendancy of urban life, fostered a belief that a decisive rupture with the past was occurring. However, the rapid pace of change brought daunting problems in its wake. Increased competition and falling profits resulted in periods of depression through the 1870s and 1880s, which persisted into the mid-1890s; inflation followed from the late 1890s. Confronted by the unbridled power of large-scale corporations, mushrooming city slums, the destruction of rural life, workers responded with a new mood of militancy, while sections of the middle class, troubled by the conditions of the poor, also questioned class inequality. Women, as well as men, felt a moral compulsion to intervene, bringing their own experiences to bear on the dissident economic and social perspectives which were emerging. And when they encountered opposition to their engagement in the public arena, middle-class and working-class women invoked motherly care, moral cleansing and class loyalty to justify stepping beyond the prescribed 'womanly' sphere.

At the same time, women's demands for access to employment and for political rights were pulling women outwards; calling into question their assumed dependence on and subordination to men. The suffrage movement inspired some women to resist other forms of injustice and inequality, and effect change in social and economic life more broadly. It also carried with it an internal promise of self-actualization and human dignity, encouraging efforts to alter personal ways of being. In moving towards a new role in the public sphere, feminists disturbed cultural assumptions about how women could be and what they could do in their own lives.

The bicycle became the symbol of this self-propelled female vanguard contesting physical and psychological spaces. 'The bicycle is doing more for the independence of women than anything expressly designed to that end', declared the British social reformer Clementina Black in the *Woman's Signal* in 1895. 'Nobody expects a woman to go cycling escorted by a chaperon, a maid, or a footman'.[3] Women's rejection of the habitual meant that constraints of gender were being stretched, intensifying tension around the manner in which female/male and personal/public activities were divided. Those who sought to keep women from taking a wider social and political role were quick to attack below the belt, caricaturing rebel women as unsexed and absurd, or over-sexed and deranged. In 1894, *Punch* derided British new women for living on 'nothing but foolscap and ink', while in New York 'Bohemian girls' were morally suspect.[4] Bicycle or no bicycle, women acting alone without men-folk to protect them were deemed liable to fall.

External demands for change were apt to boomerang back into the personal realm of being and relating, further breaching the demarcation between private and public life. Progress through education or access to employment revealed new unforeseen cultural and psychological barriers; radical movements, and the backlash these evoked, combined to relate resistance in one arena to rebellion in others. From the 1880s to the 1920s, three generations of women in both the United States and Britain can be seen challenging many different aspects of women's subordination and questioning how aspects of human experience were zoned and defined. The American social reformer Mary Beard summed up this integrated vision in 1912: 'Everything that counts in the common life is political'.[5]

The women who tried to alter everyday life and culture along with their own destinies were both dreamers and adventurers, for they explored with only the sketchiest of maps and they headed towards the unknown, courageously interrogating assumed behaviour in personal relationships and in society. They challenged gender divisions, sexual attitudes, family arrangements, ways of doing housework and mothering, existing forms of consumption and paid working conditions. They proposed new approaches to the body, alternative kinds of clothing and food; they turned their attention to how space was used in cities, to the time needed for leisure, to the purposes of work. From their rejection of the familiar came iconoclastic projects, demands and concepts. En route they criticized existing methods of education, delineated new areas of knowledge and subverted existing assumptions about culture. The American writer Kate Chopin crystallized women's extraordinary bid for new identities, new relationships and new mores in her 'new woman' novel of 1899, *The Awakening*.

The potpourri of rebels and reformers dreaming of a new day did not comprise a cohesive group or even a 'tendency'. Their revolt arose from disparate sources: they were driven by fear of moral and social disintegration, by anger against injustice, by visions of utopia and by a resolve to improve everyday living and relating. Nor were they united in outlook or intent. Some aspired to alter existing culture, others to transform the world; some wished to regulate and improve, others to release and liberate. They were, moreover, shaped by dissimilar social backgrounds. Some were upper middle class and keen to cast off privilege;

others were members of the growing in-between strata, educated yet not quite 'ladies', uprooted, mobile, and liable to be iconoclastic. Among their ranks, working-class women striving for solidarity stood along-side African-American women linking gender to their emancipation as a race.

The American and British dreamers of a new day came too from opposing political cultures. They might be women, but they were also free thinkers, anarchists, socialists, feminists, communists, moral and social reformers, liberals, progressives, labour movement women, bohe-mians, sexual radicals or eugenic enthusiasts. Their views ranged from extreme forms of individualism to advocacy of association and collectiv-ism. Some were mystics searching for inner change, while others wanted to concentrate on external reforms. There were women who considered that their sex carried special values which could improve the male public sphere, and others who saw identity as always in flux. Some emphasized social change rather than the suffrage, while others believed that the suffrage would lead to wider reform. Some believed firmly in state plan-ning, others in spontaneity and direct action. There were advocates of expanded productivity and consumption, and women who clung on to the nostrums of thrift and self-help. Some imagined technology taking over daily life, while others propounded the simplification of life.

Though the dreamers started from conflicting vantage points, headed off down contrary tracks and disagreed over solutions, many of their preoccupations overlapped and interacted. This convergence was most evident around the boundaries that marked personal and public identities. In both Britain and the United States, women who braved the public arena found themselves subverting gendered assumptions. The middle-class moral and social reformers, both black and white, who sought to tackle vice or poverty, inadvertently shifted a personal womanly role out into the new habitat of the urban slum. In the process they altered suppositions of what women could do. Along with more radical women who became involved in movements like anarchism, socialism or African-American liberation, they could discover that being active in public spheres raised many personal questions. Some began to wonder why gender issues were deferred into the indefinite future and why men in these movements often considered that the freedoms they sought for themselves were not suitable for women.

Misgivings about the cultural expectations of womanly behaviour in personal relations could also arise as part of a wider rebellion when external forces impinged upon daily life. These could be traumatic. The outer world of big business and modern industry drove through the customary lives of rural and urban women in the home, demolishing the familiar and the known; while violent attacks on African Americans led women from these communities to organize. Those who were provoked into resistance experienced the power of taking part in collective action; some went on to become active in the suffrage cause.

Changes in the position of women themselves created new spaces for heterodoxy. By the early twentieth century, women on the radical fringes of the feminist movement were exploring startling ideas about personal emancipation, and rebellious bohemian women were contesting the bounds of acceptable femininity and staking out alternative sexual identities. The 'modern' 1920s women who inherited the consequences of all these revolts along with the shock of World War One, struggled to connect a vision of equality with an affirmation of women's differing needs, to articulate a new scope for personal feelings and desires, and to translate their experiences as women into a wider democratization of everyday life.

Divisions between groupings and generations were by no means hard and fast. A surprising degree of connection occurred even between women in apparently quite distinct camps, while the strong networks they developed from the late nineteenth century formed a series of remarkable criss-crossing webs that survived over several decades. Though many of the political proposals and social policies they devised were not to be realized during their lifetimes, fragments of their utopias would later percolate into the mainstream. Through their strenuous personal rebellions these dreamers of a new day helped to shift attitudes about how women could be and live. Their galvanizing conviction that things could be better created waves which rippled into every aspect of culture, even if the outcomes were not always what they had envisaged. From amidst their contradictory experiments came new ways of being women.

Though a similar impulse for change appears in both Britain and the United States, the contexts in which they operated differed markedly. In 1880 Britain was the great economic power in the world; but America was zooming rapidly ahead and by the 1920s would be supreme. The American capitalist system, being new and unhampered by aristocratic remnants, was both more innovative and more voracious than its European counterparts. Able to draw on an endless supply of new,

young and desperate workers, the unprecedented economic development of the US reinforced values of competition and individual self-help.
A degree of mobility of talent was possible which could never occur in
Britain. The other side of the coin was that the power of big money was
unfettered, labour conflicts more violent and American employers less
willing to accommodate to trade unions, while workers in the US were
divided by race and ethnicity to a much greater extent than in Britain.[6]

Contemporary white middle-class observers watched in alarm as
wave upon wave of new arrivals poured into America's big cities. Black
migrants fleeing the rise of segregation and persecution in the South
found themselves competing for survival with the great hosts of immigrants from Europe, Syria, Japan, and Puerto Rico, who were arriving
clutching battered bags, boxes and dreams of the good life in the land
of plenty. In the North, African Americans encountered prejudice in
an insidious form as evolutionary theories of racial stages and biological
arguments of inherent racial characteristics became increasingly popular. Intellectual leaders such as Booker T. Washington and W. E. B.
Du Bois tried to counter these arguments, though they differed over
the strategies to be adopted by African Americans. While the former
cautiously sought to improve the skills of black people, Du Bois advocated a broad liberal education and the creation of a black elite of talent
to challenge white intellectual hegemony. At the grass-roots, African
Americans formed their own movements and devised ingenious self-
help projects.

The structure and course of the organizations and movements for
change in the two countries developed in somewhat different ways.
In Britain, the socialist and anarchist groupings of the 1880s and 1890s
were complemented in the early twentieth century by the creation of
a Labour Party which crucially entered into an alliance with the trade
unions. This combination did not occur in America, though the Socialist
Party gained support in the polls between 1901 and 1912. In America it
was the Populist Movement rather than explicitly socialist groupings that
advocated co-operative alternatives in the late nineteenth century, while
from the 1890s dynamic coalitions of 'Progressives' were demanding
state regulation of work and living conditions. While the social meanings of the Progressive impulse are much contested, broadly speaking its
adherents attempted to reform the harsher manifestations of competition, believing that in the long term a regulated capitalism would prove
more efficient. Women played an important part in this pressure for

moderate change and, despite not being enfranchised, influenced both municipal and state policies from the sidelines.

In Britain comparable ideas were to be found in the radical wing of the Liberal Party, or among the Fabian socialists who believed in gradual reform through the state. As well as campaigning for state legislation, Liberals, radicals, socialists, trade unionists were all lobbying for change locally. Consequently it was possible for women to form broad alliances. Radical middle-class women and working-class men joined forces on the school boards and, from the 1890s, Liberal Party and labour movement women combined on Poor Law reform. From 1907, women served on county and borough councils. Local government provided an entry into practical politics and a means of gaining access to state resources for projects. The Women's Local Government Society, established in 1888 to encourage the selection of women candidates in local government, disseminated information about demands women were making for municipal reform.[7] Working-class labour women were able to secure public amenities such as baths and wash houses through local councils. By the 1920s women were aspiring to pleasure on the rates as well as services for basic needs: in 1926 Mrs Grundy in Shipley, Yorkshire, secured an assurance from the chairman of the local baths committee that women would get Turkish baths at the same price as men.[8]

Despite the differing institutional forms, in both countries women participated in various types of self-help action in communities. Outside the scope of formal politics, the voluntary sector they helped to create enabled many women to gain an understanding of social problems. Most important were the social settlements which sprang up in many towns and cities from the late 1880s onwards. Growing numbers of middle-class reformers of both sexes were coming round to the view that the stress placed by evangelists and philanthropists on individual moral responsibility alone was unrealistic. Influenced by an emphasis within the Anglican Church on practical social action, and philosophically nurtured by the neo-Hegelian idealism of T. H. Green, they insisted instead on the structural causes of poverty such as low pay and urban slums. Though their goals were secular, they did not abandon the mentality of Christianity. Metaphors of social 'missionaries' colonizing poor neighbourhoods were prevalent in Britain when the first settlement of educated middle-class investigators and reformers was built in East London in 1888. Called Toynbee Hall after the reformer Arnold Toynbee, it was partly inspired by the example of American utopian communities. Toynbee Hall had a direct influence on the settlement movement in America, leading the reformer Jane Addams to set up a women's settlement in Chicago, Hull House, in 1889.[9] More democratic than its British forerunner, Hull House became the nerve centre for a range of causes, from women's trade unions to communal kitchens. In both countries social settlements cleared a space for a new public role for women, while stimulating ideas for social policy and legislation around welfare and employment.

Connections grew up between settlements and university social science departments. While women social investigators were marked by the same intellectual influences as their male counterparts, and troubled by the same urban problems, they were also guided by their experiences as women. The University of Chicago produced a formidable network of women who concentrated on sociology, economics and civics and worked closely with Hull House; the group included Florence Kelley, Julia Lathrop, Alice Hamilton and Sophonisba Breckinridge. These women researchers produced innovative studies of working conditions, child labour, immigration and motherhood. Not only did they relate their findings to proposals for practical action, they also shared the perspective of a social economy which put human needs before profits, a heterodoxy that hung on into the 1920s in some American women's colleges.[10] In Britain similar links developed between some universities and working-class communities. In Liverpool the reformer Eleanor Rathbone was active both in the suffrage movement and in settlement work. Rathbone later fused political and social reform when she became president of the National Union of Societies for Equal Citizenship (NUSEC) after World War One, spearheading the campaign for family allowances.[11]

The practical issues women encountered through social action inspired not simply policies but new kinds of cultural enquiry. In 1908 the social investigator Maud Pember Reeves established the Fabian Women's Group to study women's economic independence and equality in relation to socialism. It included several pioneering economic and social historians associated with the London School of Economics: Barbara Drake, Mabel Atkinson, Bessie Leigh Hutchins and Alice Clark wrote on both the present and the past of women's work and were among the first to assert professional women's right to combine work and marriage.[12] Because the range of their interests extended over social existence as a whole, they broke through the prevailing divisions of knowledge and their work spanned a range of disciplines. They began to take on not simply the way women lived their actual lives, but the cultural ramifications their challenge raised. By regarding everyday life through a gendered lens, they foregrounded what was distinct in women's circumstances, interrogating the assumption that men's experiences were necessarily universal.

Women can also be seen devising visionary alternatives marked by their experiences as a sex. Hence women in the American Populist movement, who formed the National Woman's Alliance in 1891, declared that the goal of a 'Co-operative Commonwealth' required the 'full political equality of the sexes', and resolved 'To study all questions relating to the structure of human society, in the full light of modern invention, discovery and thought'.[13] As well as claiming political and social citizenship, Populist women thought in terms of sisterhood and discussed how to change values and daily life through temperance and co-operative households, along with anti-militarism and labour organizing. Though Populism disintegrated as a movement, this gendered ethical radicalism resurfaced in the American Socialist Party in the 1900s.[14]

In Britain, the Women's Co-operative Guild and the Labour Party's Women's Labour League sought to combine an awareness of class and gender in campaigns that spanned work and community. The United States did not have equivalent political organizations on a national basis, but a similar perspective appears in local labour women's groups. In both countries women also established their own cross-class organizations for reforming working conditions. In Britain the Women's Trade Union League was started in 1874 by a middle-class woman, Emma Paterson, who had been inspired by women's trade union societies in the United States. In a situation where women workers were excluded from many unions, it sought to organize and change laws relating to women's employment. An activist in the Women's Trade Union League, the social investigator Clementina Black helped to found the Women's Industrial Council in 1894. The Council set out to conduct 'systematic inquiry into the conditions of working women, to provide accurate information concerning those interests, and to promote such action as may seem conducive to their improvement'.[15] Christian organizations such as the Mother's Union combined locally with secular philanthropic projects; in Birmingham, one such coalition – the Birmingham Ladies' Union of Workers among Women and Children – supported women's trade unions, recreation clubs, education and temperance. Further to the

Left, in the early twentieth century Sylvia Pankhurst's Workers' Suffrage (later Socialist) Federation created self-help services, while campaigning for policies and laws to improve women's lives in the community and at work, during and immediately after World War One.[16]

Birmingham Ladies Union Journal

In the United States, the pattern of white middle-class women's involvement was likely to be participation in the powerful women's clubs, or in organizations such as the Woman's Christian Temperance Union and the National Congress of Mothers, which emphasized the maternal aspects of social reform. Temperance was an extremely powerful movement in the US, and the leader of the WCTU, Frances Willard, sought to connect moral reform with social change.[17] Several innovative organizations around domestic activity were also set up. The home economics teacher Ellen Swallow Richards and the anti-poverty campaigner Helen Campbell worked in the National Household Economics Association, which arose out of the 1893 Women's Congress of the World's Columbian Exposition in Chicago. Both women campaigned for public kitchens. Richards battled against bacteria with Borax, sunlight and pure water and Campbell for homes designed for children's needs. Campbell was also active in the movement for ethical consumption, the National Consumers' League. From the early 1890s the Consumers' Leagues organized consumer power to improve the circumstances in which goods were produced, with a more radical wing emphasizing women's working conditions. They combined a strong ethic of personal responsibility with a commitment to social change. Similar values infused the American Women's Trade Union League. Founded in 1903 and influenced by its British namesake, the League brought together an impressive network of working-class and middle-class women.[18] In the US, women's organizations played an important role in gaining welfare and employment reforms from the state; some pioneer reformers battled on to influence the policies of the New Deal in the 1930s.

Though African-American women worked in organizations like the Woman's Christian Temperance Union, the General Federation of Women's Clubs and the National American Woman Suffrage Association, white women's organizations did not automatically express their needs. What is more, white reformers were divided over whether to work with black women; in some cases they refused to admit them into groups. Black women struggled to bring the politics of racial violence onto the agendas of white women's movements, while at the same time setting up the National Association of Colored Women in 1896. Their activism was steeled by the mounting racism which was part of the experience of African-American women of all classes; one of the founders of the National Association of Colored Women, Mary Church Terrell, highly educated and married to a judge, had a close friend murdered by a lynch mob. From the late nineteenth century, black women like Terrell and the journalist Ida B. Wells-Barnett campaigned against racist violence *and* for the vote. Alongside the movements of protest, African-American women also created their own mutual self-help projects which developed economic skills and provided welfare services.[19] From the experience of black American oppression came broader visions of emancipation: at the World's Congress of Representative Women in Chicago in 1893, Frances Ellen Harper not only called on women to oppose lynching and defend the right of black children to education, but urged them to help create a society which was not dominated by 'the greed of gold and the lust for power'.[20] A veteran by the 1890s, Harper had been part of both the anti-slavery and women's suffrage movements and had then participated in the Woman's Christian Temperance Union, her vision of a moral, non-acquisitive society echoing the utopianism of the Populists.

Ida B. Wells–Barnett (Sophia Smith Collection, Smith College)

The social and cultural turmoil of the late nineteenth century was marked by an imaginative fluidity in which fictional allegories and utopias could have practical consequences. Edward Bellamy's utopian novel *Looking Backward* (1888) presented a future of nationalized industry and collectivized domestic life. So great was the impact of the book that 'Nationalist' clubs were formed in many American towns. Not everyone was happy with Bellamy's ideal future; horrified by its authoritarian collectivism, William Morris, the British libertarian socialist, was provoked to pick up his pen and counter with an anti-state alternative, *News from Nowhere*. Appearing in instalments in Morris's Socialist League paper, *Commonweal*, in 1890, it portrayed a society in which the state had withered entirely, giving way to communal daily life and individual creative expression. This early contest of utopias presaged a deep division amid women as well as men over the role of the state in reshaping the everyday. In Britain, statist solutions were prevalent among both reformers and sections of the Left; American Progressives also aimed to increase the power of the state. However, individualist anarchists as well as the anarcho-syndicalist Left in the Industrial Workers of the World (IWW) were fiercely anti-state.

The American socialist feminist Charlotte Perkins Gilman was one of the many progressive middle-class Americans inspired by Bellamy's critique of market capitalism and by his emphasis on women's equality. Participation in the Nationalist clubs would lead her into an adventurous and influential life of public commitment. Breaking painfully from an unhappy marriage, she earned her own living, new woman-like, by lecturing and writing. From the 1890s she produced weighty books on the economic and social organization of daily life, along with a stream of short stories and novels which depicted new relations of gender and new modes of living. Cleverly, Gilman contrived to appeal to pragmatic reformers as well as to radicals dreaming of utopian transformation; her skill lay in elaborating the ordinary annoyances of women's lives into topics of intellectual debate, while making utopia seem like a new common sense. She was able to reach a wide readership by writing in popular magazines such as *Harper's Bazaar* or *Woman's Home Companion,* as well as in the *Woman's Journal,* which she edited. In 1909 she started her own magazine, the *Forerunner,* which was read in Britain as well as in the United States. Gilman used to refer her readers to articles in British publications like the *Englishwoman* which, from 1909, provided a forum for articles on women and the economy.[21]

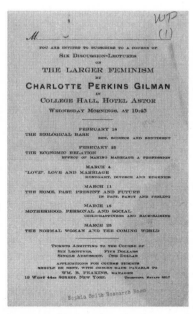

Brochure advertising lectures by Charlotte Perkins Gilman
(Sophia Smith Collection, Smith College)

Journals acted like hives around which rebels and trouble-makers buzzed away with their dreams and schemes. Among them was Ezra Heywood's *The Word*; launched in 1872, it resolutely defended the right to free speech and free love. From the 1880s the American free thought journal *Lucifer: The Light Bearer*, edited by Moses Harman and his daughter Lillian, also acted as a clearing house for 'advanced' views, including changing relations between the sexes. The free lovers' emphasis upon owning or possessing oneself struck a specifically gendered chord, attracting an intrepid group of women influenced by the heady utopian movements which had proliferated before the Civil War. They included Ezra Heywood's wife Angela, whose mother Lucy Tilton had been an abolitionist and free-love advocate, along with Elmina Drake Slenker, the daughter of a Shaker preacher expelled for his liberal views. Slenker had advertised for an egalitarian husband in the *Water-Cure Journal*; a proponent of theories of 'male continence' whereby men delayed or withheld orgasm, she envisaged love-making as 'magnetic exchange'.[22] Her friend Lois Waisbrooker, born in 1826 into a working-class background, had worked as a domestic servant and then as a teacher in black schools. A melange of women's rights, free love and spiritualism attracted Waisbrooker to the individualist anarchism which flourished in America. She possessed a mystical faith in women's purifying mission which was also characteristic of social purity reformers and some socialists and feminists.

Small groups around journals could exert an influence in campaigns. In Britain *The Adult*, a journal produced by British sex radicals in the Legitimation League, with links to American individualist anarchism, led a struggle in 1895 to release a socialist, Edith Lanchester, from the mental asylum in which she had been put by her family after choosing to live in a free union with her working-class lover.[23] Journals and magazines were not only produced by political groupings, they became a means of expressing the voices of subordinated groups challenging mainstream culture. At the turn of the century, several African American publications were beginning to express a newly confident race awareness. Writer Pauline Elizabeth Hopkins was a founding member of the *Colored American Magazine*, established in 1899 to assert black culture. Hopkins's articles on famous men and women of the 'Negro Race' helped stimulate interest in black history.[24]

From the 1890s a bohemian culture developed in New York's Greenwich Village, attracting rebels of both sexes. Villagers combined the free lovers' assertion of individual autonomy with a Romantic commitment to self-expression, but they were also engaged in many radical social causes. In the

1900s the anarchist defender of women's right to sexual freedom, Emma Goldman, produced a journal called *Mother Earth*. Like the *Woman Rebel*, edited by the birth control campaigner Margaret Sanger, it linked personal freedom with social action. In Britain, two small magazines called the *New Age* and the *Freewoman* became seedbeds for avant-garde theories of philosophic egoism and vitalism as well as rebellious ideas about sexual freedom and communal living. 'Beatrice Hastings' (the pseudonym of Emily Alice Haigh), who later moved to Paris and became involved in the Dadaist and Surrealist movements, was one of the women writers associated with the *New Age*, as were the future novelists Katherine Mansfield and Storm Jameson. The *Freewoman* was similarly situated on the iconoclastic fault-line which became evident in the 1910s. Started in 1911 by dissident feminists from the militant Women's Social and Political Union, the journal rejected Christabel Pankhurst's concentration on the vote as a single issue and explored many personal and social aspects of emancipation. Like the *New Age*, it attracted several Northern, socially 'in-between' women. The editor, Dora Marsden, came from a middle-class Yorkshire family which had sunk into poverty when her father deserted them. She had won a scholarship to Owen's College in Manchester, taught in Leeds and then returned to Manchester in 1905. Another teacher, the working-class, upwardly mobile socialist and feminist Mary Gawthorpe, from Leeds, was briefly involved with the journal, along with a lower-middle-class rebel intellectual, Teresa Billington-Greig, who had left her Blackburn home for Manchester at the age of seventeen and worked in the Ancoats settlement.[25]

These arriviste intellectuals in Britain and America were energetically reinventing both themselves and the scope of politics, debating trade union organizing, eugenics, reform of the divorce laws, celibacy and masturbation, in clubs as well as in their writing. The *Freewoman*'s London Discussion Circle marked out a new female-defined space in which women could break taboos. Men might be invited to participate, but the women set the terms. Similarly its American twin, the Heterodoxy Club in Greenwich Village, brought together 'advanced' women who were involved in art, intellectual work and radical politics. It included Mabel Dodge Luhan, whose salon was a focus for Greenwich Village socializing; and Elsie Clews Parsons, who wrote on sex and birth control and was to become an anthropologist, along with the anarcho-syndicalist and IWW member Elizabeth Gurley Flynn.[26]

Early twentieth-century radical dreamers aimed at root and branch transformation with no stones unturned. In 1912, Storm Jameson, the daughter

of a Whitby sea captain, won a research scholarship to University College,
London, where she lived in lodgings with two young men from Yorkshire.
In her autobiography she describes the irreverent mood of left-wing provin-
cials like herself and her companions. Detesting past dogmas, they were
self-consciously breaking with the past and believed themselves to be 'at the
frontier of a new age'.[27] The American anarchist Adeline Champney was
similarly uncompromising in 1903, insisting that reproduction and culture
as well as production would have to be altered: 'It must be made clear that
every institution or custom which is founded upon the present economic
system must fall.' She believed this required revision of 'our manners and our
morals'. Along with 'the socialization of the economic necessities of life' must
go changes in 'the production and distribution of the men and women of the
new day.' There were to be no couch potatoes. 'You and I and all of us must
bestir ourselves,' Champney admonished her readers.[28]

They did indeed 'bestir' themselves: living the new day in aesthetic
clothing or tailored jackets, or taking themselves off to live in social
settlements or anarchist communes. They joined unions and stood on
picket lines. They sat on local government committees, dared the night
in bohemian cafés, defied racially segregated train carriages, devised
cheap and healthy recipes for the poor, gave birth to children without
being married, fell in love with women as well as men, wrote economic
tomes, and cut off their hair. They were new, 'advanced' and modern,
maternal, bossy, charming, diplomatic and angry.

Their optimism was to be tempered but not quenched by World War
One. In 1918 the American social reformer Mary Parker Follett observed
in *The New State: Group Organization, The Solution of Popular Government*:

> We are now beginning to recognize more and more clearly that the
> work we do, the conditions of that work, the houses in which we live,
> the water we drink, the food we eat, the opportunities for bringing
> up our children, that in fact the whole area of our daily life should
> constitute politics. There is no line where the life of the home ends
> and the life of the city begins. There is no wall between my private
> life and my public life.[29]

Such grand visions of changing the everyday were not to be, but many
of the proposals and attitudes generated by the inchoate adventurers
defined modern life, and, less tangibly, impinged on how everyday relationships were seen.

Adventurers in the Everyday

What caused so many women from diverse vantage points to set about altering how daily life was lived? Part of the answer lies in force of circumstance. The lives of individual women were caught up in the large-scale economic changes which brought upheaval and suffering in their wake. Powerful vested interests were intruding into daily life, in the countryside as well as the towns and cities. The future American anarchist Kate Austin resisted when she, and the farmer she married, were evicted by the powerful River Company from the Des Moines River Basin. The federal government had granted the company land on the understanding that they would improve it. Instead, the company quickly sold it on to speculators.[1] Lizzie Holmes was uprooted from her Ohio home after a violent strike of railroad workers in 1877. In retrospect she reflected:

> 'The working classes' was a term that was just beginning to be heard and I longed to know more of the people set off as belonging to a caste . . . With my sister I went to work in a cloak factory and during the next two years passed through every phase of a struggling sewing woman's existence . . . I know of all the struggles, the efforts of genteel poverty, the pitiful pride with which working girls hide their destitution and drudgery from the world.[2]

Arriving in Chicago, she managed to find a small group, the Working Women's Union, who were struggling to persuade young women workers to organize. In 1881 the Working Women's Union was recognized by the American trade union organization, the Knights of Labor. The Knights appealed to all the 'productive' classes and were nominally committed to equality – including that of women and blacks. On 2 May 1886 Lizzie Holmes, recently married to the anarchist William Holmes, proudly headed a women's march through the garment district demanding the eight-hour day; the *Chicago Tribune* reported that despite their 'worn faces and threadbare clothing', they 'shouted and sang and laughed in a whirlwind of exuberance.'[3]

The mood of carnival release was short-lived. On 3 May, during a rally in Haymarket Square, a bomb was thrown at the police, who opened fire; 200 people were injured and an unknown number killed. The police swooped at random on activists including Lizzie Holmes, though she was later freed. Among those who would later be executed was Albert Parsons, Holmes's co-editor on a paper called the *Alarm*, which advocated taking direct action for the eight-hour working day. His wife Lucy Parsons, part African American, part Native American in descent, had also worked with Holmes in the Knights of Labor. Holmes's bonds with the Parsons meant that the impact of Haymarket was personal as well as political. Impatient for change and dismayed by the lack of revolt, she wrote in the *Alarm*: 'The spirit of justice and retribution dwells deep, if it lives at all, for it stirs no ruffles on society's surface today.'[4] Her response was to move towards anarchism, writing regularly in libertarian journals such as the *Alarm*, *Lucifer*, *Labor Enquirer*, *Our New Humanity*. Haymarket also had a profound impact on others who were not personally involved. Shaken by the news of the executions, an immigrant garment worker, Emma Goldman, who had just arrived from Russia, was also drawn towards anarchism. The Chicago Martyrs troubled the middle-class conscience too; the executions prompted the future Hull House settler and reformer Julia Lathrop to question the social order.[5]

British labour relations were less violent. Nonetheless, during the late 1880s and early 1890s, militant labour resistance radicalized both middle- and working-class women. 'New unions' extended beyond male craft workers, and sought to reach outwards to the unskilled and semi-skilled in the factories, sometimes even trying to organize scattered home-based workers. The social investigator Clementina Black, along with Karl Marx's daughter Eleanor, supported the new unionists in London, and when women at the Barton Hill cotton works in Bristol went on strike in October 1889, two local 'new women', Helena Born and Miriam Daniell, helped them to set up strike committees. Aided by the London and Liverpool dockers, the strikers won, but it was hard for many women workers involved in new unions to sustain militancy and unionization.

Emma Goldman, 1885 (Emma Goldman Papers)

Factory worker Ada Nield Chew was propelled into the public eye when, in the summer of 1894, she protested against her working conditions in a series of articles in the *Crewe Chronicle*. She complained that women could not earn a living wage and described the frustration of women waiting for work all day in the slack times, then fighting to be taken on when there was work. She revealed how women workers in the factory were forced to fund their own materials and even to pay the manufacturers for hot water to make their tea. That August, Chew and Eleanor Marx Aveling addressed a meeting of one of the 'new unions' which accepted women as members and was campaigning for the eight-hour day, the National Union of Gasworkers and General Labourers.[6] Chew later joined the Independent Labour Party and became a member of the Nantwich Board of Guardians, which administered poor relief; she supported the suffrage movement and the *Freewoman*.

Chew's protest highlighted the problem of women's low pay in labour-intensive trades which came to be known as 'sweated' work. 'Sweating' characterized factories and home-work alike, and in both Britain and America women reformers resolutely tramped up and down tenement stairs and braved dark alleys to document its extent. In Chicago, Florence Kelley led a campaign for intervention against sweating, and during the 1900s Clementina Black and Gertrude Tuckwell were able to form a broad alliance in London through the Anti-Sweating League. Along with reformers and trade unionists, the League included liberal employers distressed at the proliferation of labour-intensive work, which they saw as an archaic form of production damaging to the competitive efficiency of the economy.

If anger and guilt led women towards public action, a sense of religious and moral mission also exercised considerable sway, drawing them into movements which tried to foster sexual purity and combat prostitution. In Britain they marched in the Salvation Army and supported the National Vigilance Association, which was formed in 1886 to watch over public morals. Warning of the dangers of pornography and prostitution, women moral reformers urged working girls to join Snowdrop Bands to 'discourage all wrong conversation, light and immodest conduct and the reading of foolish and bad books'.[7] America was particularly prone to militant evangelical crusades to reclaim sinners; women played an energetic part in these, for the call to redeem overrode gender proprieties. Rescue and redemption also suffused organizations such as the women's club movement and the powerful Woman's Christian Temperance Union, which underscored the links between drink, violence and poverty.

Moral zeal could, in some instances, merge with social and political engagement. Frances Willard steered the Woman's Christian Temperance Union towards support for suffrage, social welfare and labour organizing, declaring in 1891 that when women and workers acted in combination, 'the war-dragon shall be slain, the poverty-viper shall be exterminated, the gold-bug transfixed by a silver pin, the saloon drowned out, and the last white slave liberated from the woods of Wisconsin and the bagnios of Chicago and Washington.'[8] American women reformers such as Willard not only put women at the forefront of redemption, but envisaged women bringing purer domestic values into culture, work and government. This version of women's special moral mission exerted a powerful and continuing influence upon both white and black American charitable women and social reformers. By pushing female domestic responsibilities out into the public arena and extending the scope of charitable work, they sought to appropriate motherliness and housekeeping as a source of power.

Black American reformers were inclined, however, to associate the domestic redeemer also with 'uplifting' the race. The National Association of Colored Women, formed in 1896 and led by Mary Church Terrell, integrated the concept of a special role for women with racial uplift. At the National Woman Suffrage Association conference of 1898, Terrell articulated this in a moral language both her black and white audience would understand: 'And so, lifting as we climb, onward and upward we go, struggling and striving, and hoping that the buds and blossoms of our desires will burst into glorious fruition ere long.'[9] She equated personal fulfilment with a conscious relationship with other African Americans. Her words were, moreover, rooted in the actual practice of black women reformers. Largely excluded from white charitable projects, Southern black Americans demonstrated considerable ingenuity in devising their own alternatives for survival. A black social settlement, the Locust Street Social Settlement, was founded in 1890 in Hampton, Virginia by Janie Porter Barrett. Like many African-American social welfare projects, it connected self-help with mutual aid. Providing services for everyday needs could be linked to campaigning for change. In 1908 Atlanta's Neighborhood Union, formed by Lugenia Burns Hope, incorporated educational and health services with investigation and lobbying for better schools and sanitation.[10]

A broad ethical consciousness could inspire social action among women and men alike, regardless of gender. However, some areas could be more easily justified as 'womanly'. In Britain, upper-class women's intervention as Poor Law Guardians in the care of children, the training of girls and the 'rescue' of unmarried mothers, as well as the care for the elderly and 'feeble-minded', could be presented as an extension of acceptable philanthropy. The pioneering British Poor Law reformer, Louisa Twining, argued in 1886 that since women had 'come forward to fill these posts of usefulness . . . we can truly say they have made their mark and done good service to the cause of the poor and helpless of whom women and children form so large a proportion'.[11]

A religious sense of duty and service could also be translated into socialism. Kate Richards O'Hare, who had started as an evangelical Christian in the Florence Crittenton Mission and Home in Kansas City rescuing prostitutes, became an activist in the American Socialist Party. Not only did O'Hare retain the mindset of salvation through service, she gave it a motherly twist. Facing imprisonment in 1919 under the

Espionage Act for accusing militarists of reducing women to breeding for the war machine, O'Hare made an impassioned farewell speech:

> I gave to the service of the working class all that I had and all that I was, and no one can do more. I gave my girlhood, my young woman-hood, my wifehood and my motherhood. I have taken babies unborn into the thick of the class war; I have served in the trenches with a nursing baby at my breast.[12]

The impetus to serve came also from a personal unease about class division. The Boston reformer Vida Scudder, who worked at the settle-ment Denison House among the immigrant poor, yearned to overcome the distance between classes through 'sincere and serious intercourse'.[13] The socialist and feminist Isabella Ford came from a progressive Quaker family in Leeds with a strong sense of moral obligation. Her sister Emily believed that a formative influence on Isabella's future socialism was a class the sisters had run for young women factory workers: 'This constant intimacy with girls of our own age, but brought up in different circumstances . . . was among the beginnings of her understanding what it was that was wrong with life and . . . a desire to help them to better conditions of life'.[14] Personal contact not only assuaged the separation between classes, it was seen as experientially educative.

As questions about the absolute truth of the Christian gospels mounted, partly as a result of Darwin's findings on evolution, men and women alike translated their besieged religious faith into secular contexts by establishing social settlements in the slums. For women, this social altruism was often combined with a pressing personal need to find more meaningful work. Before starting Hull House in Chicago's slums, Jane Addams and her companion Ellen Gates Starr had been uncertain what to do with their lives. Starr told her sister that Addams regarded settlement work as 'more for the benefit of the people who do it' than for the working class, and Addams was convinced that personal discon-tent with the narrow destinies available to educated middle-class women brought many of the later recruits to the settlement.[15] Social settlements provided half-way houses where women could live outside convention while remaining respectable; Hull House enabled Addams to live with her lover Starr, and offered a refuge for Florence Kelley who was flee-ing an unhappy marriage to a Russian revolutionary. Similarly, Denison House in Boston allowed Vida Scudder to penetrate the city's deprived

South End, putting her privileged Beacon Hill background behind her. Social settlers literally mapped the surrounding slum streets when they did their surveys, but they were metaphorical map-makers too, tracing new outlines for their working lives and their personal relationships.

Jane Addams (Sophia Smith Collection, Smith College)

The ethic of service not only derived from Christianity; it was also a central tenet of the Russian revolutionary tradition which emphasized the sacrifice of individual lives for the 'Cause'. Emma Goldman struggled with this self-denying creed as a young woman, and in her own life sought to find a balance between personal fulfilment and political commitment. Her dilemma troubled many other women adventurers. Revolutionaries, reformers, feminists and African-American women activists experienced conflict between autonomous needs and the pull of duty towards collective solidarities. This tension helped to shape women's challenge to everyday life and customs. It was one of the many discrepancies which provoked unease and encouraged questioning.

During the late nineteenth and early twentieth centuries, the campaigns of an earlier generation were bearing fruit in the expansion of women's higher education. This was particularly marked in the United

States, but in Britain too, late nineteenth-century women were prising open the bastions of male privilege at Oxford and Cambridge, attending University Extension lectures and entering provincial universities. As students they experienced evident absurdities: at Owens College, Manchester, in the 1880s and 1890s they were barred from the library and had to send their maids to collect books.[16] Once they graduated, some joined the ranks of teachers, clerks, 'typewriters', translators, journalists and social investigators in an effort to earn their own living, but many of the better-paid male professions remained closed to them. The incongruities in women's moves towards autonomy stimulated further revolt, as growing numbers of middle-class women found themselves with one foot in the conventional world and another in the unexplored territory of 'new womanhood'. The arrival of these 'odd women', hovering between the established parameters of class and gender, unsettled the status quo: they did not fit within the established structures of society, and their singularity inclined them to dissent.

In 1889, stirred by the Norwegian playwright Henrik Ibsen's call for individual revolt, Eleanor Marx Aveling, the novelist Olive Schreiner and Edith Ellis, who would become a new woman writer herself, gathered outside the Novelty Theatre in London after the British premiere of *A Doll's House*. Ellis records how she and her friends were 'breathless with excitement' about Nora's defiance of domesticity. 'We were restive and impetuous and almost savage in our arguments. This was either the end of the world or the beginning of a new world for women'.[17] In 1896 the American anarchist Lizzie Holmes appealed to women to brave calumny as defiant individuals: 'there is a *need* of women who are past all fear of being called "unwomanly" when a truth presents itself to be told.'[18]

On the other hand, unconventional behaviour put women in a precarious position: the consequences of deviation were much more severe than for men. Edith Lupton gravitated, via feminism and local municipal politics, to William Morris's revolutionary Socialist League in which the anarchists were gaining influence by 1890. That August, Lupton was shouted down by her colleagues for expressing a belief in 'leadership' – albeit of a spontaneous sort. In September, perhaps keen to prove her mettle as an open-air speaker on women's position in the battle for free speech, she was arrested on a charge of being drunk and disorderly. When she denied this in court, the policeman opined that if she had not been drunk she must be 'mad'.[19] Absolute defiance consequently appealed only to a minority; others resolved to cut their own pathways more strategically. Inspired by the housing reformer Octavia Hill and the social settlers at Toynbee Hall, the future Fabian socialist, Beatrice Webb, negotiated her autonomy adroitly. In 1885 she described the life she envisaged tactfully to her father: 'An interesting hard-working life with *just* a touch of adventure is so delightful, so long as one does not get stamped with that most damaging stamp, "Eccentricity".'[20]

Anxiety about reputation was not confined to the upper-middle class. In differing ways, working-class and black women knew the harsh consequences of flouting conventional gendered behaviour. Nevertheless, a desire for self-expression propelled some less privileged women to take remarkable risks. The working-class American immigrant Anzia Yezierska, who longed to become a writer, had to break with her background in a quest for self-realization which would eventually take her to Hollywood. She asked bitterly, 'Ain't thoughts useful? . . . Does America only want the work from my body?'[21] The African-American writer and campaigner Anna Julia Cooper, whose mother had been a slave, graphically described her yearning for a broader intellectual sphere: 'I constantly felt (as I suppose many an ambitious girl has felt) a thumping from within unanswered by any beckoning from without'.[22]

Such feelings led some adventurous women to try and create the conditions for 'a beckoning from without', not only through formal educational institutions, but through social action. Jane Edna Hunter formed the Working Girls' Home Association in Cleveland in 1911 on the basis of small subscriptions from a voluntary association of women. Her parents had been servants, and she became a nurse before gravitating towards law in 1925. Describing her commitment to serve African-American women, she stated:

> There was something . . . [that] kept urging and making me less content with what I was doing and calling me into a broader service . . . Then the thought came to me that there were other girls who came to Cleveland, perhaps under similar circumstances as myself and were strangers and alone and were meeting with the same difficulties and hardships in trying to establish themselves in a large city.[23]

Though this sense of personal reciprocity was particularly characteristic of black women social reformers, it also touched some of the more radical middle-class white women. Florence Kelley, who translated Friedrich Engels's *Condition of the Working Classes in England* before working at Hull House, remarked in a letter to him in 1887 that her friend Helen Campbell's understanding of poverty was typically American, coming from 'personal contact' rather than from theory.[24] In fact such an approach was not restricted to American reformers. Engels's own contacts in Manchester had after all been personal ones, while in 1883 the young Beatrice Webb observed somewhat stiffly in her diary, 'it is distinctly advantageous to us to go amongst the poor'.[25] Margaret Llewelyn Davies, the daughter of a Christian Socialist clergyman, who from the late 1880s devoted her life to the predominantly working-class Women's Co-operative Guild, was convinced of the value of personal interaction. She saw co-operation as a means of combining individual self-development with new relationships of mutuality. When she handed her friend Virginia Woolf a faded bundle of letters by Guild members, she remarked nervously that she hoped that through these accounts of hardship and aspiration, 'the women would cease to be symbols and become individuals'.[26] The co-operative women's moving life stories were eventually published by the Hogarth Press in 1930, with the title *Life as We Have Known It*.

Behind many women adventurers' impulse for a broader service and their efforts to assert their personal autonomy in a wide range of movements, lurked shadowy dreams of a new day. Some of these dreams reached back into the much older heritages of individualist radicalism and co-operative association. The American anarchist Kate Austin was brought up in a family that respected the eighteenth-century radical Tom Paine. Another anarchist and Painite, Voltairine de Cleyre, was literally a child of the Enlightenment – her father had named her after Voltaire. Margaret Sanger, the campaigner for birth control, was the daughter of a stone-cutter of Irish descent whose hero was the American free thinker Robert Ingersoll. In the mid-1880s, the British 'advanced' woman Jane Hume Clapperton demonstrated a familiarity with the work of the early nineteenth-century co-operative pioneer Robert Owen, though she believed that his mistake was to try and 'make people live together before they were fit to simply live in harmony,' arguing that change had first to come in relationships within the home.[27] At the 1898 conference of the National Woman Suffrage Association, Mary Church Terrell was carefully diplomatic in claiming both a shared and a distinct heritage, mentioning the Owenite and women's rights campaigner Ernestine Rose, along with white anti-slavery and women's rights stalwarts Lucretia Mott, Elizabeth Cady Stanton, Lucy Stone and Susan B. Anthony, as well as the black eighteenth-century poet, Phillis Wheatley.[28]

Mary Church Terrell (Library of Congress)

The utopian communitarianism of Robert Owen and Charles Fourier was preserved in American schemes for co-operative housekeeping as well as in the British Women's Co-operative Guild. In 1893, Catherine Webb called on co-operative women 'to be heralds of the dawn, rousing the world to take notice of the "good time coming".' Webb's co-operative future closely echoed that of the Irish radical William Thompson, who as early as 1825 had made an eloquent plea for women's social and political rights. Like Thompson, Webb believed that 'the day of "association and mutual helpfulness" in all stages and phases of life is slowly but surely dawning upon the world, to drive out the black night of individualism'.[29]

Strong currents within both anarchism and socialism in the last two decades of the nineteenth century shared Catherine Webb's conviction that individuals must act, while assuming, at the same time, that a utopian future was inevitably unravelling. Charlotte Wilson, who formed an

anarchist faction in the Fabian Society, was profoundly influenced by
the anarchist-communist Prince Peter Kropotkin, who had spent many
years in prison for his beliefs. In 1886 she argued the aim should be 'by
direct personal action to bring about a revolution in every department
of human existence, social, political and economic'.[30] In a less extreme
manner, some socialists were also arguing that individuals should choose
alternative ways of living in the here and now. Isabella Ford in Leeds,
writers Olive Schreiner and Edith Ellis as well as the Bristol socialists
who organized the women cotton workers, Helena Born and Miriam
Daniell, were all influenced by the ideas of the 'new life' put forward
by the British socialist Edward Carpenter. In the 1880s, troubled by
social inequality and the parasitical dependence of his own class on
working people, Carpenter decided to cut down on his needs and live
close to nature. He, in turn, was influenced by the American writers
Walt Whitman and Henry David Thoreau, stressing self-realization and
harmony with one's own 'nature' as well as with the external world.
Like the libertarian socialist William Morris, Carpenter, who wrote on
homosexuality and women's freedom, was an important inspiration for
women struggling to balance personal liberation and public commitment.[31] So too were the American Transcendentalists and Whitman.

In 1890 Helena Born and Miriam Daniell left Bristol for America.
After Daniell's early death in 1894, Born settled in Boston where she
moved in anarchist circles and was a member of the Walt Whitman
Society. While making an unsuccessful attempt to live off the land,
she told her lover, anarchist William Bailie, 'I have Morris' portrait on
the wall and Emerson's and Whitman's also conspicuous'.[32] Charlotte
Perkins Gilman's connection to the Transcendentalists was a personal
one: she was friendly with William Ellery Channing's granddaughter
Grace in the 1880s. In 1896, when she visited Britain, she was extremely
proud of the sandals Carpenter made for her and was an enthusiastic
reader of Carpenter's *Love's Coming of Age* (1896).[33] The British socialist
and feminist Mary Gawthorpe remembered how both Carpenter and
Whitman were still revered by Leeds working-class socialists in the early
twentieth century.[34]

If Ibsen, Carpenter, Whitman and the Transcendentalists were inspi-
rational sources for individual action and personal inner transformation,
some adventurers also drew on John Ruskin's organic vision of society
as an interconnected household. Ignoring Ruskin's patriarchal views
on the role of women, they interpreted his ideas in diverse ways. The

British housing reformer Octavia Hill, who believed in the endeavours of individuals rather than state intervention, applied Ruskin in her plans for housing provision and appropriated him for the Charity Organisation Society. On the other hand Ruskin's critique of laissez-faire and competitive social relations endeared him to the Independent Labour Party member Margaret McMillan, a campaigner for school medical inspections and nurseries, and to Selina Cooper, a socialist working-class activist in Nelson, Lancashire. In 1897 when Selina Cooper named her new baby 'John', it was partly after Ruskin. In the US, the anti-poverty campaigner and domestic innovator Helen Campbell was deeply influenced by Ruskin. In 1894 Campbell worked closely with Charlotte Perkins Gilman on a journal called *Impress*, in which she wrote a column on 'Household Economics'. Later more imaginatively entitled 'The Art of Living', the column was introduced by a quotation from Ruskin and heralded many of the themes Gilman would subsequently develop.[35]

In the late 1890s the Boston settlement worker Vida Scudder argued that Ruskin's dismissal of that 'unreal and unpleasant figment the so-called "economic man"', in favour of 'a man complete in all his faculties and desires, including his moral instincts', accounted for the popularity of his works in reform circles.[36] Ruskin promised the re-integration of aspects of life which had fragmented, and his aesthetic critique of capitalist production travelled into the arts and crafts movement via the socialism of William Morris. For many arts and crafts enthusiasts like the Bostonian 'new woman', Mary Ware Dennett, art was inseparable from new ways of ethical living.[37]

Regardless of their strong emphasis on the moral agency of individuals, women adventurers also assimilated more deterministic social theories. Charlotte Perkins Gilman and Helen Campbell both admired one of the founders of American sociology, Lester F. Ward. His interpretation of social evolution provided an organic metaphor of the body politic which postulated that change in one part of society necessarily affected others. This integrated perspective was attractive to Gilman because it offered a framework for connecting reform in one area of the social fabric to another. Ward's view that women were more important to evolutionary survival than men, who were merely the enablers of procreation, also appealed to Gilman and to other feminists.[38] Versions of Ward's concepts of biological necessity lingered on into the early twentieth century because they added weight to arguments that mothers required improved conditions of employment or social welfare provision.

Holding apparently contradictory strands of thought simultaneously was not peculiar to the women adventurers. A deterministic Social Darwinism exercised considerable influence within the emergent social sciences, but was frequently combined with the conviction that enlightened social scientists could sort out the problems of society. From the 1880s, Herbert Spencer's individualistic ideas of social evolution were being contested by reformers calling for more state regulation, in an effort to curb the worst effects of capitalist greed. The idea that society was evolving towards collectivism was influencing liberals and socialists alike. In differing ways they saw their role as speeding up the process.

The tension between a teleological unfolding of history and human agency was present in Marx's writings as well, though there was a tendency in the late nineteenth century to focus on the former rather than the latter. While Marx, Engels and the German socialist August Bebel all supported the emancipation of women, only Bebel stressed the importance of women's conscious agency. In Marxist groupings, primacy was always given to the proletariat as the catalytic anti-capitalist force – a view which contrasted sharply with the emphasis on women's significance in American reform circles. Personal engagement was also a sticking point. Jane Addams, for instance, was familiar with Marx's works, but her sensitivity to subjective factors in the relationships between people of differing classes and races was alien to Marx and Engels's theorizing. It proved difficult for British Marxist women such as Eleanor Marx Aveling, Annie Besant and Dora Montefiore to express discontent about male–female encounters. These remained outside 'politics', as did the personal experience of motherhood and child-rearing.[39]

In dreaming of a new day, women adventurers looked back to a heritage of radical thinking and selected concepts from their male contemporaries, but they also learned from one another. Jane Addams was reading Beatrice Webb's *The Co-operative Movement in Great Britain* soon after it was published in 1891, and Webb's work later influenced the Chicago women social theorists.[40] Arts and crafts enthusiast Mary Ware Dennett was a reader of the avant-garde British journal the *Freewoman*.[41] Labour women too were aware of books and ideas from other countries. In 1911 American labour women in the Women's Card and Label Union, which boycotted non–trade union goods in Seattle, were reading the South African socialist and 'new woman' Olive Schreiner.[42]

Women adventurers' networks extended over a range of issues and could converge in surprising ways. They also crossed boundaries as individuals took debates across the Atlantic. When Ida Wells-Barnett, the African-American suffragist and anti-lynching campaigner from Mississippi, visited Britain for a lecture tour in 1893, she was hosted by radicals, socialists and feminists. One of her lectures was delivered at the invitation of Annie Besant to the women-only Pioneer Club in London. Wells-Barnett, who was in conflict with Frances Willard because of the latter's concern to placate white Southern suffrage supporters, found allies in a club which debated feminism, anti-vivisection, anti-vaccination and temperance, and took its name from Whitman's 'Pioneers! O Pioneers'. Its members, who included Eleanor Marx Aveling, Dora Montefiore, Olive Schreiner and the 'new woman' writer Mona Caird, as well as Besant, assembled in an elegant Mayfair establishment which had formerly been a home of Lord Byron.[43]

The free thinkers and anarchists were resolutely internationalist. Lillian Harman, the daughter of the editor of *Lucifer*, came to Britain in 1898. Harman addressed a group which supported free love, the Legitimation League, who regarded her as a heroine because she had been imprisoned for living in a free-love union. Emma Goldman visited Britain several times, while Voltairine de Cleyre went to London to meet the French anarchist Louise Michel in 1897. Rose Witcop, a Jewish East End anarchist, wrote articles for Margaret Sanger's *Woman Rebel* and in 1920 spoke with Sanger on birth control in London.[44]

Personal connections were vital in communicating ideas. Harriot Stanton Blatch, daughter of the famous American radical feminist Elizabeth Stanton, lived in Britain during the late nineteenth century and was associated with the Fabians. When she returned to the US in 1902 she kept up her personal links with British social movements. Mary Beard, later a municipal reformer and historian in the US, also encountered the British women's suffrage movement while living in Oxford where, in 1899, her husband Charles founded the trade union college Ruskin Hall. Sisterhood was practical when it came to travel. Alice Hamilton, a resident at Hull House who investigated lead poisoning in industry, visited Britain in 1919 and was looked after by Margaret Ashton, a local feminist active in the Women's Local Government Society. Though feminist international networking was aided by formal organizations, such as the International Alliance of Women and the International League for Peace and Freedom which opposed World War One, these links between individuals were vitally important in disseminating ideas and policies.[45]

Sexual radicals also networked internationally, informally as well as formally. Stella Browne, a birth control advocate in Britain, met Margaret Sanger after she fled the United States, indicted for giving out information about contraception. After they parted the two women corresponded with one another; in 1916 Browne wrote to the American writer on sex and birth control, Elsie Clews Parsons, urging her to support Sanger.[46] Letters complemented direct personal encounters; they were as important as published material in spreading ideas.

Being relatively geographically mobile, middle-class women were able to establish strong direct links, but these personal bonds could also extend to working-class women in socialist and anarchist circles. The 'Crewe Factory Girl', Ada Nield Chew, admired the writings of Charlotte Perkins Gilman, which were popular in labour and co-operative circles.[47] Labour women also exchanged concepts about organizing with one another. The American trade unionist, Fannia Cohn, told the British Labour Party leader Marion Phillips in 1927:

I am extremely interested that wives of trade unionists should have an organization through which they can function just as well as middle-class women, business and professional women function through their organizations. Women of the middle class have excellent organizations in the United States and they are such a power in our social life that no political party or leader can afford to ignore them.[48]

The adventurers' inventiveness was sustained by the dynamic networks through which they organized. Ideas passed back and forth between clusters of women, interweaving, conflicting and constantly moving. Not only were they thinking in action amidst flux, but affiliations to radical and reforming organizations or networks could be extremely fluid. Individuals often straddled several causes at once, and women shifted their points of view over a lifetime. Initially anti-suffrage, Beatrice Webb changed her mind in the 1900s. The British anarchist Charlotte Wilson's trajectory is an extreme example of theoretical and organizational catholicism. In the mid-1880s she took part in the self-consciously 'advanced' discussions of the London-based Men and Women's Club about sex and society, and was a member of a group around the Russian revolutionary émigré Stepniak, the Society of the Friends of Russian Freedom. She quickly gravitated to the Marxist Social Democratic Federation and then to the Fabian Society, where she proceeded to organize her anarchist faction. In 1885 she helped to start the first British anarchist paper, the *Anarchist*, which was associated with the American Benjamin Tucker's Boston-based individualist anarchist paper *Liberty*. The following year she was editing the anarchist-communist journal *Freedom* with Kropotkin. Withdrawing from politics in the 1890s, Wilson popped up again with a new political persona during the 1900s, joining the Women's Local Government Society along with a suffrage organization called the Women's Freedom League, as well as the research group, the Women's Industrial Council. She was back with the Fabians in 1908 helping to found the Fabian Women's Group.[49]

Charlotte Wilson was unusual, but not unique. Other adventurers moved between movements, assimilated apparently contrary influences and shifted their views. Annie Besant was radicalized by free thought, later working with both the Marxist Social Democratic Federation (SDF) and the Fabians. In 1893 she converted to the spiritual philosophy of Theosophy, spending many years in India where she supported the Nationalist movement. Another 'SDFer' and feminist, Dora Montefiore, was at the same time a Theosophist and a member of the Pioneer Club, the Women's Local Government Society and the suffrage movement.[50]

Differing generations of women adventurers were affected by the prevailing preoccupations of their era. In the early 1900s the fascination with surveying and mapping which had emerged in reform circles in the late nineteenth century persisted, but it was accompanied by an intense preoccupation with scrutinizing oneself. Elsie Clews Parsons, who had worked with the settlement leader Mary Kingsbury Simkhovitch, was also influenced by the anthropologist Franz Boas's emphasis on ethnography. Observing others with a camera-eye was not such a big step from treating oneself as a document, and this is exactly what Parsons did in a series of intimate journals in which she examined her personal relationships.[51] She was indicative of a new impatient mood. In the early twentieth century an advance guard of 'modern' women were prepared to defy the sexual taboos which the older generation had, on the whole, negotiated warily.

In 1914 the creator of the Greenwich Village Heterodoxy Club, Marie Jenny Howe, writing in the avant-garde journal *New Review*, sought to accommodate the inner and outer dimensions of women's experience by linking political, economic, cultural and psychological transformations:

Feminism is woman's struggle for freedom. Its political phase is women's wish to vote. Its economic phase is woman's revaluation of

outgrown customs and standards . . . Feminism means more than a
changed world. It means a changed psychology, the creation of a new
consciousness.[52]

In the 1880s the members of the London Men and Women's Club
had struggled over how to speak about sexuality.[53] While their early
twentieth-century counterparts were likely to be more psychologically
aware, they too grappled with how to devise a language for women's
sexual desires in all their variability.[54] This endeavour was made even
harder because many of them also wanted to combine self-exploration
and self-expression with external change in society as feminists, socialists or reformers. Even for the most privileged, reconciliation was not
always possible. Mabel Dodge Luhan turned her back on her Greenwich
Village salon brimming with spiritual gurus, sexual experimenters and
revolutionary syndicalists, to head to the Taos desert in New Mexico
in 1917, declaring, 'My life broke in two'.[55] Elsie Clews Parsons also
began to look to other cultures as sources of wholeness. By 1915 she
was applying her interest in ethnography to the new cultural anthropology which was contesting the racial hierarchies embedded within the
evolutionary tradition. Parsons argued that cultural anthropology could
help an 'unconventional society' to develop by questioning accepted
systems of classification.[56] A new crop of women cultural anthropologists
would explore culture in this light during the 1920s. Among them was
Zora Neale Hurston, who chronicled the beliefs and customs of black
Southerners, and Margaret Mead, whose interest in sexual freedom led
her to enthuse about sexual attitudes and practices in Samoa.

In both countries many of the older adventurers were deeply puzzled
by the new circumstances of the 1920s. In a sense they were surrounded
by their successes. More young women were going into higher education, becoming the first generation among the middle class to assume
they would combine work and motherhood. Mobile, short-haired and
short-skirted, the new generation were casually open about ideas and
behaviour which had required martyrs in the 1880s and 1890s. Sex and
birth control were not only discussed, but demanded as rights. A distinct
lesbian identity was emerging in defiance of prejudice. The unabashed
assertion of sexual experience and the questioning of monogamy – which
before the war had marked out a minority of wild bohemians – began to
modify the sexual mores of the mainstream. In Britain, labour women
could look out at council houses and municipal swimming pools, and

occasionally even Turkish baths. In the US, too, ideas of social citizenship were alive and well at a local level, where some of the progressive advocates of city housekeeping had gained municipal influence. But while such changes in everyday social existence were imperceptibly being taken for granted, they did not correspond to the earlier grand dreams of new dawns and new days.

In the immediate post-war era, circumstances and assumptions had shifted fundamentally. Feminism had lost cohesion as a movement, and divisions which had been passed over in the struggle for the vote were beginning to emerge. Attempts were made by the American socialist feminist Crystal Eastman, among others, to draw up a broader feminist programme which could span legal reforms, equal pay, an independent income for mothers from the state, nurseries and birth control. She was trying to give weight to the specific needs of women alongside the claim for equal citizenship, and she still wanted to change personal life.[57] However, the efforts of women like Eastman who sought to unite the subjective and the social faced overwhelming political and economic obstacles.

The rifts were not only there among feminists; the women adventurers were at variance more generally. One wing had endorsed efficiency, social regulation, progress through technology; another had adopted Romanticism's elevation of the natural, the spontaneous and the simple life. Contrary impulses which before the war could ride in tandem were taking separate paths in the 1920s. For some Americans, Henry Ford promised a high-wage economy and the democratization of consumption, while others recoiled from boom-time materialism and headed for rural communes, craft workshops or Paris's Left Bank. The vibrant market economy absorbed aspects of the adventurers' faith in self-realization, which, when grafted onto the enterprise culture, stimulated private consumption rather than social transformation. Arts and crafts became a matter of form; neutralized as taste, contributing to 1920s 'modern' living in which simplification and lack of clutter were a means of streamlining existence. Similarly, enthusiasm for the 'natural' was detaching itself from any social utopia to focus on the bronzed athletic body, revolutionizing fashion and ideals of beauty. Daily life had changed, but not on the terms the innovators had imagined.

The same trends affected British society, but were constrained by long-term economic decline and by a different political context. The existence of the Labour Party, backed by the trade unions and labour women's organizations as well as Liberals sympathetic to reform, consti-tuted a much stronger lobby for state intervention locally and nationally than in the US. Though suspicion of the state persisted among both Liberals and strands of the libertarian left that had been opposed to the war, the need for state resources seemed self-evident to large swathes of male as well as female reformers. But in the 1920s, a series of bitter industrial disputes and mounting unemployment meant that the earlier glimpses of a new dawn would be tempered by severe hardship. They emerged muffled and modified by party resolutions and local govern-ment committees. Amidst the long struggle for small gains against the economic grain, hopes of democratizing relationships at work, in communities and between individuals could seem like idealistic luxuries from an unrealistic past.

Nevertheless hope died hard. In 1927 the British socialist and femi-nist Dora Russell envisioned a future in which human beings could feel 'at home in the world, not fearing change but perpetually develop-ing in suppleness and wisdom, perpetually devising new forms and new sources of delight'.[58] The dreams of a new day morphed; nonetheless they survived.

2

How to Be

Advanced women's claims to education, meaningful work and independence presented them with unique choices and decisions about personal behaviour. They questioned not simply how life might be lived but, more existentially, how they might *be*. Appearance, identity and relationships were disputed, along with the very boundaries of private and public experience. From the early 1890s the dilemmas raised by this re-creation of self, and of self in relation to society, were explored in a slew of articles and books written by women. *On the Threshold* (1895), a novel by the British socialist and feminist Isabella Ford, depicts a new woman heroine struggling with the claims of family, the decision of whether or not to marry, and her yearning for an active, independent life. The image of the 'threshold' is also there in a poem by another socialist and feminist, Dora Montefiore. She described the fin-de-siècle new woman in 1898 as 'Pausing on the century's threshold/With her face towards the dawn'.[1] The threshold not only marked the advent of a new era in terms of time; it symbolized inchoate aspirations and a powerful sense of unknown possibilities.

Being poised on the edge of the unimaginable encouraged a reliance on inner-directed defiance. The anarchist Lizzie Holmes declared in 1896: 'No barrier, no code, no superstition should stand in the way of woman working for the best thought within her, with her best strength, according to the brightest light glowing within her breast.'[2] When Helena Born died in Boston in 1902, a friend from the *Liberty* anarchist circle, Emma Heller Schumm, described the journey from respectability Born and Miriam Daniell had made when they left the protection of convention:

FABIAN WOMEN'S GROUP

Fabian Tract No. 157.

THE

WORKING LIFE

OF WOMEN.

By Miss B. L. HUTCHINS.

PRICE ONE PENNY.

Fabian Women's pamphlet (Fabian Society)

They were serving their apprenticeship in the new life of their choice. There was much enthusiasm for ideas, much storm and stress, much material hardship; but it was all very beautiful. How I longed to shelter them from the world's rough handling.[3]

Reflecting on Helena Born's life, Schumm declared, 'Hers was certainly the experimental life; there were no rut marks on her.'[4]

New selves, it seemed, could be made from old if only the will was sufficiently strong. This faith in human beings' capacity to experiment in personal behaviour simply by asserting individual judgement against established moral codes and conventions, influenced not only anarchist adventurers, but feminist and socialist new women in the late nineteenth century. 'What is thought *proper* now will very probably not be thought proper in the year 1919; *therefore*, let no mere conservative bias thwart our judgement,' predicted Jane Hume Clapperton in 1885.[5] She would be proved right. The resolve to follow inner conviction in sweeping aside the outdated clutter of conformity was reasserted from differing perspectives by rebel women on the left, in the feminist movement and in the artistic avant-garde. 'We are regimented by conventions, habits and customs and ideas persist amongst us and control us because we do not submit them to trial by our commonsense', the socialist and feminist Teresa Billington-Greig told the youth group connected to the *Clarion* newspaper, the Clarion Scouts, in Glasgow in 1914.[6]

An immediate practical difficulty when women decided to behave differently was their inability to move about easily. Fashionable apparel was of little use if you wanted to work, to walk through city slums or take off into the countryside on your bicycle. One of the delights of social work, for Mary Simmons at the Bermondsey Settlement in South London, was that she could wander happily through the streets 'with neither hat nor gloves, nor so much as even the hallmark of a sunshade'.[7] Future suffragette Florence Exten-Hann came from a socialist working-class family in Southampton. In the 1890s she and her mother were members of the Clarion Cycling Club there: 'Mother and I rode bicycles and wore bloomers, but had to carry a skirt to put on when riding in a town for fear of being mobbed.'[8] A less inhibited young Crystal Eastman was to be found hurtling through the small New York town of Glenora, on the shore of Seneca Lake, 'on a man's saddle in fluttering vast brown bloomers'.[9] Her parents, who were both Congregational ministers, believed in women's rights. Nonetheless she startled her father by the open display of 'bare brown legs' when she wore her swimming costume: 'he would not want to swim in a skirt and stockings. Why then should I?'[10]

Bloomers had a long history. Adopted initially by utopian socialists and advanced women in the mid-nineteenth century, this overtly eman- cipated clothing had attracted such obloquy and derision that the next wave of rational dressers took care to make their bloomers look exactly like skirts. The veteran American feminist Elizabeth Cady Stanton was intrigued by their ingenuity at a Glasgow suffrage meeting in 1882: 'all the garments are bifurcated but so skilfully adjusted in generous plaits and folds, that the casual observer is ignorant of the innovation.'[11] The Rational Dress Society was formed in 1888 to encourage comfort- able, healthy clothing based on reason, utility and simplification. It extended beyond women's wear, intimating a new lifestyle. By 1889 babies had been brought into the Society's remit: the advanced baby in 'simpler' dress should sport either white flannel attached with a safety- pin between the legs, or white flannel shirts wrapped in front and 'little warm bootikins'.[12]

The strict application of reason and utility were never entirely satis- factory, and Romanticism also served as a wellspring for several waves of alternative fashion. An early exponent was Mary Paley, one of the pioneering group of Cambridge graduates who became a lecturer in political economy, teaching first at the new University College in Bristol, then at Oxford and Cambridge. An admiring student compared her to Tennyson's learned Princess Ida: 'She wears a flowing dark green cloth robe with dark brown fur round the bottom (not on the very edge) – she has dark brown hair which goes back in a great wave and is very loosely pinned up behind . . .'[13] The aesthetic Mary Paley married the economist Alfred Marshall in 1877 and faded over the years into the role of great man's helpmate, earning the scorn of Beatrice Webb as an example of how definitely not to become.

If one impulse within Romanticism in style invoked a lost golden age, another emulated nature. Getting in touch with nature necessitated rethinking how to dress. After emigrating from Bristol to Boston in 1890, Helena Born explained in her lecture on 'Whitman and Nature':

> Ordinary clothes are apt to be an impediment to the appreciation of nature. For women the disqualifications of dress have been very seri- ous – happily becoming less so, not so much from a saner view of the dignity of the body as from the demands of locomotive improvement.[14]

By the turn of the century the arts and crafts movement was inspiring simplified forms of clothing suitable for locomotive, natural women. The Healthy and Artistic Dress Union, founded in 1901, propagated 'health, comfort, activity'.[15] One of its leading members, Janet Ashbee, had settled at Chipping Campden in the Cotswolds when her husband, the designer Charles Ashbee, brought the Guild and School of Handicrafts to the village. Their 'arts and crafts' community allowed scope for eccentric innovation. In the early 1900s Janet Ashbee was to be seen in a peasant smock, sun bonnet, fisherman's jacket and sandals.[16] Utopian communities fostered freer clothes along with new lifestyles, which influenced first the bohemian intelligentsia and eventually moved into the mainstream. Nellie Shaw went bare-legged and in sandals at the Cotswolds anarchist colony, Whiteway – though when her mother visited, she sat down on the road just outside Gloucester and donned 'stockings and shoes to please her'.[17]

The Healthy and Artistic Dress Union was keen to establish a countercultural aesthetic of 'graceful appearance', and promoted flowing Grecian clothes for women seeking expressive freedom.[18] The style proved popular with the American dancer Isadora Duncan and with the British pioneer of exercise and healthy food, Margaret Morris. The

Margaret Morris, 1921

wealthy American lesbian émigrée in Paris, Natalie Barney, created a
'Temple à l'Amitié' in her overgrown Parisian garden in the early 1900s,
where her women friends danced in scanty Grecian robes evocative of
nymphs close to nature.[19]

But there was more to clothes than met the eye. 'Cloth is a social
tissue; a sort of social skin,' wrote Charlotte Perkins Gilman in her 1915
The Dress of Women, arguing that the distinct costumes of men and
women were meant to ensure that 'we should never forget sex'.[20] In
the late nineteenth century the practical shirt-waister and tie subverted
these indicators. By desexualizing clothing, women could enter male
spaces – the workplace or the café at night – while signalling that
they were not sexually available. The new women who went a step
further, dressing as men and cropping their hair, found they could walk
through cities unmolested. Masculine styles were consequently at once
the badge of a geographical mobility and marked the social arrival of
the new woman in men's zones. Nevertheless, to revolt against the
conventions of appearance and behaviour meant putting oneself into
an unprotected space. Critics sneered at the plain shirtwaisters and ties
worn by Russian-Jewish immigrant working-class new women who
sat in cafés debating marriage, the family and working conditions. One
hostile observer in the 1890s derided the 'atmosphere of tea-steam and
cigarette smoke', denouncing the 'pallid, tired, thin-lipped, flat-chested
and angular' women for whom 'The time of night means nothing
until way into the small hours.'[21] To dress, act and think differently
upset cultural assumptions about gender that were deeply embedded.

Relatively small deviations in conduct could place a woman outside
the norms of socially acceptable behaviour and invoke rejection, not
only from men, but from other women. Cosmo Gordon Lang (later
to become Archbishop of Canterbury) recalled how Beatrice Webb,
while researching her book on the co-operative movement, upset the
co-operative women of Hebden Bridge in 1889 by asking if she could
smoke, then by announcing that she would go for a walk with the men
on Haworth Moor.

> The ladies were now all the more convinced that they must be at hand
> to protect their lords. We started, an odd-looking party. But the good
> women, in their long dresses and elastic-sided boots, wholly unac-
> customed to walk further than the distance between their homes and
> shop or chapel, soon gave up. They intimated to the New Woman

that they must return. 'I'm so sorry,' said she, with engaging frankness, 'but I'm going on.' Then one of the guardians of the proprieties
turned to another and said grimly: 'The impudent hussy.'[22]

Some women preferred to disregard dress sooner than defy the codes
overtly. Neither Sylvia Pankhurst nor Ada Nield Chew were particularly
interested in fashion. However, ignoring what you looked like could
also make you memorably bizarre. In the 1970s, after the passage of
more than half a century, the former trade union leader Maurice Hann
remembered Sylvia Pankhurst speaking at a meeting in a blouse that was
inside out. 'A proper scruff,' he declared to me with the admonition not
to quote him.[23] Doris Nield Chew recollected how her mother 'was
completely without personal vanity'. Indeed, her hairdresser recalled
ruefully how Chew 'crammed her hat on a head of beautifully waved
hair'.[24]

Ada Nield Chew might go 'round the world on a sixpenny tin of
Pond's cold cream', but plenty of middle-class feminists rebelled without loss of style.[25] Appropriating conventional forms of femininity offset
unconventional political action and confused male opponents. Ironically
this resulted in suffrage shoppers being courted by the new large department stores – despite the broken windows. The Women's Social and
Political Union militants, Emmeline and Christabel Pankhurst, were
studiously elegant and would have concurred with the Liberal father of
the constitutional suffragist, Margery Corbett Ashby, who advised her:
'if you want to reform anything else, do *not* reform your clothes'.[26]

In contrast, for working-class women fashionable clothes could mark
a *break* with deference. In early twentieth-century America the bright,
modern young telephone operators who formed an elite among working women brought glamour to the picket line in defiance of scabs.
They took a class pride in wearing clothes that signalled their access
to the respect and power surrounding rich women. Similarly, when
Milka Sablich, the American miner's daughter who became active in
the violent strikes of the Colorado mining industry in the late 1920s,
was taunted for wearing a silk dress, red-haired 'Flaming Milka' flashed
back: 'Miners' children like pretty things as well as anyone else!'[27] In
Britain during World War One, young women in munitions factories
earned high wages by working in conditions of considerable danger.
They responded by seeking fun and spending their money on clothes,
earning disapproving comments in the press. Such criticism provoked a

defiant letter to the *Daily Express* in November 1917 from a 'Munition Girl':

> Those who point the finger of scorn at me seem to me to be utterly without imagination. Let them put themselves in my place. Let them realise what it means, after a life of soul-suffocation, to find oneself suddenly able to breathe free air, to see the walls of one's prison house gradually crumbling, to feel the shackles of tyranny loosening from one's feet, to taste a tiny bit of ambition realised. Ambition is the same power in every walk of life, whether it aims at world domination or the possession of a small article of flesh-coloured crepe de Chine.[28]

A. Philip Randolph and his Brotherhood of Sleeping Car Porters, an organization of black workers on the Pullman trains, encouraged African-American women to stand up for their rights and stay in fashion. The union journal, the *Messenger*, opined that 'Bobbed hair is very often attractive and becoming. Bobbed brains however are a serious handicap to anyone.'[29] Randolph was encouraged by his wife, the socialist Lucille Randolph, who saw the 'new negro woman' as beautiful *and* brainy. She linked the Brotherhood's 'ladies' auxiliary', the Women's Economic Council, to 1920s modernity by holding 'bobbed hair' contests.

The semiology of the 'social tissue' was various indeed. Well-dressed suffragettes could infiltrate a venue in ladylike mode, only to smash windows and hurl axes at politicians. Workers dressed up to assert class, race and gender pride, while 'new women' donned male clothing as a means of holding gender at bay. The shirt and tie were marks of the respect due to women at the cutting edge. When in 1920 members of the Greenwich Village Heterodoxy Club made an album for the club's founder, Marie Jenny Howe, several chose photographs of themselves in white shirts and ties – including Heterodoxy's only black member, Grace Nail Johnson, who was active in the National Association for the Advancement of Colored People (NAACP) and married to the Harlem poet, James Weldon Johnson.

While male styles could denote a seriousness of purpose above feminine frivolity, by the 1920s they had transmuted into high fashion. Women added small signs of femininity to distinguish modishness from cross-dressing. The lesbian novelist Radclyffe Hall, for example, posed in male evening dress, Spanish hat, pearl earrings and a kiss-curl in 1926. The Radclyffe Hall 'look' did not indicate sexual orientation. Instead it was part of the image of belonging to a fashionable avant-garde. When Radclyffe Hall's *The Well of Loneliness* was first published in 1928, a reviewer in the *Newcastle Daily Journal* remarked on her 'aura' of 'high-brow modernism'.[30] However, the novel was quickly to be redefined as obscene and its author's dress recoded as the mark of a lesbian subculture. By 1929 the boyish styles were no longer modish, and short hair, monocles and tailored clothing came to assume a chosen lesbian identity.

The fluidity of style evident during the 1920s was personified in the insouciant flapper dancers. Yet while they appeared as the essence of ultra-modern immediacy and flux, they were shadowed by a motley crew of image-breakers who had defied the conventions before World War One. Masculine styles had been the badge of serious new women seeking sexual autonomy, but they also invoked Victorian and Edwardian erotica in which cross-dressing had been a motif. A model on a sexy postcard, dressed as Napoleon with enhanced crotch, titillated gender taboos. When, in 1910, the French writer Colette posed in men's clothes with a daring cigarette, she symbolically crashed through into the cultural space reserved for pornography and prostitution. As a 'vagabond' woman without roots, Colette pirouetted gleefully into forbidden fantasies by adopting their trappings – diaphanous nymphs, Grecian nudity, 'Oriental' slave girls, the dominatrix – and sending them up. The borderlines of feminine identity were being breached. Elsie Clews Parsons, influenced by the contemporary European thinking of Gabriel de Tarde, Ernst Mach and Henri Bergson, theorized this vagabonding before the War. In 1914 she wrote in her *Journal of a Feminist*:

> The day will come when the individual . . . [will not] have to pretend to be possessed of a given quota of femaleness and maleness. This morning perhaps I feel like a male; let me act like one. This afternoon I may feel like a female; let me act like one. At midday or at midnight I may feel sexless; let me therefore act sexlessly. . . . It is such a confounded bore to have to act one part endlessly.[31]

Instead of willing a new self through reason or seeking to uncover an innate natural self, the bohemian avant-garde had begun to play with being different selves. Women as well as men, it seemed, could be and do as the mood might take them. Crystal Eastman's brother, the writer Max Eastman, poked fun at Mabel Dodge Luhan's 'perpetual war on habit' in his 1927 novel, *Venture*. The fictional character he based on her, Mary Kittredge, 'was always just entering upon some new spiritual experiment that involved a complete break with everything that had gone before'. This restless quest made it impossible for her to settle, to be constant or still:

> Either she was getting married, or she was getting divorced, or she was testing out unmarried love ... or snake-dancing, or Hindu philosophy, or Hindu turbans, or female farming, or opium-eating, or flute-playing. There was nothing in the world that Mary could not want to do, and there was very little that she could not, in a surprisingly short space of time, do.[32]

Mabel Dodge Luhan's mercurial crazes signified a wider restlessness. The modern woman did not want to be pinned down. Elsie Clews Parsons contended in 1916 that the key objective of feminism was not political or even social rights, but the declassification of women. 'The *new woman* means the woman not yet classified, perhaps not classifiable.'[33]

In the 1920s the taboos breached by advanced thinkers and vagabond bohemians were being flouted openly by modern women who articulated a new common sense. In the symposium edited by feminist Freda Kirchwey, *Our Changing Morality* (1924), Isobel Leavenworth, an academic at Barnard, asserted women's right to experience, including sexual experience:

> Because she must first of all conform to an unpolluted archetype, and because society must be secure in the knowledge that she is indeed so conforming, she has never been able to meet life freely, to make what experience she could out of circumstances, to poke about here and there in the nooks and crannies of her surroundings [the] better to understand the world in which she lives.[34]

Though 1920s American culture fostered this kind of faith in infinitely expanding opportunities, the possibilities of opting for a plurality of identities were never equally stacked. In the Harlem Renaissance, African-American women writers briefly reached out towards dynamic self-definition, yet despite belonging to Du Bois's elite, they were constrained within a racist culture. The freedoms of the 1920s contained a catch; the radical enthusiasm for nature initiated by the Romanticism of Greenwich Village and the fashionable discovery of outsider cultures endowed black women with a spontaneous animality. This rebranding of racial difference meant that black women were being given an ascribed identity in the very era in which white women were attempting to declassify themselves. In response, some rejected sensuality outright; others grabbed the 'primitive' tag and ran with it. 'People have done me the honor of believing I'm an animal,' announced the 1920s comedian and dancer Josephine Baker. 'I love the animals, they are the sincerest of creatures.'[35] She kept dogs, cats, monkeys, rabbits, a pig, a goat and a leopard as pets.

Others tried to 'be' on their own terms. Among the American escapees to the Parisian left bank was the black novelist Jessie Fauset, who stated in 1925: 'It is simplest of all to say that I like to live among people and surroundings where I am not always conscious of "thou shalt not". I am colored and wish to be known as colored, but sometimes I have felt that my growth as a writer has been hampered in my own country.'[36] For African-American women of all classes there were manifold difficulties in being purely an individual. In Nella Larsen's novel *Quicksand* (1928), the heroine Helga Crane, who is of mixed race, recoils from the conformity of racial uplift but finds her European relatives regard her as an exotic symbol of primitive sensuality. Physically attracted to a black preacher from the South, she becomes his wife. But her resolve to improve the lives of the local women is thwarted when her own health and spirit are broken by repeated pregnancies. Hazel Carby reflects:

> As readers, we are left meditating on the problematic nature of alternative possibilities of a social self. Consider the metaphor of quicksand; it is a condition where individual struggle and isolated effort are doomed to failure. Helga's search led to the burial, not the discovery, of the self. The only way out of quicksand is with external help; isolated individual struggle ensured only that she would sink deeper into the quagmire.[37]

Whether the quest for an autonomous self was consciously willed, seen as a hidden true nature to be released or as a quicksilver of shifting selves, the yearning for a separate, distinct individuality constituted a passionate and powerful motive force in leading women to break with conformity. But there was, as Carby indicates, something more – the social self. New women not only required new ways of being individuals; they needed differing kinds of relationships with others. Charlotte

Nella Larsen (Beinecke Rare Book Collection, Yale University)

Perkins Gilman recognized that self-expression required sociability, that 'our specialized knowledge, power, and skill are developed through the organic relationships of the social group'.[38]

Organic social relating proved problematic for many fierce rebels who had been compelled to hone their new selves against the opinion of the world. And, of course, they discovered that in practice radical counter-cultures could evince competition, malice and prejudice just like the bad old world of conformity and reaction. Nonetheless their experiences of interconnection opened precious spaces for imagining, quarries for mining visionary possibilities from the known and moments when the future seemed immanent within the present. Once glimpsed these glimmered like lodestars through their lives. Mabel Dodge Luhan recalled her Greenwich Village days in terms of a fluid communalism: 'barriers went down and people reached each other who had never been in touch before; there were all sorts of new ways to communicate, as well as new communications. The new spirit was abroad and swept us all together.'[39]

Movements involved an interior culture of personal relationships which affected individuals profoundly. Women who participated in the suffrage movement found a transformative affinity with other women which could result in passionate love affairs, lifelong friendships and an overwhelming sense of empowerment. Looking back on the suffrage campaign, the British constitutional suffragist Margery Corbett Ashby recalled how it transformed perceptions. Instead of the assumption that women were necessarily 'catty and jealous', seeing 'other women as poachers on the same ground', she recalled how 'we suddenly found we were intensely loyal to other women'. The movement 'turned all the can'ts into can', affecting feminists personally and creating a new sense of collective identity.[40]

Anarchist and socialist movements, too, offered women a greater degree of equality and a broader scope for personal relationships than conventional society. Isabella Ford was drawn to the Yorkshire Independent Labour Party in the early 1890s because the woman question was linked to working-class politics; she was impressed by a visit to a Labour Club in the Colne Valley, where the men had given a tea party for the women, pouring out the tea, cutting the bread and butter, and washing everything up 'without any feminine help and without any accidents!'[41] In 1899 the new 'Clarion woman' was being hailed proudly by the *Clarion* newspaper as being able to 'look on a man's face without simpering or blushing'.[42] Hitches did occur between promise and actuality. Only a week later the columnist Julia Dawson was berating the 'miserable misoginists [*sic*]' who were trying 'to oust women from the Manchester Clarion cycling club'.[43] As Ada Nield Chew observed dryly in 1912, 'The task of taking women into account is to some reformers so appallingly difficult that they are inclined to shelve this aspect of the question and to postpone its settlement.'[44]

Nonetheless women experienced fellowship and comradeship in movements which placed a strong emphasis on creating new values, developing consciousness and making cultural institutions which reached into every aspect of life. A network of mini-utopias in the shape of cafés, clubs, choirs, theatre groups and holiday homes sustained hopes of a new day coming. Even courtships could be conducted within this alternative terrain. In 1896 Ada Nield Chew accompanied her husband-to-be George on a socialist Clarion Van propaganda tour. The van was Julia Dawson's idea and was kitted out with bunks and cupboards. George slept in a tent and was responsible for the horse who pulled them along.[45] In both Britain and the US, anarchists and socialists put great stress on education for young and old. When Annie Davison was growing up in a Glaswegian working-class

socialist family before World War One, anarchist, Marxist and socialist
Sunday Schools abounded in the city. At her socialist Sunday School she
learned to love learning, respect her teachers as well as her parents, and
remember 'that all the good things of the earth are produced by labour'.
She was taught the 'three great principles . . . Love, justice and truth',
along with a 'history, not of kings and queens, but common people'.[46]

Socialist Sunday School membership card (Working Class Movement Library)

Women gave the values of mutuality a special twist. The American
co-operative women in Seattle believed that in 'co-operation lies our
hope for the future, true co-operation that includes not merely the
matters of dollars and cents but extends to the social and home life as
well.'[47] The utopian faith in the possibility of prefiguring future social
relations in the here and now was extended in perceptive and creative
ways. Seattle co-operative women of the 1920s imagined a world without wallflowers when they decided to form a social club to enable single
girls to go out properly chaperoned. 'Especially do we desire to reach
the lonely ones who dislike to go to the public dance halls and other
public places of amusement, and as a result are deprived of the social life
which they so much desire.'[48]

African-American women also recognized that mutuality could have specific benefits for women and extend into the family. Mutual aid and benevolent associations were particularly strong in the Southern states. Along with black churches they combined practical benefits with a culture of co-operation which included informal neighbourhood networks and formal institutions. In the early 1900s in Richmond, Virginia, inventive African-American women formed a chain of mutual aid groups, which included the Children's Rosebud Fountains, established by the Grand Fountain United Order of True Reformers to teach the children to 'bear each other's burdens . . . to so bind and tie their love and affections together that one's sorrow may be the other's sorrow, one's distress be the other's distress, one's penny the other's penny.'[49] Survival and solidarity were irretrievably linked; moreover they intimated a better future.

Glimpses of alternative relations not only nurtured the quest for other kinds of being; they strengthened resistance. The American Women's Trade Union League member Pauline Newman who, along with many other women from immigrant backgrounds, worked from the age of twelve at the New York Triangle Shirtwaist factory, learned through the friendships she formed at work that 'you are no longer a stranger and alone'.[50] Mary Heaton Vorse was a bohemian radical when in 1912 she went to report on the textile strike in Lawrence, Massachusetts, where workers from many different ethnic backgrounds united to confront not only their employers, but police and company guards. The assignment changed the course of her life. Vorse recalled:

> Before Lawrence, I had known a good deal about labor, but I had not felt about it. I had not got angry. In Lawrence I got angry . . . Some curious synthesis had taken place between my life and that of the workers, some peculiar change that would never again permit me to look with indifference on the fact that riches for the few were made by the misery of the many.[51]

Amidst the hurly-burly of strikes, pickets, committees and meetings, radical and reforming movements brought women into new social relationships; they learned through doing of what might be. In turn-of-the-century Tampa, Florida, Italian and Cuban cigar workers who were influenced by anarcho-syndicalism sought to bring together male and female workers of all nationalities and colours in 'complete moral and material solidarity'.[52] Momentarily they were touched by that elusive utopian hope of making the whole world anew, and experienced the joy of boundaries dissolving.

The anarchist Emma Goldman believed autonomy and mutuality were integrally connected. The key problem for women was 'how to be one's self and yet in oneness with others, to feel deeply with all human beings and still retain one's own characteristic qualities.'[53] She gave equal weight to women's personal quest for liberation and their relational needs, in social movements as well as in friendship and love. Living the connections was harder than theorizing, as Goldman herself knew all too well. If the pull between a fragile sense of autonomy and wider solidarities caused recurring tension, sexual relationships with men were apt to blow the carefully assembled independence apart. Charlotte Perkins Gilman had hesitated when Walter Stetson proposed in 1882. 'I like to go about alone *independently*.'[54] Two years later she did marry him, but being a wife and mother provoked a mental breakdown and physical crisis which she documented in *The Yellow Wallpaper* (1890), a stark, innovative short story chronicling her claustrophobic desperation. In the year that it was published, she wrote to a friend, 'I haven't any heart but a scar. . . . Now I guess I will shut the door of my heart again; and hang on it "*Positively* no Admittance except on Business!"'[55]

Apart from a small minority of rebels, late nineteenth-century women adventurers tended to navigate carefully around the shoals of love and desire. Many were absorbed like Mary Paley, many more remained celibate and some, like Jane Addams, lived discreetly with other women. Some found a modus vivendi, at a cost. The young Beatrice Webb was shaken by her desire for the sexually attractive and dominating Joseph Chamberlain, opting instead for Sidney Webb. She told her sister Kate Courtney that her marriage would be subordinate to her work. When her sister remonstrated, 'That is rather a question for your husband,' Beatrice replied, 'No: it is the question of the *choice* of my husband.'[56] She wrote in her diary in May 1890:

> How absolutely *alone* and *independent* my life has become: not *lonely*, for I have many friends and fellow-workers and do not feel the need for more sympathy than I get; quite the contrary, in most of the relationships I willingly give more than I receive. But that terrible time of agonizing suffering seems to have turned my whole nature into steel – not the steel that kills, but the surgeon's instrument that would save.[57]

Action in the external world seemed to require a cauterization of wandering emotions and sexual passion. Later generations were more up-front and combative. 'Let us turn away from the antiquated advocacy of work in lieu of love, as an alternative to love, and let us look to work for the sake of love, as a means of salvation for love,' declared an optimistic Elsie Clews Parsons in 1913.[58]

In 1924 the American Jungian psychologist Beatrice M. Hinkle noted how modern women were not satisfied with rhetorical abstractions about freedom. Instead, they were 'demanding a reality in their relations with men that heretofore has been lacking'.[59] She celebrated the way in which women rather than men were becoming the active agents in altering sexual relationships.

Signs of this new assertive mood had already been evident in the pre-war years, when women had started documenting their responses to sexual partners in terms which would have been inconceivable to the earlier generation. In 1911 Elsie Clews Parsons gave a fictionalized account of her estrangement from Herbert Parsons in *The Imaginary Mistress*, exploring shifting subterranean emotions:

> The old sense of oneness with him which I had ridiculed as a conjugal tradition but which had been a profound and joyful reality for me had disappeared. He became alien and at moments I had the pain of feeling that our physical intimacy might become not merely indifferent but repugnant. This change in me did not affect the surface of our life at all – at least in his eyes. He did not notice. He was quite content.[60]

In the *New Age* in 1912 the defiant and beautiful 'Beatrice Hastings' described how contempt for a man had destroyed a sexual relationship. 'He becomes my spaniel.'[61] She was soon to be the Parisian correspondent for the *New Age*, smoking hashish and haunting cafés such as the Dôme and the Rotonde with her lover, the artist Amadeo Modigliani. This time she had not found a spaniel; they fought one another passionately and noisily in the cafés and streets of Montmartre.

Early twentieth-century feminists explored the ambivalence of women's wants. Two Greenwich Village writers, Susan Glaspell and Neith Boyce, married to men who supported feminist emancipation, examined the gaps between women's desires to change their lives – including sexual relations – and the contrary feelings such longings engendered.[62] Their work was part of a wider questioning about whether psychological shifts in sexual and gender relations could ever be control-led or predicted. In 1913 Elsie Clews Parsons concluded in her *Journal of a Feminist* that 'the problem of sex feminists have not faced is primarily a psychological problem'. She had decided that woman's 'impulse to subjection . . . self-surrender is one of the dominant characters of her passion'.[63]

The resolve to reveal what had been concealed by exposing the messy actuality of sexual relationships combined with a new psychologi-cal awareness to bring out problems earlier generations could not have envisaged. Confusion erupted over what exactly women wanted in their sexual relationships with men. Early twentieth-century women rebels were beset by a contradictory inheritance. They were at once daughters of reason and daughters of nature, as attached to the primitive as they were to being modern. They wished to use their intellects *and* to remain open to all those heady romantic feelings of infinite energy and elemen-tal receptivity. They felt a need for the intimacy, mutuality, warmth and sensuousness which seemed to have been excluded in the drive for self-possession. More and more women found themselves living out the incongruities which were arising from the changing relations between the sexes. By the 1920s the subjective voice had hit the mainstream. In 1927 the British journalist Leonora Eyles confessed in *Good Housekeeping* how becoming a divorcee had led her to question deeply-held assump-tions about independence, adding, 'It is necessary to strike the personal note.' She told readers she had married 'a man who was not a very strong character', and managed everything by doing 'without him'. But this had left him feeling that he was not needed.[64]

Problems were evident in the labour movement too. Eyles noted in the left-wing *Lansbury's Labour Weekly* how 'the new woman, the comrade woman' was 'tending to admire the weaker, gentler, less active type of man'. They in turn were fastening 'on to the aggressive woman'. Unforeseen snags were appearing from efforts to reverse gender roles, and Eyles observed the new relations bringing hostility. Men were sore because women seemed to be encroaching on the places they held sacred. Eyles urged women not to inflame sex antagonism by 'putting on airs of superiority about our earnings and our abilities'.[65]

In 1925 the African-American social investigator and journalist Elise Johnson McDougald, writing in a special issue of *Survey Graphic* dedi-cated to black intellectuals, was also inclined to hold out an olive branch. She noted some conflicts in relationships between 'the masses of Negro men . . . engaged in menial occupations', and 'Negro working women' who were tasting 'economic independence' and rebelling against 'the domineering family attitude of the cruder working-class Negro man'. But she contrasted these to 'the wholesome attitude of fellowship and freedom' evinced by younger, educated 'Negro men', advising women to 'grasp the proffered comradeship with sincerity'.[66]

The possibilities of new personal relationships interacted with external circumstances. McDougald was writing in a period when hopes of changing race relations were not stirring only among members of the young black intelligentsia like herself in the North. Black and white Southern American women were beginning at last to organize together, and black women were laying out their terms. They were agitating for nurseries, playgrounds and recreation centres along with better education for black children. They also challenged segregated accommodation on public transport and lynchings.

In contrast, among the white metropolitan intelligentsia in the United States, the pull to public engagement was slackening. The suffrage had been won, but World War One had divided radicals; there was a red scare after the Bolshevik revolution, isolating those who joined the Communist Party and making it harder for independent leftists to form coalitions. Radical 1920s women were edgy and undermined; a feeling of exhaustion is evident in the autobiographical essays written by radicals and reformers for the *Nation* which Freda Kirchwey gathered together in 1926–27. Surrounded by a buoyant consumer culture, several women expressed their longing for a more hedonistic self. Garland Smith, in rebellion against her Southern Presbyterian background, described a love of dancing, early intimations of sexuality, her interest in Freud and Ellis. 'I am at least free now from the old distortions and repressions.'[67] They were beginning to feel that they could no longer find self-realization simply through taking part in movements for external change. Ruth Pickering, a journalist who had been a member of the Heterodoxy Club in Greenwich Village, said she had 'traded . . . exhilarating defiance . . . for an assurance of free and unimpeded self-expression'.[68] The preoccupation with the personal impinged on how feminism was conceptualized. Dorothy Dunbar Bromley, writing in *Harper's* in 1927, decreed that the 'Feminist – New Style' who was 'truly modern' no longer felt the need to renounce marriage and children for a career; a 'full life' required combining work with emotional and domestic fulfilment.[69] Beatrice M. Hinkle internalized the feminist quest for freedom. Women's struggle against convention was, she wrote, essentially 'the psychological development of themselves as individuals'.[70] Adventuring was being recast as a purely inward affair.

In response, a determined radical minority mounted an effort to reconnect how to 'be', personally, with the transformation of society. The faith in self-realization inspired by the American educational philosopher John Dewey persisted into the 1920s, travelling in tandem with a new psychological awareness. In Britain, 1920s feminists such as Dora Russell and Stella Browne, active in campaigning for birth control in the labour movement, explicitly combined economic and social demands with an interest in culture and psychology. In the United States, Crystal Eastman resolutely continued to write about both the inner and outer forms of subordination. In 1920 Eastman defined the 'problem of women's freedom' as being 'how to arrange the world so that women can be human beings, with a chance to exercise their infinitely varied gifts in infinitely varied ways'. This was not 'the whole of feminism', she conceded, but 'enough to begin with'. When some of her friends protested, 'Oh don't begin with economics! Woman does not live by bread alone. What she needs first is a free soul,' Eastman carefully asserted a balance. She agreed it was true:

> Women will never be great until they achieve a certain emotional freedom, a strong healthy egotism, and some un-personal sources of joy – that in this inner sense we cannot make woman free by changing her economic status. What we can do, however, is to create conditions of outward freedom in which a free woman's soul can be born and grow.[71]

In 1926, in *Concerning Women*, another radical modern woman, Suzanne La Follette, similarly argued the need to challenge both the economic and psychological aspects of women's 'subjection'.[72] Emma Goldman too was not prepared to abandon the link between the outer society and her personal experience. When in 1927, aged fifty-eight, she was planning her memoirs, she told the bohemian Hutchins Hapgood: 'I want the events of my life to stand out in bold relief from the social background in America and the various events that helped to make me what I am: a sort of conjunction between my own inner struggle and the social struggles outside.'[73] Yet in using her own life as a document Emma Goldman was aware of how she would be judged. Though she left a

trail for posterity through letters documenting her passionate and painful love affair with the hobo philanderer Ben Reitman, Goldman knew
that the exposure of her personal vulnerability and her sexuality would
not be understood in the America of the late 1920s. Both her politics
and her gender laid her open to derision. The woman who had defied
so many boundaries was forced to concede that there were some she had
to negotiate. Goldman confided to her former lover and companion, the
anarchist–communist Alexander Berkman: 'We all have something to
hide. Nor is it cowardice which makes us shrink from turning ourselves
inside out. It is more the dread that people do not understand, that what
may mean something very vital to you, to them is a thing to be spat
upon.'[74]

The translation of personal intimacy and sexual desire into the public
realm of the social and political proved to be one of the most difficult
aspects of women's freedom.

3

The Problem of Sex

Forgotten 'free lovers' dreamed up many of the assumptions eventually destined for 1920s modernity. In the late nineteenth century, high-minded clusters of free lovers were bringing individualist ideas of the inviolability of the person to their conceptions of personal relations; Lillian Harman insisted in *Lucifer* in 1897 that ownership of oneself was integral to women's inner 'self-respect'.[1] Placing a great emphasis on 'self-control', free lovers also believed that a frank and rational approach to love would prevent much unnecessary suffering, and enable people to understand and control their feelings. Sarah Holmes, who became one of Helena Born's friends in Boston, was, like Born, associated with Benjamin Tucker's journal *Liberty*. Writing under the pseudonym 'Zelm', she insisted in 1889 that 'Honesty is the best policy in love, because it is the only policy that ever gets love – love being the sympathy of those who can understand our real selves.'[2] Unlike the twentieth-century moderns, however, free lovers did not seek out unconscious motivations. Instead they took as their mentor the Russian writer Nikolai Chernyshevsky, whose novel *What Is to Be Done* (1863) adopted a highly rationalist stance toward alternative ways of living and loving.

In their campaigns for honesty, frankness and the right to knowledge, free lovers were confronted by a resolute foe. The campaigner for social purity Anthony Comstock had managed to get a law passed in 1873, banning the distribution of 'obscene' literature through the mail. The 'Comstock Law' meant that free-love advocates could be criminalized; the editor of *Lucifer*, Moses Harman, Lillian's father, went to jail several times for defending women's sexual freedom, including the right to resist rape in marriage. As late as 1905 Moses Harman was back in prison, for publishing articles by the birth controller Dora Forster on 'Sex Radicalism'. Forster argued that the worst kind of prostitution occurred in conventional marriages in which women were taught to use their bodies for economic and social advantage. She asserted that few married women experienced sensual enjoyment, and maintained that sex should not be restricted necessarily to one partner. She also defended sexual play in childhood, and advocated sex education.[3]

Women free lovers wanted to democratize personal relationships and extend possibilities of choice and control. When in 1898 Lillian Harman came to speak in London to the British free lovers in the Legitimation League, she put the case not simply for 'freedom in sexual relationships' but for extending the spaces for wider forms of personal encounter between men and women. She considered that the tendency for women's 'expression of friendship' to 'be construed into an invitation to flirtation' distorted relations between the sexes. She wanted women to be able to define whether relationships were to be sexual or not, rather than simply having to respond to the terms set by men. Women's freedom was one aspect of a wider 'freedom in *social* relationships'.[4]

The women free lovers' campaigns for the right to knowledge involved not simply access to information but self-knowledge, an inner awareness which could foster empathy with others. Writing in *Liberty* in 1888, Sarah Holmes connected self-control to 'self-understanding'. Replying to a worried young anarchist whose girlfriend Minnie had been shocked by his views on free love, Holmes explained to him how Chernyshevsky had demonstrated that a troubled love was not real love. We could not rely on our 'natural, spontaneous feeling', because 'We are taught the traditions of slavery'. Constant struggle and 'watchfulness' were needed 'against lapses and mistakes'. In believing he loved Minnie 'instead of some woman who was a theoretical free lover' he was, she suggested, emotionally ambiguous about his own free-love ideas. She then proceeded to propound to him the alternative Holmes ideal of 'free love'. Love was part of a process of harmonized development through which a person grew '*wholly* . . . not unevenly', and it required 'latent sympathy in ideas'. She thought that love became 'a quiet, gentle, normal, life-giving impulse and power only as fast and as far as this sympathy is found and its free expression made possible. It becomes a troubled, wild, anxious, life-destroying fever and madness as fast and as far as this sympathy is lost sight of, or jarred upon, or intercepted in its manifestation.'[5]

Similarly idealistic, perfectionist aspirations to wholeness, harmony and control recur in the writings of other free-love women. Elmina Slenker proposed 'Dianaism', a non-penetrative sexuality advocated by Tolstoy, as a means of gaining wisdom and poise. In December 1889, she assured readers of Ezra Heywood's *Word* that this was not a 'cold, apathetic, distant, unnatural Love' designed to deny sex feeling.[6] Eight years later in *Lucifer*, Slenker – who believed as did many feminists in this period that women were more spiritual than men – was still explaining Dianaism: 'The little touches, pats and caresses tokens of love. The clasp of the hand, the glance of affection, the tone of the voice, and all that speaks of genuine kindliness and friendliness; this we offer in place of the overmuch sexing, that is murdering millions of wives and scattering syphilis all over the world.'[7] Accepting that 'the masses' would move slowly towards Dianaism, she suggested that meanwhile small groups could set an example by adopting alternative ways of making love. Drawing on a metaphor of thrift, common in nineteenth-century free-love discourse, Slenker advised readers of *Lucifer* that they should 'Conserve the life forces and not needlessly waste them in mere paroxysms of pleasure'.[8] Other women in free-love circles were also interested in changing sexual practices. Alice B. Stockham, a friend of Lillian Harman, argued in *Karezza: Ethics of Marriage* (1896) that copulation should not be regarded as simply a means for procreation; rather it should be 'a blending of body, soul and spirit'.[9] Prolonged intercourse without orgasm for either men or women, Stockham maintained, was both pleasurable and a form of soul union.

However, women's supposed spirituality proved contentious. While some women free lovers agreed with Slenker that the 'sex instinct' was stronger in men, others angrily asserted women's physical desires. In 1897 Dora Forster told a London meeting of radical sexual reformers at the Legitimation League that the suppression of desire resulted in 'morbidity', insisting that women 'suffer as much from enforced celibacy as men'.[10] Amy Linnett challenged Elmina Slenker in *Lucifer* in the same year, taking up the cudgels on behalf 'of our younger radical women . . . who are not ashamed to avow the deliciousness of their sex, as Walt Whitman put it'.[11] When a male contributor argued in the journal that October that women were the moral regulators of sexual relationships, Elizabeth Johnson responded indignantly that 'woman' should have the 'right to use her functions as she pleases'. She declared: 'Stop setting woman on a pedestal, recognize her as an equal and half the problem would be solved.'[12]

Within the lofty discourse of free love it was somewhat difficult for women to assert an active desire which might make them seek more than one man. But Rosa Graul raised the question of women choosing differing fathers in her utopian novel *Hilda's Home*, serialized by *Lucifer* in 1897:

> if a woman desires to repeat the experience of motherhood, why should it be wrong when she selects another to be the father of her child, instead of the one who has once performed this office for her? Why should the act be less pure when she bestows a second love, when the object of this second love is just as true, just as noble, just as pure-minded as was the first one? Why should an act be considered a crime with one partner which had been fully justified with another?[13]

She added bravely, 'My words are backed by personal experience and observation, experience as bitter as any that has been herein recorded.'[14] On her visit to Britain in 1898, Lillian Harman also defended variety. 'I consider uniformity in mode of sexual relations as undesirable and impracticable as enforced uniformity in anything else. For myself, I want the right to profit by my mistakes.'[15]

The aim was the right to be happy *and* to make independent choices. In 1891 the anarchist Lillie White, Lizzie Holmes's sister, defined this as a self-conscious awareness of individual autonomy: 'When women learn that their best and highest object in life is to be independent and free, instead of living to make some man comfortable; when she finds that she must first be happy herself before she can make others happy, we shall have loving, harmonious families and happy homes.'[16] For White, an assertion of self was necessary in order to bond as equals.

Despite the rationalism in both the free-love tradition and the radical utilitarianism of Chernyshevsky, anarchist women also insisted on romance. Clashing in the pages of *Liberty* in 1888 with the Russian anarchist Victor Yarros, who believed in conventional family life, Sarah Holmes insisted that in the future 'the love of men and women will not take the form of violets first, and beefsteak but no violets ever after.' Her 'most yearning wish' for her own daughter was that

> she may never, in all her life, look into the eyes of an old-time lover and say: *You used to bring me violets.* I want men and women to keep their love as fresh as the baby-life to which such love gives birth; to be

true, honest, strong, self-sustaining men and women first; and then to love; to love one or to love many – fate and the chances of life must settle that – but, one or many, I want each love to be as full of its own essential fragrant essence as a violet's breath.[17]

Elmina Slenker was a great enthusiast of Diana-style marks of tenderness, while Rosa Graul expressed a desire for romance in *Hilda's Home*. In Graul's co-operative community of the future, '*liberty*' meant '*life will be a constant wooing*'.[18]

Echoing the early nineteenth-century utopians, the anarchist Kate Austin suggested that free love carried a promise of what might be. Writing in *Firebrand*, she argued in 1897:

> We all know that no golden key will unlock the casket of love, and that oft-times free love is the priceless possession of the poorest man or woman on earth. Many insist on saying 'free love is not practicable under present conditions'. Now I am not afraid to say that free love is all there is of love, that it was born of life and has always been with us, and is all that sweetens our onward march. If love is put in a cage, or fettered in any way, it is no longer love, but a ghastly nameless thing, that blasts the living and curses the unborn.[19]

Women advocates of free love were, however, all too aware that it was easier to express new ideals of sexual relationships than to live them. Lizzie Holmes's novel *Hagar Lyndon* (1893) detailed the practical obstacles her heroine encountered when she sought to be free, to love passionately and to survive in a hostile world. Eventually she was compelled to renounce passion for autonomy. When the journal *Discontent*, produced in the anarchist Home Colony in Washington, serialized a free-love novel by Nellie M. Jerauld, Holmes wrote a letter pointing out that free-love couples could be as demanding and possessive as married ones; moreover they, too, could be forced to stay together by economic pressures, especially after they had children.[20]

Although free-thinking and anarchist women were on the whole hopeful about the possibility of mutual understanding between men and women, they could be critical of men's gender blindness. In 1895 Edith Vance, a convinced free thinker associated with the Legitimation League, raised the differing consequences of heterodoxy for two Leeds members, the Dawsons, who lived in a free union:

I did not know until I had a talk with Mrs Dawson afterwards . . .
what a very great deal she has to endure, it is very easy – perhaps it
is fun to you gentlemen – to be twitted about your connection with
the League. You can bear it with fortitude, and perhaps rather like it
than otherwise, and if the conversation gets too bad, you can knock
the man down but Mrs Dawson is not in a position to thus deal with
her slanderers, men or women, and in most cases the women are the
worst.[21]

Women in free-love circles knew from experience that abstract 'free-
love' prescriptions could overlook the complexities of actual situations
and needs in relationships, and that refusing marriage was no guarantee
of happiness. Not only was it evident that cultural attitudes were far
less forgiving towards women's sexual deviance than men's, but some
suspected that enthusiasm for autonomy and the value of 'experiences'
could be cynical male ploys. Nellie Shaw describes how a man who
arrived at the Whiteway Tolstoyan anarchist community in the British
Cotswolds during the early 1900s, advocating 'varietism', was sent pack-
ing. Autonomy was about women expressing their individuality within
monogamy, as far as she was concerned.[22]

The dilemmas and arguments continued in the early twentieth
century, though the context changed. The American anarchist Voltairine
de Cleyre regarded sex as one aspect of experience, and believed in a
state of permanent flux and autonomy. Writing in *Mother Earth* in 1908
she plumped for 'ecstasy' rather than permanent free union. 'Never allow
love to be vulgarized by the common indecencies of continuous close
communion.'[23] The problem was, when freedoms conflicted who was
to decide? Jealousy too proved particularly resistant to free-love reason-
ing. Women advocates of free unions might insist they were motivated
by a higher, inner-directed morality rather than old-style competition
for men, but their rivals were not necessarily convinced.

Some of the free lovers' assumptions about the need for self-ownership
and greater choice and control were shared by the 'new women' writers
of the late nineteenth century. In 1888 the British novelist Mona Caird
was insisting on the need for a 'full understanding and acknowledgement
of the obvious right of the woman to *possess herself* body and soul'.[24]
New women, however, were inclined to be more sceptical than anarchist women about the possibility of co-operating with men; as Caird
declared, 'The enemy has to be met and fought within men's soul'.[25]

Voltairine de Cleyre (Labadie Collection, University of Michigan)

Like anarchist free lovers, new women like Caird believed that women's dependent status was deeply embedded not only within existing family relations, but in established institutions such as the church and the state; however, their strategies for change differed. While free lovers stressed individual direct action in defiance of the law, Caird was prepared to accept that self-ownership required legislative reforms such as female suffrage, equal parental rights, and divorce, along with marriage as a free contract, co-education and the abolition of segregated patterns of work. Like the free lovers, though, Caird asserted that woman's self-possession involved the right 'to give or withhold herself . . . exactly as she wills'.[26]

Self-ownership, greater equality in sexual relationships, interconnections between personal behaviour and external political demands, along with free love, were all being discussed in the socialist movement during the late nineteenth century. Edith Lanchester's free union in defiance of her family in 1895 brought the issue of sexuality out into the open and caused ripples of controversy. However, prominent women socialists, whose position was already socially and culturally precarious because of their politics, were inclined to be wary. As the Independent Labour

Party activist Margaret McMillan put it, 'Marriage is bad and Free Love is worse'.[27]

Many women who sought to live more autonomously were inclined to associate sex with danger. Meridel LeSueur, who would become a novelist, came from a left-wing background in the Mid-West and her mother was a feminist. As a young woman in Greenwich Village before World War One, she met and admired Emma Goldman, but contrasted Goldman's frank acceptance of sexual pleasure with the attitudes of her mother's generation.

> Many of them felt sex was a humiliating force, symbolic of their repression – of marriage and child-bearing – and it represented to them violence, rape, and enslavement. Many of them at that time felt a woman had only two choices: living her own life with a career and calling as a radical, or marriage with sex and children.[28]

In the late nineteenth century the conviction that women needed to be protected from male sexuality encouraged women reformers in both countries to become involved in efforts to eradicate prostitution. An unintended consequence was that over-zealous police harried women they thought were not 'respectable'. In Britain in 1885 a broad coalition led by the supporter of women's rights, Josephine Butler, secured the abolition of the Contagious Diseases Act which had sanctioned forced physical examinations of women whom police suspected of prostitution. The National Vigilance Association was formed as a result of the campaign. However, divisions arose between women concerned to protect working-class prostitutes from destitution, and vigilance campaigners who wanted to close brothels by force. Among the latter was Laura Ormiston Chant, a supporter of the Liberal Party, women's suffrage, temperance and social purity. Although initially distrustful of state intervention, Chant and other social-purity activists began to shift from simply campaigning to seeking changes in local and national government policy. In the 1890s Chant, with allies from the British Women's Temperance Association, successfully put pressure on a coalition of Progressives on the London County Council to restrict licences to music halls that featured acts of which they disapproved. In 1901 a vigorous campaign against prostitution was mounted by Progressives, evangelicals, feminists and temperance supporters against prostitution; it targeted the women rather than their male clients, an approach which caused conflict among social-purity feminists.[29]

Social purity was also a powerful force in the United States. The Woman's Christian Temperance Union could mobilize women on a mass scale, while women's clubs and women in social settlements combined with members of the Christian League for the Promotion of Social Purity and the Mothers' Congress, not only in the campaigns against prostitution but in attempts to regulate theatres, dance halls and the new cinemas. As in Britain, voluntary groups began to press for municipal and legislative intervention. Some moral reformers also came to realize the need for practical services to support and retrain prostitutes. The Florence Crittenton homes provided a refuge for young girls as well as training them in domestic service and nursing.[30]

If the reformers' zeal could be coercive and repressive, the social-purity movement nonetheless contained several subversive sub-texts. Some moral campaigners demanded equal moral standards for men and women, while their efforts to curb incest, rape and violence within families broached the question of the extent to which relations within the family were to be regulated. Moreover, by marshalling powerful emotive arguments, they generated a public discussion of hitherto unmentionable topics such as venereal disease. The social purity regulators, like their antithesis the free lovers, contrived to bring sex into the public arena.

When social-purity women spoke out on platforms and in committees, it was evident that the boundary between women actively asserting their allotted 'female' role of moral purification in a public context, and breaking through the prevailing conventions about the woman's sphere, could be frangible. Indeed, Chant's efforts to close brothels led to her being castigated as a 'new woman'.[31]

From the 1880s, moral reformers who went into the urban slums to rescue the poor from drink, vice and family violence could find themselves moving on to other social issues. In both countries, social purity contributed to the emergence of broader reform coalitions which sought to tackle urban problems in the early 1900s.[32] The attempt to redeem could shake assumptions. When the future campaigner against lead contamination, Alice Hamilton, braved a brothel in Toledo to rescue a prostitute, she found, instead of the victim she had expected, 'a woman of mature years, handsome, dignified, entirely mistress of herself' in a house that was 'luxurious but vulgarly ugly'. The meeting was an occasion for mutual incomprehension. The young idealistic reformer heard

the calculating voice of a tradeswoman. 'I might make a good sales-
woman . . . for I spend my time persuading men to spend money on
what they don't really want.' For her part, the prostitute was appalled
by Hamilton's altruistic settlement life in the Chicago slums: 'That is
not the sort of thing I could possibly do,' she observed with disgust.[33]
The reformers' values could also be challenged. From 1910 the upper-
middle-class Bostonian Fanny Quincy Howe regularly corresponded
with a Jewish prostitute and morphine addict, Maimie Pinzer, who told
Howe she regarded divorce as 'a lot of foolishness and a marriage cere-
mony the worst lot of cant I ever heard'.[34] Such encounters resulted in
a steep learning curve.

As moral reform fused with wider action in communities, perspectives could subtly alter. By 1915, when the radical Mary Beard wrote
Woman's Work in Municipalities, reformers were looking at preventative
action and trying to understand the social and cultural bases of moral
problems. So while club women in Pittsburg, Kansas were busy securing
the censorship of 'all films depicting scenes of crime, drinking scenes,
and suggestive "love scenes"', more imaginative reformers sought not
simply to ban, but to influence the content of the new leisure industry
in an effort to ensure pleasurable improvement.[35]

The new approach of positive intervention also led them to embark
on sex education. Beard reported that by 1914, women's meetings were
being held to discuss teaching 'sex hygiene'. Speaking to the Council of
Jewish Women, Dr Rosalie Morton pointed out that women must take
on the issue in their own homes rather than leaving the topic of sex to
men alone. In the past she claimed women had been 'too sentimental,
they have been too ignorant of their limitations in the world of practical
affairs; they have lacked well-balanced judgment as to how it was best
to teach, how it was best to help'.[36] The Women's Municipal League of
Boston began to give sex lectures, 'realizing the physical misery which
is resulting from ignorance in regard to matters of sex, and the spiritual
degradation following the wrong conception of the high purpose of the
sex function, to which must be added the loss of efficiency in human
ability'. The League believed that there were too many dangers to justify
'a further continuance of . . . silence'.[37]

Sex was a social issue, not simply a personal one. In both the US and
Britain, sex hygienists approached the topic in terms of efficiency and
regulation. Warning of the dangers of promiscuity in lurid terms, their
emphasis was on the interests of the body politic, which they equated

with the heterosexual family and parenthood. Nonetheless they too
were part of a profound cultural shift. In the late nineteenth and early
twentieth centuries, private intimacies were coming out into the public
gaze and becoming a topic for public discourse.

This transposition presented a dilemma about how to discuss sexual
practices and relationships. The free lovers Ezra and Angela Heywood
advocated words in common use. Angela Heywood wrote in 1887:
'Such graceful terms as hearing, seeing, smelling, tasting, fucking, throb-
bing, kissing, and kin words are telephone expressions, lighthouses of
intercourse centrally immutable to the situation; their aptness, euphony
and serviceable persistence make it as impossible and undesirable to
put them out of pure use as it would be to take oxygen out of air.'[38]
Common usage or not, the Heywoods had to write 'c—, c— and f—'
or go to jail.[39]

In 1897 the British free lovers in the Legitimation League were
puzzling over the existence of 'two forms of speech or language in
connection with sex matters'. One was scientific and the other 'the
bald, rugged phrases of the gutter and the market-place'. In an article
headed 'Wanted: A New Dictionary', the League asserted that raising
'the discussion of sex matters to a higher plane' required the 'formulation
of a vocabulary'.[40] This anxiety about language partly expressed a recognition of the practical threat they faced. They had to position themselves
on the 'higher plane' if a line between sexual radicalism and obscenity
was to be drawn. This strategy was not always successful. In the late
1890s the police were hounding the League; they seized Havelock Ellis's
Studies in the Psychology of Sex: Sexual Inversion, despite its academic tone,
because it was published by a press used by the League. A later generation of women sex reformers, the birth controllers Margaret Sanger and
Marie Stopes, adapted this 'higher plane' tactic by developing a high-
flown prose style.

For 'advanced' women the search for a new language of sexuality
was part of a wider struggle for a self-defined cultural space. Between
1885 and 1889, the female members of the Men and Women Club
in London found themselves confronted by a group of radical men,
who had adapted Darwinian evolutionary theories in an abstract and
distanced manner to the discussion of sexual questions. The men set
the terms of debate. One woman member, Maria Sharpe, reflected
that she and the other women 'even in general discussion . . . had
to learn a partially new language before they could make themselves

intelligible'.[41] While the women in the club expressed frustration in curbing their subjectivity, they also discovered that 'objectivity' could provide a useful cover for personal feelings. Yet Sharpe still felt embarrassed when she returned the books she was reading on prostitution in the British Museum.

The free thinkers and anarchists in the US created a similarly hardwon space for the study and discussion of sexuality. In 1891 Lizzie Holmes affirmed the value of the voice *Lucifer* gave to radical women, and upheld women's own experiences against received knowledge:

> It is the mouthpiece, almost the only mouthpiece in the world, of every poor, suffering, defrauded, subjugated woman. Many know they suffer, and cry out in their misery, though not in the most grammatical of sentences. . . . A simple woman may know nothing of biology, psychology, or of the evolution of the human race, but she knows when she is forced into a relation disagreeable or painful to her. Let her express her pain; the scientists may afterwards tell why she suffers, and what are the remedies, if they can.[42]

The creation of an explicitly female counter-cultural space in which to articulate wants and desires continued to preoccupy early twentieth-century women writers seeking to understand and alter sexual customs and behaviour. The editor of the *Freewoman*, Dora Marsden, deplored 'the failure of language' to express a new sexual awareness among women.[43] She spoke for a group of rebel feminists who believed in tackling sex head-on, rejecting what she dubbed 'the great soporifics – comfort and protection.' Echoing the heroic individualism of the anarchists, she declared that free women would stand alone, convinced of their own strength, and claim all experience. For Marsden this could involve being 'content to seize the "love" in passing, to suffer the long strains of effort and to bear the agony of producing creative work'. She believed that through asserting their power as individuals, women would learn 'that their own freedom will consist in appraising their own worth, in setting up their own standards and living up to them'.[44] Similar ideas circulated in Greenwich Village where Mabel Dodge Luhan, too, was demanding the right 'to encompass all experience'.[45]

This mixture of aggressive will and sexual appetite appalled some women. Olive Schreiner complained to Havelock Ellis that the

Freewoman 'ought to be called the Licentious Male . . . It is the tone of the brutal self-indulgent selfish male.'[46] Conflict erupted on the *Freewoman*'s letters page with a feminist, Kathlyn Oliver, expressing the view that 'freewomen' would not be 'slaves of our lower appetites'.[47] When a 'New Subscriber' wrote in defending women's right to sexual experience, Oliver assumed the correspondent to be male. But it was the Canadian birth control campaigner, Stella Browne, quoting Havelock Ellis on 'auto-eroticism'.[48]

Ellis's diligent observation documented a wide range of sexual practices and wants – including his wife Edith's attraction to women. Ellis's method of case studies, combined with his stance as a scientific observer, established an idiom for talking about sex. Instead of appealing to either morality or an ideal of free love, he had devised a standpoint from which he could catalogue and consider what his subjects declared as their wants. The study of sex psychology created a platform of 'objectivity' which could provide a reference point beyond subjectivity and be a means of comprehending feelings and behaviour which did not 'fit'. However, in creating a new terrain for sexual expression he, along with other sex psychologists, also defined and constrained women's varied experiences and desires; both by imposing their own categories and by the ponderous scientific terminology which pinned down individuals according to type, rather in the manner of nineteenth-century natural science's specimens of butterflies. Nevertheless, Ellis's assumption of the role of the distanced expert gave a new, secular, scholarly significance to personal testimony. He helped to establish a conduit for sexual observation which broke with the confessional and the peep show: observation of sexual feelings and behaviour was transmuted into a field of study. An important space had been opened.

Even Ellis had found that his writing on homosexuality and lesbianism could be castigated as 'obscene', and any public assertion of same-sex desire remained well-nigh impossible. Instead women tentatively expressed their emotions in private correspondence. Edith Ellis, an anonymous witness in her husband's volume on 'inversion', confided in the socialist and sexual radical Edward Carpenter, whose openly lived homosexuality gave him a kind of gender neutrality. Following the death of her lover, Lily, in 1905, Edith Ellis wondered why she was getting headaches after years without them, and concluded that 'the need of the lusts of the flesh – like mine – was the reason.'[49]

Edith Ellis (Carpenter Collection, Sheffield Archives)

Women communicated their own responses to sympathetic male friends, explicitly distinguishing those who evinced a capacity to observe and listen, and they made a selective use of the writings of male sexologists in relation to their own perceptions. When in 1915 Stella Browne gave a paper at the newly formed British Society for the Study of Sex Psychology on 'The Sexual Variety and Variability among Women', she explained carefully:

> I have tried to say nothing in this paper, that was not known to me, either through my own experience, or the observation and testimony of persons I know well. My conclusions are based on life, not on books, though I have been confirmed in my personal opinions and conclusions by some of the greatest psychologists, especially Dr Havelock Ellis, whose immense research is fused and illuminated by an inspired intuition.[50]

Stressing the need to relate experience and theory, Browne also explicitly addressed the need for women to devise a new discourse. 'The realities of women's sexual life have been greatly obscured by the lack of any sexual vocabulary. While her brother has often learned all the slang of the street before adolescence, the conventional "decently brought-up" girl, of the upper and middle classes, has no terms to define many of her sensations and experiences.'[51]

Like the rebel free lovers, Browne challenged the idea that women did not possess a 'sex impulse', arguing instead that women's desires were diverse, differing not only between individuals but in the same individual over time. She did not believe their varied sexual needs could be expressed or satisfied within either patriarchal marriage or its corollary, prostitution. While Browne, the modern woman, absorbed earlier arguments from the sex-radical tradition, she was well read in contemporary European sexual theory, and familiar with the new philosophic trends which stressed energy and flux. Like her counterparts in Greenwich Village, she was aware of the new context psychoanalysis was creating for personal testimony. Browne and her contemporaries not only invoked reason; they were seeking a space for a more complex cultural expression of contradictory feelings.

Interest in sex psychology and psychoanalysis was part of the wider contemporary preoccupation with self-observation. In 1916 Elsie Clews Parsons, reflecting on subjective knowledge, noted: 'At times testimony about the private life takes on a sufficiently public significance to free it from ridicule or the charge of bad taste.'[52] Greenwich Village bohemians, male and female, were fascinated by the dual processes of self-examination and self-revelation. Intimacies were common knowledge, corresponded about, written about in novels and plays and openly discussed. Christine Stansell comments on how their 'talking about sex' was created by an 'amalgam of feminism, cross-class fascination with working-class mores, and a belief in the power of honesty between the sexes'.[53] The bohemian and anarchist Hutchins Hapgood, who had pioneered the impressionistic documentation of 'outsiders' in the 1890s by writing on immigrant life, wanted to apply the same conscious scrutiny to sex. He and the novelist Neith Boyce set out to be sexual chums. 'I begin to feel we are a couple of sports', Boyce declared in 1899.[54] But when they had children, it was to be Hapgood who retained the freedom to roam in a quite conventional manner. 'Varietism', Boyce concluded in 1905, using the free lovers' terminology, was so 'crude and unlovely – and besides it takes the zest out of sinning.'[55]

Emma Goldman, whose eclectic openness caught the mood of the Village perfectly, acted as a crucial intermediary between free lovers and twentieth-century bohemians. Goldman possessed a unique capacity to look backwards, outwards and forwards. She was familiar with the little clusters of American free-thought and free-speech groups, as well as Russian writers such as Chernyshevsky, while being equally well versed in Ibsen, Nietzsche, Shaw, Carpenter, Ellis and Freud.[56] Even as the Villagers took over some of the watchwords and demands of the free lovers, they re-routed and transposed the old ideals, shaping them into the new set of assumptions about sexuality which would surface in main-stream culture during the 1920s. Confident in the infinite possibility of 'being' amidst a booming America vibrant with energy, the bohemian rebels stressed release and expression rather than the conservation of energy, Slenker-style. The free lovers' 'self-control' morphed into Margaret Sanger's term 'birth control', and their interest in therapeutic cures and closeness to nature fed into a concern to manage the body through diet and exercise, in accord with the early twentieth-century American 'can-do' approach to mind and body.

Greenwich Villagers resolutely set out to break down the taboos between the hidden world of forbidden sex and a new, sexually radical culture. Emma Goldman personified the new mix. Goldman's letters to her lover Ben Reitman combine lofty transcendent imagery with a language designed to arouse. The two lovers devised an effusive code designed to confuse the censorship of the mail, and the juxtapositions are bizarre. Goldman declares that she wanted to drink from his 'fountain of life'. She wanted to make him 'go mad with joy and ecstasy . . . I know how to induce you, and if I could draw, you would see, but this way you wait until Oh let it be soon, please, please, come right on. I want you.'[57] Christine Stansell suggests that Ben Reitman represented the Romantic fantasy of the primitive. By embodying a forbidden power he released a carnal self within Goldman.[58] In her agonized relationship with the unfaithful Reitman, Goldman reversed gender roles by becoming the Romantic artist while he was cast as the temptress. Her more down-to-earth friend Almeda Sperry, a former prostitute, berated her for romanticizing Reitman. She revealed how Reitman had 'asked Hutch Hapgood to suck one of my breasts while he sucked the other so I could have two orgasms at the same time . . . he also asked me how many men there are in this town that I had not fucked yet.' Sperry told Goldman, 'For a woman of your knowledge you are strangely innocent. . . . I understood him thoroughly as soon as he grabbed my arm as we walked down the street. I used the same kind of language he did.' She called the language '"fuck" talk'.[59] To Ben Reitman, Sperry, once a prostitute, was always a prostitute.

Men still set up the boundary posts; they defined the terms of freedom. Meridel LeSueur relates how when she arrived in Greenwich Village as a young woman, Emma Goldman took her to Mabel Dodge Luhan's weekly salon. The young Mid-Westerner felt humiliated when, after refusing 'the amorous advances of some famous male writers', she was 'laughingly dubbed the Corn Virgin from Kansas'. She was left feeling 'culturally rebuked'.[60] Class stereotypes also held fast. Agnes Smedley, from a working-class background in Colorado, became a socialist and supporter of Indian nationalism through contact with Indian immigrants in California. She moved to New York in the spring of 1917, but felt uncomfortable and inarticulate among Greenwich Village intellectuals who, in idealizing the working class as embodying raw experience, assumed that working-class women were naturally sensual.[61]

In fact, many working-class women had strong inhibitions about sex. Margaret Llewellyn Davies referred with regret to 'the heavy curtain' which falls in working-class women's lives upon marriage, encouraging Women's Co-operative Guild members to speak out rather than regard sex and the family as aspects of life which could not be changed.[62] The Yorkshire socialist and feminist Mary Gawthorpe moved in radical political circles herself, but was all too aware of the gulf in sexual attitudes. She reflected in her autobiography *Up Hill to Holloway* that her father had given her mother sufficient grounds for a legal separation. But custom and cash made this inconceivable. 'Mother still believed that you had made your bed and would lie on it. Or at least she thought she believed that.'[63]

However, a radical minority were resolved to choose their own sexual destinies. Feminism encouraged small clusters of lower-middle-class and working-class women to try and relate their sexual feelings to new sexual theories. The diaries and letters of Ruth Slate and Eva Slawson chronicle the aspirations of two young Londoners who were not highly educated but were bursting with ideas. They read widely, attended meetings on left politics, on ethics, on aesthetics, and were interested in 'The Sex Question'. Eva Slawson found Edward Carpenter's *Love's Coming of Age* 'full of suggestion', and in 1911 she was attending the *Freewoman* discussion group. But the two young women were circumspect, sufficiently cognizant of power to select who they could be honest with. Ruth Slate reminded Eva, 'When you were sleeping with me . . . you said "Be careful to whom you give your confidences, for people do not see things as you mean them".'[64] Eva Slawson became involved with a working-class woman called Minna, and this new relationship made her think that 'too much spiritual and physical love is reserved for sexual union. We ought to be able to mingle soul and body, woman with woman, man with man – glorifying, caressing, embracing with the whole body – not simply the touch of hands and lips.'[65]

A few working-class women made an outright break with respect-ability. The anarchist Rose Witcop, who came from a strict Jewish working-class immigrant family in East London, lived in a free union with the anarchist-communist Guy Aldred and became a birth control campaigner. Ada Nield Chew had gradually grown apart from her husband George Chew, though to live separately was a decision that took her a long time. Her daughter recalled how shortly 'after his death she said pathetically and almost in bewilderment, "You know, I'm happier without him."'[66] Alice Dax, whom D. H. Lawrence portrays as Clara in Sons and Lovers, was an intellectual working-class woman, active in the suffrage movement in the Midlands village of Eastwood, interested in new ideas about personal freedom and the simplified lifestyle. Unlike Lawrence she never escaped into a wider world; she and many women like her were forced to temper their dreams of freedom.

Personal discomfort with convention could draw working-class women to labour organizing and radical political ideas. In 1918, Mary Archibald, an American clerk, active in the Seattle Woman's Card and Label League, which pledged consumers to buy from stores which stocked union label products, described herself in the Seattle Union Record as: 'A square peg in a round hole. I was not domestic by nature. . . . And this is my quarrel with marriage – there are too many square pegs in round holes.'[67]

Becoming involved in radical politics could bring an expansion of personal possibilities. There were movement love affairs. The American trade union leader Rose Schneiderman met Maud Swartz, an Irish-born printer, at a suffrage rally in 1912 – they became lifelong partners. Another woman trade union organizer, Pauline Newman, fell in love with an upper-middle-class woman, Frieda Miller, who left her job as a research assistant at Bryn Mawr College to become secretary of the Philadelphia Women's Trade Union League. When Newman wrote to her friend Rose Schneiderman for advice in 1917, Schneiderman urged her to take risks for 'joy', reflecting: 'There must be thousands of women who feel like us, eurning, eurning [sic] all the time for warmth and tenderness from a loved one, only to be worn out and settled down to the commonplace everyday grind.'[68]

In the post-war world, the risks for joy seemed rather more feasible. Modern 1920s women seemed to have shifted the rules of the game. Elsie Clews Parsons, writing on 'Changes in Sex Relations' in Freda Kirchwey's 1924 collection *Our Changing Morality*, wanted to know 'What of the actual sex life?'[69] Dorothy Parker, one of the New York writers who met to talk at the Round Table literary gatherings, started to write about sex in humorous verse which sent up sincerity and squeezed a brittle humour out of the perplexities of modern love. Round Table women talked sex with a new twist – they joked about it, not just together, but in male company. When Frank Adams arrived for a Round Table lunch after playing tennis with his shirt open showing curly black hair, Peggy Leech stared and quipped, 'Well, Frank – I see your fly is open higher than usual today.'[70]

The new frankness was not confined to the intelligentsia. Popular, confessional 'true' romance magazines took the delights of self-revelation into the mainstream. Advertisers discovered the new 'sex appeal' and packaged the promise; an advertisement for Camel cigarettes showed a young man lighting a woman's cigarette accompanied by the caption 'Pleasure Ahead'. Mae West, famous for her witty sexual innuendos, wrote and performed in the 1926 Broadway hit musical *Sex*.[71] 'Sex' suddenly seemed to be overt and everywhere. Greenwich Village's pre-World War idealization of 'outsider' groups had focused initially on ethnicity and class. However, by the 1920s jazz and the blues were transporting a lyrical and metaphorical sexual imagery from the culture of poor blacks to fashionable white audiences. Much was lost in translation; it passed through a prism of incomprehension. The white intelligentsia, in casting off their Protestant guilt, was inclined to envisage a uniform black America which they constructed as a primitive 'other'. This put educated black women seeking independence and sensual expression in a difficult predicament. Erotic affirmation could simply confirm racist stereotypes.[72]

Despite the razzmatazz of the 1920s, resistance to sexual radical ideas continued to be powerful at many levels in both societies. In the US, Comstockery was far from exhausted and moral reformers in organizations such as the Woman's Christian Temperance Union, which had lobbied successfully for prohibition in 1919, exerted considerable sway. In Britain the Catholics steadfastly opposed birth control, the Anglicans' Church Penitentiary Association favoured the disciplined regime of rescue homes for the contrite unmarried mother, while non-conformists were wary of any loosening in sexual attitudes. The moral guardians comprised a formidable redoubt. In 1925 the socialist feminist Dora Russell castigated the London County Council in her book *Hypatia* for turning down 'the suggestion of sex-teaching in elementary and secondary schools'.[73] Four years later the writer Vera Brittain complained in *Halcyon or the Future of Monogamy* (1929) that the London County Council was still rejecting sex education. Exasperated by 'the superstitious identification of virtue with ignorance',[74] Brittain quoted the American campaigner for birth control, Mary Ware Dennett: 'At present sex knowledge is being conducted on a boot-leg basis'.[75] However, while rebels in the Labour Party and the Women's Co-operative Guild challenged violence and rape in marriage and argued for sex education, for the rights of unmarried mothers, and control over fertility, the majority of Labour women pushed diplomatically for the democratic equality of companionate marriage. Radicals and reformers alike were confronted by a gap between their aspirations and lived realities.

Dora Russell was distressed by 1920s working-class women's low expectations of sexual pleasure. Women told her, 'He doesn't bother me', or 'He bothers me all the time.' She reflected: 'They evaded sexual relations as far as they possibly could because they were terrified of having more children. Rejecting their husbands' advances was the only means they had of protecting themselves.'[76] In *The Woman in the Little House* (1922), the popular writer and journalist Leonora Eyles quoted a woman as saying, 'I shouldn't mind married life so much if it wasn't for bedtime.'[77] From talking to working-class women Eyles deduced that much sexual unhappiness arose because the education they had received from the church, from schools and from the press was completely inadequate. This was compounded by material circumstances: bad housing, bad food, a harried, rushed life and too many pregnancies.[78]

It was also the case that working-class women, having been defined by the Victorian middle class as more animal than the refined and lady-like middle class, aspired to a 'respectability' in which ignorance was the mark of virtue. For working-class men who shared the same assumptions, the implications were frustrating. A collier confided to Eyles: 'A nice girl like Kit – she knows nothing, and it makes it blooming hard for a fellow with a girl like that – the way they lead you on without knowing where they are going.'[79] The dread of pregnancy also contributed to women's fear of sex. Annie Williams, a young Welsh woman in service in 1920s London, relates how ignorance fostered a complicated mix of desire and anxiety. She slept with her future husband Douglas before they married: 'And he used to say that I was the hot bitch then, because I used to plead with him to stay.' They used withdrawal, and 'Every month it was murder, I was waiting for my periods and all this, and I thought the only thing to do is that I'll have to get married, you see.'[80]

The socialist paper *Lansbury's Labour Weekly* provides intriguing glimpses of the sexual uncertainties of young working-class men and women in the 1920s. 'Martha', who wrote on 'Problems of Real Life', took a stern line. In 1925 she rebuked 'a most foolish and mistaken young man' who had written in about his 'problem'. 'You *can* control yourself if you want to. The trouble with you and boys like you is that you don't want to. You think that girls are only made for your convenience, and that every impulse is to be followed to the bitter end.' She referred him to Kipling's advice to get a large hoe and shovel and to dig until he 'gently perspired'.[81] In contrast, Leonora Eyles aimed to popularize some of the ideas of the earlier generation of sex reformers like Havelock Ellis and Edward Carpenter for a 1920s audience, by serving them up in the idiom of romance literature. She assured her labour readers that sex was not just for procreation, and warned that sexual denial could lead to 'nervous breakdowns' and 'neurasthenia'.[82] In March 1925 she called on women to value their bodies: 'Not many women nowadays think half enough of their bodies. They think that bodily love is just one of the side-issues of marriage, part of the man's "rights". What tragic nonsense. If only a woman could realise that this is something tremendous that she is bestowing, her man would think so too.'[83]

That September she resolved to tackle 'Doing Wrong' because so many young people were writing in about sex, although 'I know my older readers don't much like me to discuss it, and although George Lansbury tells me to do so as rarely as possible.' She remarked that since the war, 'so many ideas have gone by the board'. Young people were saying, '"The love of the body is a happy and beautiful thing. Why should I deny it? Why should I wait till I am married?"' The main reason Eyles gave women for waiting was the terror of having an illegitimate child who would be looked down upon, because they had 'given way' to their emotions. Eyles adopted an intimate and subjective voice to get alongside her readers: 'And we are all having such a devil of a fight with our emotions, and most of us are getting on top of them, so that we hate those who can't control themselves. There may be a little jealousy in it – I don't know.' After this laborious preamble, her own opinion was startlingly subversive. 'I do most honestly say that I see no wrong in the love of two young people for each other. And I don't see any logical reason why a civil or religious marriage should make holier something already holy.' Then, quickly hedging, Eyles added that she could not advise sexual intercourse, because young people often did not love the actual person but the bodily 'thrill'. Bodily thrills, it was implied, were a step too far. Moreover, Eyles pointed out pragmatically, following through on the 'thrill' could tie people down. Instead girls should regard their bodies as a 'beautiful secret'.[84]

The sexual freedom of the 1920s was implicitly framed within an assumption that heterosexuality was the norm. Though many women in reform circles in the late nineteenth century and early 1900s had been involved in relationships with other women, their sexual choices were necessarily discreet. Ironically, for women attracted to other women, the bohemians' success in disseminating sexual disclosure into mainstream culture would prove to have disadvantages. Margaret Anderson, a friend of Emma Goldman's and editor of the *Little Review*, a journal which pioneered work by the modernist avant-garde, had lived with her lover Jane Heap, but retreated to a utopian colony in New Jersey after the war. During the 1920s several lesbian writers and artists joined the literary coterie Natalie Barney had established in Paris. They were partly fleeing the commercialization and standardization of their own country, but Paris held another attraction. In Andrea Weiss's words, 'It left its foreigners alone'.[85]

Shari Benstock suggests that Gertrude Stein's interest in subverting 'grammar' was partly about her own efforts as a lesbian to shift the parameters of gender. Stein's story of her encounter with her lover and companion, Alice B. Toklas, in 'Didn't Nelly and Lilly Love You' in 1922, jumbles 'he', 'she', 'we' and 'I'.[86] Even those within her own milieu could find this bewildering. As Andrea Weiss observes,

> The resulting ambiguity could be maddening to some, as it was to Natalie Barney, who nonetheless realized that Gertrude's 'obscurity' functioned as 'the better part of discretion'. Gertrude's seemingly

opaque style made possible her 'improper' and audacious subject matter, so carefully disguised at times that the lesbian centre of her writing was never fathomed. Having read steadily through 'Didn't Nelly and Lilly Love You', Natalie Barney claimed she couldn't 'make out whether they did or didn't'. The chances being two against one they didn't.[87]

If ambiguity enabled an avant-garde to explore sexual alternatives, there remained the question: what about the rest? By the 1920s women in 'advanced' circles could obtain sexological material fairly easily, but for the majority there was a lack of information about lesbian sexuality. The furore aroused by Marguerite Radclyffe-Hall's *The Well of Loneliness* was partly because the book reached a middlebrow audience. The trial meant that both the book and its author came to be defined as notorious. However, notoriety also made for visibility, and launched a lesbian sub-culture in a Radclyffe Hall idiom.[88]

The crystallization of an explicit lesbian identity threw into new relief relations between women in which sexual feeling was amorphous and fluid. The British writer Vera Brittain, her husband Gordon, and close friend Winifred Holtby, all lived together from the mid-1920s. The arrangement was most convenient for Vera, though sometimes tense for Gordon and Winifred. It looked as if a crisis was looming in 1929 when Gordon decided he wanted to have an affair. Affairs, declared Gordon, were perfectly modern. Vera Brittain's letter to him reveals the complexities of 'honesty' and the psychological contortions which could ensue when the personal collided with the political. Vera the modern woman accepted Gordon's point about affairs; her concern was that her efforts to demonstrate that marriage and a career were perfectly possible would be jeopardized. Gossip might 'smirch or spoil or render less dignified . . . our relationship [and] the success of our marriage matters to the world, to society, to politics, to feminism . . . one happily married wife and mother is worth more to feminism . . . than a dozen gifted and eloquent spinsters'.[89] So many men had died in the war that marriage had become a competitive achievement. It enabled a modern woman to hold advanced views yet keep her mainstream middlebrow audience.

Vera Brittain's *Halcyon or the Future of Monogamy* was published in 1929, just after *The Well of Loneliness* had been banned as obscene. Though Brittain was not enthusiastic about the novel, she remarked that its censorship indicated a fear of enabling 'women with homosexual tendencies to recognise and understand them'.[90] Brittain argued that the trial, along with the attempt in the US to ban a pamphlet on sex by the birth controller Mary Ware Dennett, indicated that a rearguard reaction was consolidating.[91] Despite the extraordinary shifts in attitudes and behaviour during the 1920s, radical women found themselves uncomfortably isolated and still exposed to attacks from their opponents on several fronts. The space gained for the expression of sexual heterodoxy was exceedingly fragile.

The 'modern' feminist women of the 1920s responded by stressing the need to change education and culture. They defined themselves as members of an emancipated minority, but they were in a vulnerable situation for many women did not accept the sexual changes they were advocating. As the impetus of the suffrage movement declined, this sense of belonging to a specific, distinct type accentuated the divide between them and other women. 'Moderns' were inclined to assume that sexual knowledge and experience gave them an edge. In 1927, Dora Russell insisted: 'Women *are* unsexed at present by a steady and merciless process of elimination that leaves them atrophied or self-denying, advocating repression for others. Perpetual watchfulness against the snares of sex dries in them the springs of affection and sympathy.'[92]

Sexual competition is highly combustible, and this categorizing of other women as sex-starved infuriated anti-feminists and feminists alike. An irate Charlotte Perkins Gilman protested against the 1920s' 'wild excitement over sex'. By accepting they were 'just the same as men', she considered that women were having to adapt themselves to 'the overdeveloped sex instinct of men'. She was of the opinion that modern feminists were misleading women with new inventions like psychoanalysis, a theory thought up by 'the ingenious mind of man' in order to retain the power that older systems of control 'no longer assured him'.[93] Whereas an earlier generation might have wrestled with the balance between inner and outer aspects of being and existence in religious or broadly spiritual concepts, the new generation was casting the dilemma in psychological terms. Their scrutiny kept raising those awkward questions about inner desires which did not 'fit' the outer framework of assumptions, contributing to a wider cultural uncertainty about the relationship between personal perceptions and public action.

Nevertheless, the 1920s saw a courageous and far-reaching redefinition of sexual radicalism which extended into the public sphere. Echoing the aspirations of free-love iconoclasts and new women, Crystal Eastman's

programme of demands launched at the feminist Woman's Party annual
meeting in 1921 sought:

> To rid the country of all laws which deny women access to scientific
> information concerning the limitation of families. . . . To re-write the
> laws of divorce, of inheritance, of the guardianship of children, and
> the laws for the regulation of sexual morality and disease on a basis of
> equality. . . . To legitimatize all children.[94]

In her 1926 *Concerning Women*, Suzanne La Follette connected women's
sexual freedom to a critique of culture. She asserted that 'the whole mass
of taboo and discrimination arrayed against the unwedded mother and
her child is the direct result of the subjection of women.'[95] Aware that
the unmarried mother was condemned by women as well as men, she
believed this was because marriage remained most women's only option.
The woman who did not marry threatened 'the economic value of the
"virtuous" woman's chief asset'.[96] The implications of the changes sought
by Eastman and La Follette presented a fundamental challenge to religious
institutions, to the family and to existing patterns of work.

Elsie Clews Parsons (American Philosophical Society)

The utopian impulse persisted too in the glimpse of a transformed sexuality. Against an old-style morality of duty and fidelity, in 1924 Elsie Clews Parsons asserted a new culture of 'reciprocity in passion, emotional integrity, and mutual enhancement of life'. The new sexuality she envisaged would be 'all kinds of relations for all kinds of persons . . . with respect or tolerance for the individual and without hypocrisy'.[97] Parsons turned her psychological understandings outwards in an attempt to theorize how a new sexual consciousness would arise. Denying that 'rationalistic propaganda' would bring change, she argued that external pressures such as housing congestion, fear of an over-populated world and the growth of urbanization would break down religious objections to non-procreative sex. She believed new forms of sexual culture had been held back 'because the technique of contraception is still in the experimental stage, perhaps because in popular consciousness the morality of contraception in itself is not fully established.'[98]

Birth control was the critical battleground.

4

'What Every Girl Should Know'

When, O, when will the great mass of humanity learn and realize that in ENFORCED MOTHERHOOD . . . is to be found the chief cause of the degradation that gives birth to human woe. When will they see that enforced motherhood is the curse resting upon and crushing out the life energies of woman; while on the other hand, the consciousness of being the mother of a DESIRED babe, a child conceived in a happy, a loving embrace, needs no other blessing, no other sanction, than such act itself bestows.[1]

When Rosa Graul made this passionate appeal against enforced mother-hood in her novel *Hilda's Home* in 1897, she voiced a subversive idea; that women should be able to exert choice over fertility. This concept of the individual woman's rights over her body would constitute an impor-tant strand in 'birth control' campaigns in the early twentieth century.

Ideas about 'voluntary motherhood' sprang from the radical individu-alist tradition of rights which exerted a wide-ranging influence on very different reform movements in the United States. Free lovers, feminists and social-purity activists alike debated voluntary motherhood – which did not necessarily mean supporting contraception. Indeed they were inclined to suspect that contraceptives would *restrict* women's control over their own persons, and instead favoured changing attitudes and practices. Celibacy, self-control, the woman as regulator of sex and non-penetrative forms of sexual pleasure were among the alternatives being proposed at the turn of the century.

Free lovers Lois Waisbrooker and Elmina Slenker were among those who distrusted contraception. In Waisbrooker's view, 'The sex fountain is the source of power and consenting to tamper with it to please man diverts that power to man's use.'[2] Elmina Slenker considered the solution to involuntary motherhood to be 'Dianaism' – the non-penetrative sexuality which she thought would stop all abortions and infanticides, and enable women to 'have none but wished-for children'.[3] The Heywoods were influenced by the leader of the Oneida Community, John Humphrey Noyes, who argued for intercourse without ejaculation or 'coitus reservatus'. They were, however, also prepared to support women's right to use contraceptives; Angela Heywood advocated the vaginal syringe from the early 1880s.[4]

Angela Heywood (Kate Sharpley Library)

In the late 1890s, when fierce opposition to both continence and Dianaism erupted in the pages of *Lucifer*, free lovers divided over contraception. Amy Linnett disputed the Dianaists' assertion that the 'free woman' only used contraception to please her lover, insisting that the desire for sexual relations was mutual and not confined to men. Linnett said contraceptives meant that a woman could 'please herself' sexually. Declaring a war of the generations, she attacked her older opponents with the tart comment, 'Perhaps the fact that I am not yet thirty instead of seventy has something to do with my feeling in this matter.'[5] Though the idea of a woman's right to experience pleasure had been part of early nineteenth-century radicalism, it was still an explosive desire for a woman herself to articulate in the 1890s. Linnett was breaking a powerful taboo in openly advocating contraception so that women could enjoy sex.

While feminist movements in both Britain and the US were extremely wary of topics which might damage their respectable image, 'voluntary motherhood' as a means of women exercising greater autonomy in sexual relationships was being raised. The daughter of the American radical feminist Elizabeth Cady Stanton, Harriot Stanton Blatch, wrote a paper on 'Voluntary Motherhood' in 1891, in which she placed women's control over reproduction in a wider social and economic context. Blatch contended that women should have control over conception and child-rearing, while also having access to a good education and means of financial independence. As she was living in Britain at the time and was in the middle of a difficult pregnancy, the paper was read to the National Council of Women of the United States in her absence.[6]

While proponents of voluntary motherhood put the stress on the individual woman's right to control her own destiny, from the early nineteenth century radicals had also argued that control over reproduction could benefit society, especially the poor. They based their case on the theories of the eighteenth-century economist, Thomas Malthus, who had maintained that fewer children would alleviate poverty. Annie Besant's popular tract *The Law of Population* (1877) approached 'limiting the family' as a social question and stressed how it would reduce poverty.[7] Jane Hume Clapperton drew on Malthusian ideas in *Scientific Meliorism and the Evolution of Happiness* (1885):

> The issue of artificial checks to reproduction promises, in my opinion, to effect eventually all that is desirable, and seems to me the *only possible method* by which society can reach to the foundation of its miseries, its poverty, its pauperism, and check these *at the source*.[8]

While some radicals accepted family limitation, others suspected that Malthusian population control substituted restricting fertility for changing the ownership and distribution of wealth. The argument continued on into the twentieth century. In the early 1900s, the Malthusian League's propaganda was explicitly targeting 'working men and women'; large families meant children could not be well cared for and the mothers' health suffered, while in the long term fathers faced more competition in the job market. Slanting its approach in an anti-capitalist direction, the League posited that the people who benefited from large families were:

(1) those who want to keep up *cheap labour*; (2) those who think an *enormous standing army* is necessary; (3) those who prefer that the poor shall always exist, so as to have a class ready to do all the disagreeable work of the world; (4) those who think that this world doesn't matter, and no matter how miserable we are here, we're sure of a good time in another world.[9]

Unlike the free lovers' individualist approach, the 'Malthusians', or 'Neo- Malthusians', put the economy, the state and industrial relations in the foreground, presenting sexual reproduction as an integral part of society. Instead of a discourse of rights over one's person, they emphasized the need for economic and social policies to control population. Despite efforts to combine the two ways of looking at fertility in the late nineteenth century, the conflict rumbled on into the twentieth.

Another influential current, the eugenicists, also focused on the social implications of reproduction, claiming that the reorganization of fertility was the key to national efficiency. Eugenic ideas had originated in the American utopian milieu where perfecting and controlling all aspects of life and social relationships had appeared to be a possibility. John Humphrey Noyes developed his own idiosyncratic approach to changing sexual practices at the Oneida Community in New York State (1848–1881). Concern about women's suffering in childbirth led him to seek ways of separating what he called the 'amative' side of sex from propagation. The result would be a system of tight cultural regulation over sexuality. Only the older men who had learned to have intercourse without ejaculating were permitted to have non-procreative sex with young women. The young men were confined to older women. Those who wished to have children applied to Noyes and a committee who decided which mates would be best for the community. The children were cared for communally. Though Noyes's selection process was haphazard, he bequeathed the idea of 'stirpiculture' to the free lovers who saw it as part of their efforts to perfect personal and social existence. The Heywoods were enthusiastic advocates and so was Moses Harman, who in 1901 asserted 'the right to be born well'.[10] This phrase circulated widely, and was being repeated by the municipal reformer Mary Beard as late as 1915.[11]

A term for the study of selective breeding, 'eugenics' was coined by the British scientist and geographer Francis Galton in 1883. The first cousin of Charles Darwin, Galton produced a social theory which complemented the competitive struggle for existence in the natural world. His aim was to produce 'better' people. Eugenics presented a supposedly scientific answer to social problems, and Galton's proposition that a better future could be secured for the whole nation by engineering reproduction possessed a strong attraction for the growing strata of middle-class professionals. In a period when the working class was pressing for change in the organization of production, eugenics provided an alternative promise of progress without seriously upsetting the status quo. The loaded question was, of course, who decided who was 'fit' and who was 'unfit'. Given their own breeding pool, eugenic theorists tended to equate 'fitness' with the white Anglo-Saxon middle class, and worried that the 'wrong' people were having the most children. There were thus two aspects to eugenic propaganda: positive and negative. On the one hand eugenicists wanted the 'best' stock to reproduce itself, while on the other they sought to restrain those they saw as 'unfit' from bearing children.[12]

The appeal of eugenics reached right across the political spectrum. It was adopted by social reformers, such as the Progressives in the US and the Fabians in Britain, who believed in the need for evolutionary change, but feared class conflict. It found favour too with imperialists concerned to strengthen the imperial race in Britain, while eugenic warnings about dilution and swamping played on the fears of Anglo-Saxon Americans facing the mass immigration of workers to the US. At the same time eugenics could be embraced as a positive force by feminists and socialists campaigning for better conditions of motherhood, while birth controllers and advocates of free love could similarly back up their cause with eugenic rhetoric. Eugenic arguments were mixed with environmental ones to support a variety of causes.[13] For advocates of mothers' pensions, mothers needed resources from the state in order to build up 'the race' and free women who chose their partners would, according to Charlotte Perkins Gilman, eliminate the lower type of male.[14]

On the other hand, the possibility of elite new women exercising choice by rejecting fertility could present a threat to eugenic plans. Harriot Stanton Blatch introduced a menacing observation into her 1891 paper on 'Voluntary Motherhood': 'more and more the best women turn from the work of motherhood and join the ranks of competitive labour, or seek in society and politics a field for the free play of their ambitions.'[15] This idea of a 'birth strike' intrigued utopian novelists in the late nineteenth century; it figures in *The Strike of a Sex* (1891), written by George Noyes Miller, the son of John Humphrey Noyes, and in Lois Waisbrooker's *A Sex Revolution* (1894) as a metaphor for women's sexual power.

During the 1900s, anxiety about a real 'birth strike' was causing widespread concern because the middle- and upper-class birth-rate was in decline. In practice it was tricky for the state to intervene in the procreation habits of the privileged, while negative eugenic propaganda against the 'unfit' tended to feed into a social panic rather than policy. However, Britain's 1913 Mental Deficiency Act did reflect eugenic attitudes. Children and young people could be classified as feeble-minded and moral defectives for failing in school and for delinquent behaviour. Delinquency included young unmarried women who became pregnant; it was commonly assumed that their children would be degenerate.[16] In 1915 Mary Beard recorded discussion about the segregation and sterilization of the 'feeble-minded' in the US, though doubts were expressed by women reformers about whether *all* unmarried mothers could be viewed as feeble-minded.[17]

Critical voices were being raised against eugenic authoritarianism from the 1890s. Lizzie Holmes, Lillie D. White and Voltairine de Cleyre all combated eugenic ideas among free lovers and anarchists, while Lois Waisbrooker, who had been initially enthusiastic, shifted her position after observing the popularity of eugenics among the Progressive social reformers in the early 1900s. She came to believe 'that as long as mothers were both independent and loving, eugenics could be forgotten.'[18] There was, moreover, dissent within the Progressive camp. Alice Hamilton's experience of working at Hull House from 1897 convinced her of the need for birth control. But she was not

> moved much by the plea that the upper classes are being submerged by the lower and that the poor must be kept from breeding too fast. We know that ability and character are not a matter of class and that the difference comes from the unfair handicaps to which the children of the poor are subject, and we would remedy matters by working for equality of opportunity for all children, instead of trying to encourage the propagation of one class and not of the other. The arguments for

birth control which most appeal to us are based on the welfare of the
women of the poorer classes and the welfare of their children.[19]

Instead of eugenics Hamilton invoked the old radical arguments of the
poor needing knowledge and power, coupling these with change in the
social environment that produced poverty.

Environmental rather than eugenic arguments prevailed among
socialists advocating birth control, on the grounds that it would help
working-class women and improve family life. Though some socialists
maintained that socialism would make contraception irrelevant, others
were beginning to think otherwise. In response to the demand for information, Julia Dawson, a columnist on the British socialist paper, the
Clarion, recommended a birth control tract in 1896 which demonstrated
how to make pessaries from cocoa butter and quinine.[20] The working-
class socialist and feminist from Derbyshire, Hannah Mitchell describes
in her autobiography *The Hard Way Up* how she decided to marry in the
mid-1890s because of 'the newer ideas which were being propounded
by the Socialists'. Among these new ideas was 'limiting the population
as a means of reducing poverty'. Pragmatically Mitchell combined the
social and economic case with individual rights: 'although birth control
may not be a perfect solution to social problems, it is the first and the
simplest way for the poor to help themselves, and by far the surest way
for women to obtain some measure of freedom.' As a young woman
Mitchell had resolved that she was not going to join the ranks of 'pretty
merry girls who had married on a small wage and whose babies had
come first'. She dreaded their destiny, which was to become 'slatterns
and prematurely aged women'.[21] Her aspirations were shared by other
thoughtful working-class women radicalized by socialism and feminism.
By the early twentieth century, the Neo-Malthusian Alice Vickery,
who was active in the propaganda drive in working-class areas of South
London, presented her audiences with both individual *and* social reasons
for birth control. Vickery also made a point of engaging with women
in labour organizations in 1912, addressing the Women's Co-operative
Guild in Tottenham, North London on how 'married persons' could
limit births.[22]

In the United States the penalties for propagating birth control information were so severe that only the most intransigent sexual radicals, such
as Moses Harman, were prepared to risk repeated prosecutions. Some
were broken by repression; in 1900 Ida Craddock committed suicide

rather than face another term of imprisonment.[23] However, by 1910 European Neo-Malthusian ideas were being debated in the American Socialist Party. The catalyst was Antoinette Konikow, a doctor born in Russia and educated in Germany, who contended that smaller families would enable workers to avoid extreme poverty and thus fight more effectively for social change. In 1913, Konikow used Engels's writings on reproduction to argue for the 'wonderful interdependence of the manifold factors of human life, especially the factor of sex relations with the basic ones of economics'.[24] This emphasis upon reproduction and production as linked structures complemented the individualistic strand in radicalism which emphasized self-possession. But Konikow's influence was limited, partly because many American Socialist Party members adhered to social-purity assumptions about sex, and partly because assertions of the individual's capacity to act held a greater appeal than her Marxist concepts of reproduction and production, which could appear abstract and remote. Many Marxists continued to oppose birth control because it was considered to be a diversion from the class war.

By the early 1900s, however, feminists, anarchists, anarcho-syndicalists and socialists in many countries were discussing the link between controlling fertility and women's control over their bodies, invoking Nietzsche's celebration of the will, sex psychology and anarcho-syndicalist ideas of control and direct action. Theories about reproductive freedom were transmitted through international networks which included Madeleine Pelletier and Hélène Brion in France, and Alexandra Kollontai in Russia, as well as Stella Browne in Britain. In Germany the League for the Protection of Motherhood and Sexual Reform approached reproduction as a totality, advocating chosen motherhood, contraception and maternity reforms.

Emma Goldman was quick to make the connection between birth control and women's sexual and social liberation. She had become convinced of the need for information about contraception while working as a nurse among immigrant women on the Lower East Side. In 1900, through her anarchist friend Victor Dave, she attended a secret Neo-Malthusian conference in Paris where she learned about the latest contraceptive methods. Though Goldman spoke in support of free motherhood and 'Family Limitation', she did not outline methods of contraception until 1915, because she knew it would mean jail and prevent her from supporting her numerous other causes.[25]

Goldman influenced the young Margaret Sanger, who in 1913 also sought Dave's advice in Paris. From a working-class Irish Catholic family in New York, Sanger was only sixteen when her mother died after bearing eleven children. A resolve not to follow in her footsteps, and contact with poor women as a visiting obstetrics nurse on the Lower East Side, persuaded Sanger that birth control was a priority. In 1912 she wrote a series of articles on sex for the socialist paper the *Call*, under the heading 'What Every Mother Should Know'; when these were censored under the Comstock Law, the column appeared blank, with the defiant heading 'What Every Girl Should Know' followed by the word 'Nothing'.[26] Influenced by the anarcho-syndicalist group Industrial Workers of the World (IWW), in 1914 Sanger started her revolutionary magazine *Woman Rebel* which proclaimed sexual liberation along with the total transformation of society. In the June issue Sanger introduced the term 'birth control' as a counterpart to the IWW's slogan, 'workers' control'.[27] Arraigned under the Comstock Law for the contents of the magazine, Sanger defiantly produced the pamphlet *Family Limitation* which gave instructions on contraception and birth control methods

Left to right: Margaret Sanger in court with her sister Ethel
Bryne, 1916 (Sophia Smith Collection, Smith College)

and that October, before her trial, she fled to Europe. Feminists, socialists, anarcho-syndicalists and anarchists, including Mary Ware Dennett, Kate Richards O'Hare, Elizabeth Gurley Flynn and Emma Goldman, rallied to Sanger's support.

In her 1915 article 'Comstockery in America' in the *International Socialist Review*, Sanger put forward a class-based argument for birth control, declaring that her *Woman Rebel* had not seen it as a 'panacea' for all social wrongs but 'as the most important immediate step which should be taken toward the economic emancipation of the workers'. At the same time she made a gendered case for the rights of working-class women:

> The fewer children she had to cook, wash and toil for, the more leisure she would have to read, think and develop. That freedom demands leisure, and her first freedom must be in her right of herself over her own body; the right to say what she will do with it in marriage and out of it; the right to become a mother, or not, as she desires and sees fit to do; that all these rights swing around the pivot of the means to prevent conception, and every woman had the right to have this knowledge if she wished it.[28]

During her stay in Europe, Sanger studied the history of birth control campaigning, and in her article she paid tribute to Moses Harman as well as to the British Neo-Malthusians, Charles Bradlaugh and Annie Besant. She also connected to networks of sexual radicals and birth controllers, meeting Edward Carpenter, the East London anarchist Rose Witcop, and her free-love partner Guy Aldred, as well as Marie Stopes. A particularly close friendship developed between Sanger and Stella Browne, the socialist and feminist who had insisted in the *Freewoman* in 1912 that 'our right to refuse maternity is . . . an inalienable right. Our wills are ours, our persons are ours'.[29] When Sanger left Britain for Paris in September 1915, Browne wrote: 'I simply won't believe that I shall never see you again. We are going to meet again some day and in the meanwhile I'll do what I can, though it won't be as much as I should like to do . . . It has been one of the *biggest* and one of the *dearest* things in my life to have met you and known you.'[30] However, the most crucial meeting for Sanger was with the sex psychologist Havelock Ellis. Ellis fell in love with the vibrant young American, and his intellectual outlook tempered her anarcho-syndicalist views. He argued she should concentrate on birth control and criticized her faith in direct action.

Ellis was not the only reason for the shift in Sanger's thinking when she returned home. During World War One, the political atmosphere in the US changed dramatically. After America joined the allies in 1917 it was no longer just a matter of the mail being censored under the Comstock Law: thousands of American leftists were being given long prison sentences for opposing the war. The generally repressive climate persisted in the Red Scare of the post-war era; direct action tactics met with harsh reprisals. Several birth control activists served time in US prisons: Agnes Smedley, the socialist and feminist supporter of Indian nationalism, went to jail on charges of espionage and distributing birth control literature; as did Kitty Marion, a British suffragette who prop-agandized about contraception to her fellow prisoners. In 1919, after serving time in prison, in bad health and without the radical networks through which she had been able to distribute her magazine the *Birth Control Review*, Sanger modified *Family Limitation* by cutting out her recommendation of birth control as a method of direct social action, and eliminating references to abortion.[31] She also shifted to the position that birth control information should be given by doctors and nurses. In October 1919 the Supreme Court upheld Sanger's conviction, but agreed that physicians and druggists would not be prosecuted.

In 1922 Sanger developed an alternative framework for her approach to birth control, equating it with modernity rather than with workers' control over production. In her book *The New Motherhood* she challenged the masculine bias in sexual morality, and called on women to regard birth control and maternity as part of a wider self-determination which challenged established attitudes and conventions. While still acknowl-edging the need for a working-class movement, *The New Motherhood* was presented as part of a wider human cause: 'American womanhood is blasting its way through the debris of crumbling moral and religious systems towards freedom'.[32] Sanger gained an international reputation with her ideas of self-determination and self-fulfilment, though when she was about to go to India in 1924, Agnes Smedley cautioned her that 'it is better not to stress the woman freedom viewpoint until you have a foothold'.[33] Smedley, who was familiar with educated Indian attitudes, was aware that the benefits to 'the race' and the improvement of chil-dren were more acceptable to Indian Neo-Malthusians.

Although Sanger attracted the most attention, hers was not the only political trajectory in America. Antoinette Konikow was still campaign-ing and providing information on birth control, which she linked to a broader Marxist programme. In Massachusetts from 1919 Blanche Ames's Family Welfare Foundation connected birth control to the welfare of mothers and children, while the former arts and crafts enthusiast Mary Ware Dennett set up the Voluntary Parenthood League in the same year. Dennett held that both parents should decide about contraception, and used civil liberties arguments to defend their right to knowledge. She was suspicious of state-led population policies, opposed eugenics and believed information should be given not only by the medical profession.[34]

In 1915, dissatisfied with the existing works on sex hygiene, Mary Ware Dennett had written an essay for her two teenage sons. Published in the *Medical Review of Reviews* in 1918, it was then circulated as a pamphlet, *The Sex Side of Life: An Explanation for Young People*. Dennett gave a clear account of sexual intercourse, menstruation and birth control and was affirmative about sexual pleasure. 'Sex union is the very greatest physical pleasure to be had in all human experience, and it helps very much to increase all other kinds of pleasure also.'[35] In 1929 the cautious and respectable Dennett was tried for sending her pamphlet through the mail. The judge asked the carefully screened jury (anyone who had read Havelock Ellis having been excluded) to consider the 'probable reasonable effect' of 'The Sex Side of Life' upon the 'decency, purity and chastity' of 'the family which is the common nursery of mankind, the foundation rock upon which the state reposes'.[36] The jury's verdict of guilty provoked a storm of protest, indicating that public opinion was changing. Comstockery was being forced on to the defensive, though it fought a resolute rearguard action. Time would be on the side of the moderate demand for information about sex, but to reformers in both Britain and the US during the 1920s, obscurantism seemed powerful indeed.

In Britain, the legislative context was somewhat different from the American one. There was no equivalent to Comstock, and birth control ideas were being disseminated to the middle and working classes by the Neo-Malthusian New Generation League. Nonetheless the obscenity laws could be invoked. In 1922 the anarchists Rose Witcop and Guy Aldred deliberately tested the legal situation by publishing Sanger's *Family Limitation*. It was duly seized in their London home that December, and they were charged with distributing obscene literature. As working-class anarchists living in a free union, Aldred and Witcop were vulnerable and marginal. Despite support from Dora and Bertrand Russell and the Neo-Malthusians, *Family Limitation* was declared obscene. Dora Russell recalled in her autobiography, *The Tamarisk Tree*, that a lawyer explained this was probably because of a diagram which showed a pessary being placed in a vagina. The obscenity lay in the possibility that the finger was not the woman's own. An amazed Dora Russell remarked, 'Not having a sufficiently "dirty mind" this had simply not occurred to me.'[37]

In the foreground, left to right: Stella Browne,
Dora Russell and Bertrand Russell, 1923

In 1924 Rose Witcop published *Family Limitation* again, in defiance of the ruling, but she was an exception. On the whole left-wing birth controllers in Britain eschewed the direct-action tactics of the Americans, in favour of a campaigning approach within the labour movement. When, towards the end of 1922, Nurse E. S. Daniels from the Neo-Malthusian League was sacked from her job as a health visitor in Edmonton, North London, for giving advice on birth control, a campaign was mounted in her defence, mainly through the socialist press and women's labour meetings. In January 1923 Stella Browne wrote to the socialist magazine the *New Leader* insisting that birth control advice should be available in all maternity and child welfare centres. Dora Russell followed up with a letter on the Aldred-Witcop case for good measure, while the feminist

Evelyn Sharp, a friend of Edward Carpenter, told readers that opposition to birth control was a form of class prejudice.[38]

Throughout the 1920s Browne and Russell took the issue into labour women's organizations all over the country. Labour Party women voted over and over again at their own 'women's conferences' for birth control advice to be made legal in welfare centres, only to be defeated at the Labour Party conferences. The Labour leader Ramsay MacDonald insisted that birth control was a private, not a political, issue and the women's organizer, Marion Phillips, who appeared 'massive and terrifying' to a young Dora Russell, fiercely defended the Labour line: 'Sex should not be dragged into politics. You will split the Party from top to bottom.'[39] To socialist feminists like Russell, sex was already part of politics – but the Labour leadership were aware of their dependence on a strong Catholic lobby, and refused to budge on birth control. The eventual outcome would be a compromise. The Ministry of Health issued a memorandum in 1930 saying that information could be given to married women on medical grounds, if having another child would harm the woman's health.[40]

The shift in public attitudes to birth control in Britain had been greatly influenced by the popular impact of the writings of Marie Stopes. Among Stopes's seventy works were *Married Love* (1916), *Wise Parenthood* (1918), *Radiant Motherhood* (1920) and *Contraception: Its Theory, History and Practice* (1923), along with a polemical play, *Our Ostriches* (1923). The versatile Stopes even produced a film, *Maisie's Marriage*, in which a chubby, enquiring, wanted baby emerges from an unfolding rose. The censor cut the baby and the birth control message. Resolving to go beyond propaganda, Stopes set out to test whether there was a demand for birth control advice among working-class women. In 1921 she opened the first birth control clinic in Britain, in Holloway, North London, and the following year took out a writ for libel against the Catholic Dr Halliday Sutherland, who had said contraception was a plot to reduce the numbers of working-class voters. She lost the case but the publicity increased the sales of her books, making Stopes a national figure. Her celebrity, along with her popular style, enabled her to reach a mass audience.[41]

Stopes sympathetically addressed working-class women's fears about sexuality: 'You begin to dread what used to be your chief joy.' Explaining that 'men who are husbands need what is wrongly called the "husband's right"', she assured them that contraception would mean they did not have to be anxious 'that some bad girl will get him'.[42] She urged her women readers to ask for guidance at their maternity welfare centres:

> You *may* find that they refuse. But never mind; be brave, and think that even by asking for this information you are making it easier for other women in the end to get it, because until all the women in the country ask for this knowledge, until they insist on getting this knowledge, women and unwanted babies will go on suffering as they have suffered in the past, and are suffering now.[43]

Stopes was careful not to upset too many taboos at once. Unlike left-wing socialist campaigners she was not trying to transform society; her propaganda addressed existing attitudes. She always preferred to act as an individual, leaving the background organizing to others. In 1931, when the National Birth Control Association was formed, Stopes was on the executive along with experienced feminist campaigners and social investigators Dr Helena Wright, Eva Hubbock and Margery Spring Rice. But Stopes chafed under committee-style politics, declaring 'I'm not the Cabin Boy in this movement. I'm the Admiral.'[44] The other women listened politely and carried on regardless.

Eugenic ideas still permeated birth control propaganda. In *Radiant Motherhood* Stopes stated that fertility should be encouraged among those likely to 'give rise to healthy, well-endowed future citizens'; it should be discouraged among those likely to produce 'weakened, diseased or debased future citizens'. It was the 'duty of the community to make parenthood impossible for those whose mental and physical conditions are such that there is well-nigh certainty that their offspring must be physically and mentally tainted if not utterly permeated by disease'.[45] In 1919 Margaret Sanger also appealed to the eugenic lobby, by endorsing the 'elimination of the unfit'.[46] She accepted restrictions on the reproduction of the poor and the sterilization of the mentally ill, while resisting any measures to ensure a higher birth-rate among the 'fit'. Though she called for immigration control, Sanger did not, however, equate immigrants with the eugenically 'unfit'.[47] In *Woman and the New Race* (1920), which contained a preface by Havelock Ellis, Sanger stressed the environmental factors which had forced people to migrate and insisted that free motherhood was vital for the 'foreign and submerged mother . . . to enable her to prevent bringing to birth children she does not want'. She maintained that free motherhood 'withholds the unfit, brings forth the fit; brings few children into homes where there is not sufficient to provide for them'. Sanger envisaged an 'American race containing the best of all racial elements', which she thought 'could give to the world a vision and leadership beyond our present imagination.'[48] In Britain, Stella Browne gave the eugenic case for birth control an unusual twist by declaring birth control would 'produce a new race fitted to carry out Communist and Feminist ideals.'[49] Browne saw the individual making the choice, not the state. In bolstering their case with eugenic theories, birth controllers assumed that controlling reproduction would result in progress and a better society.

However, the repressive implications of eugenics were also challenged within the birth control movement. The Workers' Birth Control Group, formed in 1924 by socialists including Dora Russell, was anti-eugenics. Russell commented in 1974, 'You usually found that the so-called worst stocks were the poorer people and for that reason we completely dissociated ourselves from eugenics groups.'[50] By 1926 the British Communist Party paper the *Woman Worker* had come around to supporting birth control, as a way of helping working-class families out of poverty and freeing women for engagement in political activity. But eugenics was ridiculed: 'Some say we breed too many lower class humans – the unfits who go on the rates – that's you and me Flo! Not a word about the unfit conditions which produce the "unfits".'[51]

In the United States, progressive African Americans were faced with a dilemma, because eugenic arguments were used to restrict the black birth-rate. The black nationalist Marcus Garvey rejected birth control, which he believed would lead to the extinction of African Americans. W. E. B. Du Bois opposed 'eugenic sterilization', but argued in 1921: 'the future woman must have a life, work and future independence. . . . She must have knowledge . . . and she must have the right of motherhood at her own discretion.'[52] Birth control information was carried in the black press, and discussed at meetings. In 1918 the Women's Political Association of Harlem called upon black women to 'assume the reins of leadership in the political, social and economic life of their people', and announced that birth control was to be one of the issues debated.[53] Birth control was also treated sympathetically by black women novelists Nella Larsen and Jessie Fauset, who protested against the assumption that a woman's place was at home producing a large family.

In Britain and the US, the birth control clinics and the propaganda of birth controllers revealed a widespread desire among women to control their fertility. Amidst all the uncertainty about sexuality and identity in the 1920s, one thing was clear – many women wanted birth control. When Leonora Eyles got a job on *Woman's Own*, one of the new mass-market women's magazines appearing between the wars, her secretary Jessie Stephen remembered how any article on birth control would be followed by floods of mail.[54] Stephen was a veteran of the pre-war Glasgow suffrage and socialist movements; she had worked with Sylvia Pankhurst as a birth control campaigner immediately after World War One, and had then joined the Workers' Birth Control Group. She belonged to a network of working-class women active in the local campaigns for birth control and in the new clinics springing up around the country. They linked class with gender, rejecting any lingering suspicions of Malthusianism, and presented birth control as part of a wider labour movement struggle. Mrs Lawther from Blaydon, Co. Durham, urged miners to support the Labour Party women's campaign for birth control advice in maternity centres, reminding them of the help women had given to them when they were on strike in 1926.[55] Attending a conference of labour women in Britain in 1925, the American socialist feminist Crystal Eastman was delighted to note that when 'two firm young socialists . . . rose to explain that birth control was an economic issue that would not survive the social revolution, an earnest woman responded with adamant conviction, "Even in the coop-erative commonwealth I think a woman will want to choose her time and say how many."'[56]

Birth control's new visibility between the wars revealed the hidden suffering caused by abortions performed under dangerous conditions. Mrs E. Williams wrote in *Lansbury's Labour Weekly* in 1925: 'It is almost heartbreaking to listen to the women who come to me day by day seek-ing my advice. They tell me of the terrible amount of drugs which they have taken, enough to rot the inside of the strongest, to try to prevent a child being born.'[57]

Alice Hamilton had noted before the war how American working women did not regard abortion as a crime.[58] Similarly, in 1929 in *Mother England* Marie Stopes reported: 'In three months I have had as many as twenty thousand requests for criminal abortion from women who did not apparently even *know* that it was criminal.'[59] Marie Stopes used this as an argument for birth control; but Stella Browne had been an advocate of abortion as early as 1915, putting the case for its legalization in a paper to the British Society for the Study of Sex Psychology. She continued to argue for abortion as a necessary complement to contraception through the 1920s, and was a founder member of the Abortion Law Reform Association in 1936.

Dora Russell reflected retrospectively on the 'intense anger and frustration' she had felt 'at the attitude of the opponents of our modest requests on birth control' within the Labour Party hierarchy.[60] However, the case for birth control was not quite as 'modest' as she implied. Though it would find broad support as 'family planning' during the 1930s, its roots were in a decidedly unrespectable libertarian sexual radicalism and in the transformatory schemes of early nineteenth-century utopian socialism. Links to theoretical heterodoxy were evident in 1923 when Stella Browne went to lecture to workers in South Wales, telling her audiences that birth control was part of a new sexual ethics. She connected these new values to better housing, education and employment, and summoned Nietzsche, Ellis and Marx to support her case.[61]

Browne struggled to extend the syndicalist belief in willed action into the circumstances of human reproduction. She saw women's control over procreation as part of a wider process of creative, liberatory revolution. In 1922 in a letter to the *Communist*, she declared that 'Birth control for women is no less essential than workshop control and determination of the conditions of labour for men . . . Birth control is woman's crucial effort at self-determination and at control of her own person and her own environment.'[62] The slogans 'workers' control' and 'birth control' foregrounded active individual agency in the wider struggle to transform society. This new sexual politics of women's right to self-determination was surfacing in France and Germany among anarcho-syndicalist and left Communist women, who linked it to demands for workers' control over production. It was endorsed by the Soviet advocate of women's emancipation, Alexandra Kollontai, and influenced Sanger, Konikow and Eastman in the US, as well as Browne in Britain.

Birth control was also seen as a means of altering mores. In 1924 Elsie Clews Parsons suggested that changes in reproduction might effect the kind of changes in values and culture which Marxists assumed would arise from transforming production. She declared:

> Birth control makes possible such clear-cut distinctions between mating and parenthood that it might be expected to produce radical changes in theories of sex attitude or relationship, forcing the discard of many an argument for personal suppression for the good of children

or the honor of the family, and forcing redefinition of concepts of honor and sincerity between the sexes.[63]

Parsons was unusual in defining sexuality as an autonomous structure; however, other campaigners were alert to the significance of detaching sex from biological procreation. In *The Right to Be Happy* (1927), Dora Russell asserted that the confusion about sexual relationships could be greatly reduced by recognizing that the widespread demand for contraception required a change in how sex was regarded: 'Most of the trouble flows from our absolute refusal to separate the instincts of sex and parenthood in our social and economic structure'.[64] This separation would have far-reaching implications in the second half of the twentieth century for rethinking same-sex relationships as well as heterosexuality.

Several layers of heresy were thus wrapped up in the birth control bundle, and so was a fundamental contradiction. The idea of a woman's right to determine her own fertility was rooted in the individualist belief in the inviolability of the person. As the socialist feminist Teresa Billington-Greig put it in 1915, an undesired baby was 'a terrible infringement of the personal rights of the mother'.[65] This radical tradition was reinforced by the individualism which asserted the will and would have no truck with collectivities; nation, state, society, race or class. Rejecting eugenic arguments about reproduction contributing to the national stock, the editor of the *Freewoman*, Dora Marsden, remarked: 'It is surely a fallacy to hold that sex is primarily experienced with the motive of continuing the race. From the first protozoa up through the scale of life, it has been experienced for its own satisfaction.'[66] Against calls for women to reproduce for the good of society, Helen Winter stated 'As a Freewoman . . . I care nothing for the continuance of the race nor the reproduction of any man; my desire is to continue *myself*.'[67]

But there were other women, especially in the labour movement, who insisted that reproduction was a social as well as an individual matter. They accordingly adopted a very different approach in the 1920s, demanding state resources both for the provision of birth control information and for the welfare of mothers and children. This division was carried over into debates about policies that would benefit mothers in rearing children. How to balance the needs of individuals with the interests of society was an unavoidable conundrum. 'Now we can begin', declared the optimistic Crystal Eastman in 1920, after the vote was won.[68] Quite how was to prove less clear as the decade wore on.

5

Motherhood

When Dora Russell examined the maternal death rate in the early 1920s, the statistics were startling: 'We found that the *average* death rate of mothers was then four to five per thousand births. By contrast the death rate of miners from fatal accidents was 1.1 per thousand miners actually engaged in mining. Leah L'Estrange Malone and I then coined the slogan: "It is four times as dangerous to bear a child as to work in a mine . . .".'[1] Concern about infant and maternal mortality had been gaining momentum from the late nineteenth century, and by the early 1900s proposals for reform were circulating internationally. From 1904 the pioneering German League for the Protection of Motherhood and Sexual Reform presented integrated policies for child-bearing and child-rearing, while supporting birth control and abortion. After the 1917 Russian revolution, Alexandra Kollontai declared mothering a 'social function' and introduced eight weeks' maternity leave, nursing breaks at work, free pre- and post-natal care and cash allowances. When the International Congress of Working Women held a Maternity Convention in Washington DC in 1918, among its proposals were full maintenance payments and free medical care for six weeks, before and after childbirth. Along with birth control, motherhood had become a terrain of struggle.[2]

These large-scale, ambitious policies had grown out of an accretion of small interventions. In Britain the dangers associated with infancy and maternity had led charitable organizations to send 'health visitors' out to mothers in their homes during the mid-nineteenth century; by the 1890s this philanthropic activity was being taken on by local authorities. But it quickly became evident that while advice might be useful, poverty and the hard work women were doing, before and after giving birth, were contributing to mortality. As a result, ad hoc maternity and child welfare centres were set up; these not only gave advice but provided a range of practical services such as meals for pregnant women, mothers and young children.[3] An early initiative was taken by the socialist and feminist Charlotte Despard. After she was widowed, she settled in Nine Elms, South London, where her charitable attempts to educate her working-class neighbours on baby care and diet evolved into a mother and baby clinic which she set up in her own home, employing a nurse to assess the babies.[4] The understanding she gained contributed to the creation of clinics elsewhere.

By the early 1900s maternity and child welfare centres were being started by local health officers, by councils and by women's voluntary efforts. Funding came from the government, local councils and in some cases from the co-operative movement. Under pressure from women in St Pancras, London, the Medical Officer for Health opened a school for mothers along with a clinic employing health visitors. In 1908 the feminist and labour activist in the Women's Co-operative Guild, Sarah Reddish, a Poor Law guardian in Bolton, persuaded the local co-operative movement to follow the St Pancras example. She and other members of the Guild were aware of international experiments in maternity provision; they went to Ghent, in Belgium, to investigate 'the pioneering "Consultations for Mothers"', before establishing Bolton's School for Mothers, with tea and biscuits 'to show friendliness and good feelings'.[5] Within the year the co-operative movement found itself supporting five clinics which the local council was eventually persuaded to take over. In another Lancashire textile community, Stalybridge, Anne Summers, the charitable wife of a wealthy iron founder, formed a school to teach motherhood which turned into a Maternity and Child Welfare Centre.[6] The infant mortality rate in the northern mill towns was exceptionally high, and every practical initiative on behalf of mothers served to reveal the problems of mothers and infants.

A pattern emerges of voluntary action being gradually augmented by local authorities.[7] This was by no means an automatic process. Behind the scenes, Labour women activists energetically applied political pressure. Aware that 102 babies out of 1,000 were dying in the town during their first year and that a combination of poverty and illegal abortions put working-class women's lives at risk, the secretary of the Women's Labour League in Nelson, Lancashire, Harriette Beanland, wrote to the Labour Party in 1913 urging that 'Baby Clinics' be adopted as policy, complementing the Party's advocacy of school clinics and medical inspections in schools for older children.[8]

Despite the need for such provision, working-class women often felt a deep-rooted suspicion that medical experts would despise their own knowledge of mothering based on experience. Consequently, in 1913, when the Women's Labour League set up a mother and baby clinic in a working-class area of London, they were determined to show that information need not be given in a patronizing way. They argued for a clinic on the same grounds as the birth controllers, invoking the nineteenth-century radical working-class argument of the right to knowledge.[9]

The suffragette and socialist Sylvia Pankhurst was hostile towards state involvement and believed in self-help projects. In 1915 her East London Federation of the Suffragettes collected money from wealthy supporters and bought a pub, 'The Gunmakers' Arms', which they renamed 'The Mothers' Arms', using the former bar as a reception centre and providing medicines, milk and nutritious food, including fresh eggs from the country. Domestic science lessons were offered and a nurse employed to weigh the babies and assess their progress. The Pankhurst venture pioneered combined provision: a nursery run on first Tolstoyan and then Montessori lines was housed in the same building. Self-help, however, proved problematic. Pankhurst's suspicions of the state forced her to depend on wealthy feminists in running these projects, which also absorbed a considerable amount of energy. The ELFS found itself tussling with the babies' inability to digest milk and with an embarrassing case in which a nurse was accused of stealing from the centre.[10] Problems such as these inclined reformers to seek state support for the maternity welfare centres, which spread rapidly in the early twentieth century; however, the existence of self-help projects like The Mothers' Arms undoubtedly helped to demonstrate the demand for provision.

Once established, a maternity clinic could become the basis for a network of services. Women devised schemes which became part of social policy provision, such as health visiting and 'home helps', who provided free domestic service for mothers after they gave birth as well as helping the elderly and ill.[11] Piecemeal local responses were inevitably uneven and women campaigners, linked through the Women's Local Government Society, began to press for systemization of provision both nationally and locally. Elected as Manchester's first woman councillor in 1908, Margaret Ashton persuaded the Council to establish a Maternity and Child Welfare Committee, which she chaired.[12]

Maternity welfare centres continued to act as catalysts for further change and, during the 1920s, were at the eye of the storm over birth control advice. However, the welfare clinics were not in themselves a solution to all the dangers of maternity. Gaps in medical knowledge combined with broader economic and social factors contributed to the maternal death rate. Local councils found it cheaper to set up a clinic than to deal with the more costly problems of the inadequate sanitary systems in industrial towns.[13] Nevertheless the whole range of voluntary measures, and their institutionalization, reinforced the argument of there being a social responsibility for reproduction, in relation both to maternity care and maintaining the future generation.

In the early twentieth century the Liberals were bidding for the male working-class vote through social reforms, and working-class women's organizations sought to ensure that women's interests were not overlooked. When the Liberals proposed legislation in 1910 on national insurance, the Women's Co-operative Guild began a campaign for non-wage-earning married women's maternity, sickness and invalidity to be incorporated. However, the bill which was drawn up did not include full sick pay for women, and it made maternity benefit the property of the man. While the Labour Party's Women's Labour League was prepared to accept this, the Women's Co-operative Guild protested, mobilizing 700 women on local councils and Poor Law boards, along with members of nursing and midwives' associations, health visitors and sanitary inspectors, to sign a statement insisting that maternity benefits should belong to women themselves. Eventually Lord Robert Cecil, a Conservative sympathetic to women's issues, amended the Bill to enable the husband to receive the benefit on the authorization of the wife.[14]

World War One was the turning-point in agitation for state support for maternity. Panic about racial 'degeneracy' contributed to a public mood which enabled labour organizations to push for reforms. Breaking the silence around pregnancy and childbirth, the Women's Co-operative Guild published *Maternity: Letters from Working Women* (1915), edited by the indefatigable Margaret Llewellyn Davies. Far from idealizing motherhood, the writers documented how they dreaded the arrival of another baby. They recorded miscarriages, infant deaths and the lack of time to rest. Their moving testimonies intensified concern about maternity.[15] Suddenly in wartime, mothers having babies and the survival of infants became a matter for 'the nation'. In 1915, municipalities were given power to set up maternity committees. Three years later the Maternity and Infant Welfare Act empowered local authorities to finance services such as maternity hospitals, hospital provision for children under five, home helps and nurseries for children under five without fathers. From 1919 grants were also available for voluntary groups doing similar work. As a result, in post-war Britain a patchwork of state and voluntary services would be co-ordinated by the Maternity and Child Welfare Committees.

Even though the wartime state's welfare provision had developed in a top-down way, a strong democratic current ran through the labour movement, and this was braced by a gendered class feeling. The Women's Co-operative Guild and the Women's Labour League reckoned that neither men, middle-class women, nor the state could be relied upon to safeguard their interests, and pressed for working-class women's representation on the Maternity and Child Welfare Committees. Consequently the demand for state resources merged with the resolve to influence the services provided. The long, hard struggles for maternity provision bred both profound fortitude and a sense of democratic entitlement which enabled labour women's organizations to carry on defending services right through the 1930s depression.[16]

In 1890s America, the cause of maternal welfare was taken up by large and powerful charitable organizations. The Charity Organization Society in the US, as in Britain, emphasized individual effort, admonishing mothers to adopt habits of order, cleanliness and thrift. A coalition of club women, suffrage and social-purity activists created the National Council of Women, and municipal councils of women were formed. The Mothers' Congress of the Christian League for the Promotion of Social Purity and the Woman's Christian Temperance Union combined charity with a religious message, while the National Congress of Mothers dispensed advice on maternity, child welfare and the rearing of children through Parent-Teacher Leagues and women's clubs. The National Congress of Mothers sought to strengthen women's position in the home, while at the same time providing practical services such as kindergartens. From the 1910s they prioritized child health, setting up centres for babies, and began to seek state funding.[17]

Black American women reformers also intervened in efforts to improve motherhood. The National Association of Colored Women (NACW), formed in 1895, sought to reshape prevailing ideas of motherhood by making black women moral guardians of race uplift. In 1900, the Chicago Afro-American Mothers' Council told mothers to: 'Instruct their girls in all matters pertaining to their future welfare; not to let them roam the streets by day or by night, but they must keep close to their daughter and make constant companions of them, and wield such a refining influence over them for good that there will be no danger of them ever wandering from the path of rectitude.'[18] This extra sense of the need for motherly supervision arose in response to both the actual dangers of sexual violation facing young black women, and to racist stereotypes.

The formation of the social settlements enabled women to investigate and spread awareness of the needs of poor women and children. In 1909 Alice Hamilton conducted a Hull House survey of 1,600 working-class families, immigrant and native-born, which showed that infant mortality was higher in larger families. Progressive social reformers began, as they did in Britain, to press for training for midwives, education on breastfeeding and 'milk stations' to ensure pure milk in poor immigrant areas. They invoked ethical arguments to justify reforms for mothers and children and made an economic case by pointing to the long-term social costs of failing to intervene.[19]

Though African-American middle-class reformers placed a strong emphasis on mothers as a vital moral force, they were more likely than the white middle class to accept pragmatically that women had to earn money. Through their women's clubs, they therefore created a wide range of services for children and young people as well as mothers. These included day nurseries, kindergartens, orphanages, working girls' lodgings and extra schooling for children.[20] African-American women also formed settlements. The pioneering Clotee Scott Settlement in Chicago was founded by women's club member Clotee Scott, who described the settlement as 'the living home for the children while the parents are at work'.[21] By the early twentieth century, black settlements were inclined to stress the provision of improved social opportunities for children from poor black neighbourhoods rather than moral reform.

In 1912 the establishment of the Children's Bureau, headed by Julia Lathrop from Hull House, meant there was a small national budget for mothers and babies. Lathrop united conservative and progressive groups by focusing on infant welfare, and these links with people active on the ground enabled the Bureau's funds to reach out to the local level. In 1916 it launched National Baby Week with the backing of the powerful General Federation of Women's Clubs. As in Britain, the onset of war helped to bring infant and maternal mortality to the fore, and health clinics were set up. After the war Lathrop played a crucial role in the campaign for the 1921 Sheppard-Towner Act, which established federal welfare provision for instruction in prenatal and infant health care for mothers. A formidable coalition included the National Congress of Mothers and Parent-Teacher Leagues, the National Council of Jewish Women, the National Association of Colored Women, the Woman's Christian Temperance Union, as well as the Women's Trade Union League. Welfare policy in the United States was profoundly gender-inscribed. However, over the course of the decade the supporters of Sheppard-Towner and the Children's Bureau would face powerful opposition from the right to the very principle of public provision.[22]

While it proved particularly difficult in the United States to make the case that the well-being of mothers and children was the responsibility not only of individuals but of society, neither was it easy in Britain. Reformers used a range of ingenious tactics to overcome opposition. When in 1899 Charlotte Despard, serving on the Nine Elms School Board, was told by the Board's male members that there were no finances to feed starving schoolchildren, she responded with an upper-class form of direct action; bringing in saucepans, a cooking stove, tables and benches and presenting the Board with a fait accompli. She then used similar direct action to introduce medical inspection, providing a nurse from her own self-help baby clinic to diagnose schoolchildren's bad teeth and rickets.[23]

British women employed the same approaches to children's needs that they used around maternal welfare. They mixed voluntary and public provision, they extended their areas of activism from one issue to another, they established local Labour–Liberal alliances, and supported women's enfranchisement. Margaret McMillan, whose socialism was inspired by Ruskin and Morris, exemplified this strategic flexibility. Between 1894 and 1901 she campaigned as an Independent Labour Party member on the Bradford School Board for a school clinic and meals for schoolchildren. When the Conservatives' 1902 Education Act dissolved the School Board and assigned control over elementary schools to urban district or county councils which did not yet include women, the pragmatic McMillan worked to secure national School Medical Inspection with Robert Morant, a progressive Liberal reformer whom she knew from the London settlement, Toynbee Hall. Medical inspection became compulsory in 1907, partly as a result of the social panic about working-class health stimulated by the Boer War. However, the diagnosis of illness did not imply that the schools provided medical care, and McMillan agitated next for an Act requiring local authorities to provide treatment. The compromise was to be a clause in the Education Provisions Act in 1908 which enabled but did not require local authorities to provide treatment. With financial backing from the American soap millionaire Joseph Fels, and support from Robert Morant in the Ministry of Education, McMillan started her own clinic, first in Bow, and then from 1910 in Deptford, South London, by which time local authorities were able to pay for the medical treatment of schoolchildren.[24]

In combining self-help, state and charitable resources, McMillan was able to make use of national networks. In the case of nurseries, however, the move into the state sector would take much longer than it did for other kinds of educational services, such as medical inspection and school meals. In 1918 it seemed that an Act drafted by the Liberal historian H. A. L. Fisher would ensure nursery schools within the state system of education. But the transfer from the Board of Education to the Ministry of Health made nurseries costly, because of the high ratio of teachers to children, and few local authorities were willing to give grants. Nevertheless, McMillan's utopian vision of childcare influenced the teachers she trained. In 1928, the Bradford Education Committee accused Mary Chignell from the Deptford Centre of taking socialist propaganda into the nursery. They must have been mystified by her transcendent response, with its echoes of new-life utopianism. The nursery school, she declared, should bring a 'social rebirth, a reinterpretation of life and society, of human tradition'.[25]

In both countries, arguments endorsing society's responsibility for motherhood were being applied to demands for maternity grants, as well as for resources for information and centres. The claim for cash from the state extended to a demand for an allowance or 'pension' for mothers who were bringing up children, and this proved to be the most controversial aspect of the social maternalist case. Before World War One, British labour movement women had begun to debate the idea of a weekly payment by the state to mothers for every dependent child as well as payment in kind – free milk and bread – to supplement the work of the welfare clinics. Support for mothers' pensions also came from feminists and social reformers aiming to secure independence for women and to take low-waged working mothers out of the sweated labour market. The demand became a lifetime's cause for the feminist Eleanor Rathbone, whose work on the Liverpool Board of Guardians and efforts to organize homeworkers had convinced her that poverty, rather than bad mothering, perpetuated problems in working-class families.[26]

During World War One the government paid Separation Allowances to the dependents of men in the services.[27] Working-class women came to appreciate the regularity of these allowances, which also began to legitimate a mother's entitlement to resources from the state. In a 1918 letter to *The Times*, Eleanor Rathbone proposed 'a simple extension of the system which has worked so admirably during the war of separation allowances paid direct to the mother who bears and rears the children, and proportional in amount to their number'.[28]

Eleanor Rathbone

After the war, labour women's organizations pressed the Labour Party for a policy of payments to women who were without male breadwinners. This was adopted as Labour Party policy in 1918, although not the extension of 'pensions' to unmarried women, which some labour women were advocating. In 1924 Labour was about to draft a bill for Widows' and Orphans' Pensions but lost office before it could be implemented. Nevertheless the Conservatives, with an eye on female voters, introduced Widows' Pensions the following year.[29] In her 1925 *Hypatia* Dora Russell pressed for a wider allowance, arguing that women needed 'recognition of their work – the most dangerous of trades', by 'endowment from the community'.[30] During the inter-war period, Eleanor Rathbone and the Family Endowment Society continued to campaign for allowances for mothers. They were prepared to accept contributions from employers – a proposal opposed by trade unionists, who suspected the allowances would be used by capital as a means of controlling men with families and result in lowered wages. Their fears were not without grounds. In 1926 the Royal Commission on the Coal Industry recommended wage cuts for single men, accompanied by family allowances to supplement the income of men with children.[31]

Some feminist and socialist women suspected that instead of the greater degree of independence envisaged by Rathbone, Mothers' Pensions would be used to reinforce the notion that women's place was in the home. Her proposal also provoked the anxiety that men would vanish and leave mothers to parent alone, while support from a male breadwinner appeared a more attractive proposition to many working-class women than state handouts, which were redolent of the humiliating Poor Law system. However, Eleanor Rathbone and the Family Endowment Society did not give up, and after the General Strike and the miners' lockout of 1926, poverty was so acute that some of the suspicion of state benefits diminished. Between 1927 and 1930, a Joint Committee of the Labour Party and the Family Endowment Society took evidence; their final report recommended a state payment for children 'in order to lighten the burden that now falls on the mothers who are trying to bring up a family on a hopelessly inadequate income'. The emphasis had shifted, from women's autonomy as mothers to the relief of poverty. Nonetheless the report was free of the judgemental condescension which had characterized the Poor Law:

> We are convinced that the money so disbursed would be spent both wisely and economically, since it is our view the mothers themselves are best able, because of their experience and training and their overwhelming personal interest, to apportion this expenditure in the way most calculated to secure the well-being of their children. No public authority, can, in our view, make money go as far in the provision of food, clothing and healthy surroundings, as can the mothers who have learned economy in the hard school of experience.[32]

The Committee wanted the state allowances to be paid through the Post Office, and to include illegitimate as well as legitimate children. In

1945 Family Allowances were finally to be introduced on these terms, as a universal benefit which avoided the shame of Poor Law provision.

Similar debates were taking place in the US. Before World War One, the need for state allowances for mothers and children had been identified by networks of women's civic groups including the General Federation of Women's Clubs and the National Congress of Mothers, as well as by Progressive reformers around settlements such as Hull House.[33] Their policy proposals drew on direct experience. The social reformer Mary Beard described how observation of the ineffectiveness of charitable relief for widows with young children led to 'a demand for public aid for mothers', because otherwise the children would be cared for in a few charitable 'orphan asylums' or put to work. She pointed to the cost of orphanage care as well as the social cost of 'broken-down physiques, undeveloped minds, wrong associations and delinquency'.[34] Clara Cahill Park, a member of the Massachusetts Commission on Widows' Pensions, said she had started out 'with a blind faith in philanthropic methods', but had become critical because charitable efforts were 'not exact, and not careful', or 'mitigated by that human sympathy which would atone for human faults'. She added, 'State aid, to my mind, is an advance, as showing the policy of the nation, to conserve its children and its homes, and in recognizing the mother as a factor in that campaign, for the welfare of all.'[35]

Although the mainstream feminist organizations did not endorse mothers' pensions, socialist feminists Crystal Eastman and Harriot Stanton Blatch, who were in contact with British feminists and socialists, pressed for payment for mothers, as did Katharine Anthony, who wrote the introduction to the American edition of Eleanor Rathbone's 1918 Family Endowment Committee report. Katharine Anthony was also familiar with German and Scandinavian debates, in which state endowment was envisaged as one aspect of a new approach to motherhood. She was among a minority of American reformers who argued for the rights of children born to unmarried women.[36]

Actual provision was to be circumscribed. Payment for mothers had been put forward as a policy proposal in 1909 at a White House conference on the Care of Dependent Children, with a proviso which was to be of considerable significance: payment was to go to the 'children of reasonably efficient and deserving mothers who are without the support of the normal breadwinner'.[37] Mothers' pensions were introduced on this limited basis in various states before the war. During World War

One, US women did not get separation allowances, though by 1919 thirty-nine states had created Mothers' Pensions schemes. These represented a major breakthrough in acknowledging that care for children was the responsibility of society as well as individual families. However, these small payments were to be used as a lever to enforce particular views of motherhood. As Gwendolyn Mink observes, 'evidence of smoking, lack of church attendance, poor hygiene, male boarders, or faulty budgeting, could result in withdrawal of a mother's allowance.'[38] Social workers exercised considerable power in determining who were fit mothers. The result in practice was that both foreign-born and African-American women were less likely to qualify than women of Anglo-Saxon origin.[39] During the 1920s, 'mothers' pensions' increasingly became part of social casework, erasing all traces of earlier concepts of universal entitlement. Even under the New Deal in the 1930s, when mothers' pensions were replaced by Aid to Dependent Children and administered by Roosevelt's Social Security Administration, they never acquired the legitimacy of contributory benefits.[40]

In both countries, the meaning of state endowment was interpreted in very different ways by its supporters. One strand stressed social efficiency. Reform around reproduction was presented as being in the long-term interests of state and society. As Eleanor Rathbone put it in 1918:

> After all the rearing of families is not a sort of masculine hobby, like tobacco-smoking or pigeon flying. If nations are to continue to exist they must reproduce themselves, and the cost of doing so must be paid for somehow by the nation.[41]

Other advocates stressed basic social needs, the possibility of economic independence, and greater honour and respect for mothers as the recipients of state endowment. In an Independent Labour Party pamphlet, *Socialists and the Family: A Plea for Family Endowment*, the 1920s birth control campaigner Dorothy Jewson insisted that 'Of all the services claiming attention and demanding national help and protection there is none of more importance to the nation than that of bearing and rearing healthy children.'[42] Another Labour Party activist, Dorothy Evans, said in 1925 that women wanted 'some form of remuneration for mothers for the state service of rearing children'.[43]

British labour women tended to couch their demand for state endowment in terms of mothers' contribution to society as a whole. However, in 1920 the American socialist feminist Crystal Eastman also stressed women's rights as individuals. Caring for children should be recognized as work 'requiring a definite economic reward and not merely entitling the performer to be dependent on some man'.[44] Eastman regarded motherhood endowment as giving women a choice between home and work, and argued that cash payments should be complemented by child-care and equality in employment. Linking mothering and employment, Eastman's propositions built in the possibility of extending women's capacity to determine how they should live.

Nonetheless, state payments troubled libertarian leftists in both countries. Ada Nield Chew argued in 1912 that the proposal would be utilized by the state to 'command obedience'.[45] In the US, Benita Locke took up the cudgels in Margaret Sanger's anarchist journal, the *Woman Rebel*. In a 1914 article entitled 'Mothers' Pensions: The Latest Capitalist Plot', Locke argued that such payments would restrict women's options. While conceding that Mothers' Pensions advocates were well-intentioned, she warned that the 'effect of social reforms . . . is often the reverse of that intended by their sponsors'.[46] Stella Browne, who supported family allowances, opposed Eleanor Rathbone's emphasis on marriage or the morality of the mother as conditions for receiving the allowance. She saw such stipulations as an inadmissible extension of the state's control over personal behaviour: 'Why should the child or children be made to suffer if its two progenitors refuse to turn a brief – though possibly worthwhile – illusion into a permanent incompatibility?'[47]

The push towards seeing motherhood as a social activity in which intervention was possible contributed to a growing self-consciousness about how to mother. Carrica Le Favre's *Mother's Help and Child's Friend* (1890) combined advice about bathing babies and letting fresh air into rooms, with exhortations about the importance of 'moral sunshine' in making for 'domestic happiness'. She stressed that women's rights involved responsibilities, and aimed to reconcile women to motherhood by raising the 'esteem' in which it was held.[48] The message of such mothering manuals, anxiously perused by the enlightened, was that motherhood was a skilled activity which had to be learned.

Calls on women to seek alternative ways of mothering proved particularly popular in the United States, where self-help health movements proliferated and 'mind-cure' flourished. Alice B. Stockham, a feminist interested in spirituality and free love, followed up her 1896 alternative sex manual *Karezza* with her 1911 *Tokology*, covering pregnancy, childbirth and infant care. Stockham mixed common sense with mind control. Pregnant women were advised to avoid 'tight lacing', to take thermal baths, to adopt 'fruit diets' and deep breathing, to have massages, walk upstairs, stride up hills, do gymnastics and, when the baby was born, to breastfeed.[49] Stockham exhorted them to live active, socially useful lives, and in the event of ailments or pain, to abstract their thoughts. She concluded *Tokology* with the assertion that the 'mind, the real self' determined life. Hence Stockham's advice to would-be mothers was: 'Learn to subordinate the body.' Both parents, in her opinion, needed to 'lose sight of selfish interest, and strive to the utmost for all conditions that shall favour the highest good of offspring, "for to be well born is the right of every child".'[50] Moses Harman's phrase was thus to enter that modern and popular genre – the childbirth advice manual.

The utopian promise of the ideal offspring lurked behind all these proposals for better mothering. In Charlotte Perkins Gilman's ideal future, the children are all mysteriously 'eager, happy, courteous'.[51] This faith in harmony extended even to infants; an optimistic Rosa Graul promised that anarchist co-operatives would foster exemplary babies. Precociously aware of how much they all were wanted, 'they were wonderfully good babies.'[52]

In the early twentieth century, the Swedish feminist Ellen Key's exaltation of the fulfilling aspects of motherhood exerted an international influence. Key's conception of expressive mothering combined social demands for childcare provision and state payments for mothers, with the individualistic assertion of a woman's right to fulfil her potential as a person. Key argued that women's difference from men should be the basis for the reform of motherhood, and that women's subordination was founded on their economic dependence on individual men. Her mystical celebration of mothers, elaborated in *The Century of the Child* (1900) and *Love and Marriage* (1904), redefined how to mother, and delineated how mothering could be endowed with new values.

Charlotte Perkins Gilman adopted a contrasting perspective, though she too wanted to change how mothering was seen and what it entailed. Gilman believed that the individual home confined women, and that they could make much better use of their mothering skills by moving outwards into society. In *Moving the Mountain* (1911), Gilman outlined the conditions necessary for her new motherhood.

a. Free, healthy, independent, intelligent mothers.

b. Enough to live on – right conditions for child-raising.

c. Specialized care.

d. The new social consciousness, with its religion, its art, its science, its civics, its brilliant efficiency.[53]

Gilman was searching for opposing social values to a competitive, male-dominated capitalism. She located these not in an ideal of existing mothering, but in the potential it contained. In her ironic utopian work *Herland* (1915), Gilman depicted an all-female community which had established a maternalist co-operative haven based on nurture. Three male visitors, accustomed to the struggle for existence and the confinement of mothering within the domestic sphere, were deeply puzzled:

> We are used to seeing what we call 'a mother' completely wrapped up in her own pink bundle of fascinating babyhood, and taking but the faintest theoretic interest in anybody else's bundle, to say nothing of the common needs of *all* the bundles. But these women were working all together at the grandest of tasks – they were Making People – and they made them well.[54]

Gilman argued for new conditions for mothers, while suggesting that mothering carried values which were relevant to men as well as women, and could be translated into a universal social alternative. Like Key, Gilman combined individual fulfilment with social reorganization and a vision of community. Her ideas were influential in Britain as well as in America. In the *Daily Herald* in 1912, Mabel Harding dismissed 'early Victorian platitudes about a woman's place being the home, and her only true vocation that of wife, mother and housekeeper'. She asserted, like Gilman, that the home was not 'encompassed by four walls, no longer is a woman confined to her own narrow circle'. Instead a woman now had duties to the 'bigger family of the city and the state'.[55]

Motherhood, for and against, aroused strong passions. While some radical women believed that changing motherhood was a crucial element in improving women's lives and position in society, others were wary of highlighting biological or cultural difference; they considered that concepts of a gendered citizenship for mothers undermined a universal right based on a common humanity. Moreover, amidst all the talk about socialization, it was unclear whether the aim was to enhance or minimize

mothering as an aspect of women's lives. For some women adventurers, it was simply a trap. In 1892, Lizzie Holmes's sister, the American
Populist and Secretary of the Kansas Freethinkers' Association, Lillie D.
White, advised women to ignore 'wifely and maternal ties and burdens'
and to 'unlearn . . . any duties of any kind to gods, men or communities'.[56] Writing in the *International Socialist Review* in 1911, Georgia
Kotsch, from the radical West Coast wing of the Socialist Party, considered that 'the mother function' and the 'mother instinct' were the 'last
citadel' of masculine psychology's way of managing women.[57] The anarchist Voltairine de Cleyre similarly repudiated the mother instinct and
defended the childless.[58] A 1912 contributor to the *Freewoman* deplored
the way women tended to go to pieces intellectually when they became
mothers.[59] 'Beatrice Hastings' (Emily Alice Haigh), who wrote in the
avant-garde *New Age*, also held motherly nurture in contempt. Ticked
off by a proponent of breastfeeding, she exploded, 'I don't care a
tacking-thread whether women feed their children or not'.[60] She wanted
a bohemian, independent identity and sexual freedom.

The American socialist feminist Harriot Stanton Blatch tried to cut
through the polarities and the passion by arguing that the key question was how to balance work and mothering.[61] Similarly Ada Nield
Chew carefully distinguished between domesticity and mothering in the
Freewoman in 1912: 'The confusion arises from the fact that the maternal
part is mixed up in some minds inextricably with what are regarded as
equally sacred duties – duties to houses and clothes, to pots and pans and
to food. We can never think clearly about this matter till we accustom
our minds to regard women as individual human beings.'[62] In 1915 the
Greenwich Village bohemian socialist and feminist, Henrietta Rodman,
stressed the creative benefits of mothering: 'The baby is the great problem
of the woman who attempts to carry the responsibilities of wage-earning
and citizenship. We must have babies for our own happiness, and we
must give them the best of ourselves – not only for their own good,
not only for the welfare of society, but for our own self-expression.'[63]
Yet this enthusiasm for expressive motherhood did not imply constant
contact: 'The mother of the past has been so busy with her children that
she hasn't had time to enjoy them . . . The point is not how long but
how intensely a mother does it.'[64]

The problem was how to achieve the desired equilibrium. In practice,
women's personal solutions ranged from leaving children with relatives
or servants to living communally and sharing childcare. But by World

War One a few middle-class American feminists and reformers were raising the sexual division of labour, both in their own personal domestic arrangements, and as a social issue with policy implications. The consciously modern Crystal Eastman wanted fathers to be involved with looking after the children, though her proposition of 'marriage under two roofs', whereby the man and woman lived in separate places when children arrived, suggests that sharing childcare would have presented difficulties for the unconventional semi-detached couples.[65] The connection between changing childcare and changing both men and women's work was acknowledged in 1918 by 300 delegates from social reform organizations at the Women's Legislative Congress in Chicago, who argued for a shorter working week 'so the father can give personal care to the child'.[66]

By the 1920s, progressive child-rearing theories in Britain were also beginning to count fathers in. However, when it came to the crunch, old habits died hard. Leonora Eyles described this graphically in the mid-1920s. When baby wakes and cries:

'Feed him,' says father, and turns over dragging most of the clothes with him. Mother, afraid of a row, and distressed at spoiling the breadwinner's night, feeds him. And in an hour's time he wakes again, and is sick. Usually by this time both mother and father are wet and uncomfortable. Mother sleeps with one eye open, so that father shan't be disturbed. And next day she gets up at the call of the alarm clock, red-eyed, fuzzy-headed, nervy, tired to death to begin the new day.[67]

Some supporters of childcare provision implied that mothers were not up to the task. Children, it was thought, would benefit from seeing less of their biological mothers. Charlotte Perkins Gilman's conviction that isolated individual mothers in the home were so backward and inefficient that they held back their children, led her to argue for collective forms of childcare outside the home. She believed that once small children were in contact with trained and enlightened carers, they would find alternative role models with a wider view of life and society.[68] In *Women and Economics* (1898), Gilman criticized the attitude of 'absolute personal ownership' towards children, making the rights of children another plank in her platform for change in the home.[69] In 1912 the American socialist Georgia Kotsch advocated collective responsibility for childcare on similar grounds, stating that under socialism 'the rearing of the children' would not 'be left to the haphazard chance of the individual mother', but be recognized as a specialized activity.[70] Kotsch, echoing Gilman, firmly told mothers they had to acknowledge their children's rights as individuals to the best form of upbringing. This meant accepting that they were not always the best carers. Mothers for their part had a duty to 'employ time' hitherto devoted to their babies in other ways. 'That baby which you call yours is not wholly yours,'[71] Kotsch informed them.

In the same year, Ada Nield Chew put the case for nurseries in a less authoritarian style. She proposed 'beautiful baby gardens, quite near to the homes of the parents', so babies could get the best of both worlds, adding, 'A baby loves and thrives on a sunny mother, and the company of other babies is as dear to its baby soul as is the company of other children as they grow older.'[72] Chew regarded the nursery as an opportunity for small children to associate, as well as helping mothers. However, leading Labour Party women Marion Phillips and Averil Sanderson Furniss endorsed nurseries in 1919 because they gave 'children a better training both for mind and body' than working-class mothers could. In their view, it was 'not good either for mothers or children that the little ones should always be under the care and within the sight and hearing of their mothers'.[73]

Women adventurers were divided on how children should be cared for and educated. While one wing emphasized the need for rigid training by applying method and system in raising the perfect offspring, others favoured libertarian approaches which derived from anarchist practice and from progressive educational theory. Louise Michel, the anarchist survivor of the Paris Commune, had established a free school in London when she was released from imprisonment; a teacher there, Agnes Henry, equated kindergarten educational theory with anarchism.[74] Learning through observation and 'doing', along with the cultivation of the senses, were being advanced by progressive educationalists in many countries as alternatives to training, discipline and rote-learning. Such ideas were influential in both America and Britain. In *Moving the Mountain* (1911), Gilman conceived a utopia of baby gardens and child-centred communities where none of the children wore glasses, because 'Much of the instruction was oral – much, very much, came through games and exercises; books, I found, were regarded rather as things to consult, like a dictionary, or as instruments of high enjoyment.'[75]

Margaret McMillan's centre for children in South London constituted a hybrid, combining Louise Michel's anarchist ideas of spontaneous development with the educationalist Édouard Seguin's enthusiasm for garden schools, plus a dash of regulatory social hygiene.[76] Her approach influenced both the state nurseries in Britain and the progressive school movement. In 1926 Dora and Bertrand Russell took their children to McMillan's 'open-air nursery', and applied her approach in the school they started. The Russells, who had studied the theories of Pestalozzi, Froebel, Montessori and Piaget, as well as the psychological work of Freud and Adler, thought that children should not become bookish and academic too early. In Dora's words, 'There is a period of doing, feeling, observing the world'. They decided the Montessori material was too rigid, preferring 'the McMillan style of providing the child with all kinds of materials by means of which it would find its own way'.[77]

Margaret McMillan

In the early years of the twentieth century, progressive theories about child development were part of a wider challenge to educational methods mounted by the American John Dewey. Influenced by Hull House, Dewey linked education to a wider social awareness and stressed learning through 'doing'. Charlotte Perkins Gilman gave this approach a gendered slant. In *The Home* (1903), she pointed out that children learn not only through formal teaching but through example. In order to break the pattern by which girls perpetuated the isolation and restricted outlook of the mother, they needed to experience a different upbring-ing.[78] In *Moving the Mountain* (1911) she envisaged that education could minimize gender divisions: 'from infancy to adolescence – all through these years of happy growing – there was nothing whatever to differenti-ate the boys from the girls! As a rule, they would not be distinguished!'[79]

Margaret McMillan Nursery Camp

Anarchists were especially critical of the authoritarianism in exist-ing schooling. In 1892 Lizzie Holmes described schools as fostering 'blind obedience'. She wanted an alternative which would encourage 'the development of the human faculties, the rounding out of indi-vidual character . . . [and] the opening of the way to fresh and fullest activities'.[80] Anarchists regarded education as a process of drawing out spontaneous capacity, and recognized the value of play and closeness to nature. Voltairine de Cleyre imagined boarding schools in the country-side, linked to farms where children could 'learn in free contact with nature'.[81] In 1909 Goldman echoed Lizzie Holmes's approach, declaring that 'if education should mean anything at all, it must insist on the free growth and development of the innate forces and intelligence of the child'.[82]

Both anarchists and socialists stressed the need to create a new culture. Annie Davison remembered her non-sectarian father sending her to the Partick Socialist Sunday-school in Glasgow, as well as to the anarchist one where she learned about fellowship, internationalism, the rights of labour, love, truth and justice.[83] The American working class created a similar counter-culture which prefigured new relations of fellowship; each wave of radical immigrants brought their own customs. In the Finnish socialist halls, children not only learned formally, they experienced a big alternative family and called all the adults 'aunties' and 'uncles'.[84] Implicit in the alternative culture of the socialist and cooperative movements was the idea that the upbringing of children was a social responsibility. Though not setting out to change gender roles, this radical culture did imply that both mothering and fathering could change.

'Modern' feminists of the 1920s were beginning to argue that new mothering required not simply the practical participation of men, but a new form of fathering. In *The Right to Be Happy* (1927), Dora Russell made the case for a democratic, shared parenting: 'If we are to admit rights of parents at all, then those rights must be for father and mother, if both desire them.'[85] Along with other 1920s modern women, she searched for a cultural solution to fixed gender ideas about women's peculiar propensity to care for children. 'What is needed for mutual happiness seems to be not a decline of paternal or a mere intensification of maternal feeling, but the "fusion" of paternal and maternal "feeling"'.[86] She would find in her own life with Bertrand Russell that democratic parenting presented problems if a couple separated; power between men and women in society at large was not equally weighted. Moreover, though she wanted to reject the existing confines of the motherly role, Russell also wanted to validate mothers. She sought to overcome the tension by defining a new 'maternal feeling' which would be a self-conscious, rather than instinctive, force. 'Women are rediscovering the life of instinct in the light of scientific knowledge. But when they return to it they do so in a mood quite unlike that which tradition would teach them.'[87]

For Dora Russell, and for the American 'moderns' like Suzanne La Follette and Crystal Eastman, 'the new motherhood' required state resources and legislation along with economic independence and changes in working time. It also involved a new culture of sexual freedom and gender equality. They campaigned for practical reforms while trying to keep the way open for new definitions of mothering and fathering. However, their outlook was precariously situated, for the possibilities of transforming social relations were being assailed economically and politically. The most basic needs of women as mothers would be under threat in the depressed years of the 1930s.

6

New Housework: New Homes

In 1903 a jubilant Charlotte Perkins Gilman hailed two decades of progress in what she called 'household science' and 'home industry' – a sustained theoretical and practical reassessment of the home and women's domestic role which was reaching out into society. 'We are founding chairs of Household Science, we are writing books on Domestic Economics; we are striving mightily to elevate the standard of home industry.'[1] This 'household science' had been pioneered by Ellen Swallow Richards. A farmer's daughter and former schoolteacher, Richards became the first woman graduate from the Massachusetts Institute of Technology where she was later to teach. First published in 1882, her book, *The Chemistry of Cooking and Cleaning*, presented domestic work as a scientific area of study. Along with other inventors of the new academic subject of 'home economics', Richards regarded women's activity in the home as the basis for a much wider social responsibility for the lived environment. The new thinking dissolved the demarcations between the household and life outside the home. The world, she announced, was 'everybody's house' and consequently good housekeeping required a science of the environment. She found a new word for this: 'oekology', later simplified into 'ecology'.[2]

The inspiration for a science of the household came from direct contact with the broader problems of society. Among the pioneers was Gilman's mentor Helen Campbell who, along with Richards, founded the National Household Economics Association, which grew out of the Woman's Congress of the World's Columbian Exposition in 1893. The institutional framework developed from hands-on experience. Her involvement in the Populist movement during the 1880s led Campbell to establish a diet kitchen, then a school, while investigating working-class

Richards testing the algae on Jamaica Pond, Boston
1901 (Sophia Smith Collection, Smith College)

conditions in Washington DC. In the early 1890s she was in the feminist
wing of the Nationalist movement which was inspired by Edward Bellamy's
utopia, *Looking Backward*, before working closely with Gilman in the mid-
90s. Campbell's writing on poverty and housekeeping merged Ruskinian
ideas of the social economics of the household with the Progressive reformers' preoccupation with efficiency and the elimination of waste.[3]

From its inception, the new subject area of home economics contained a
strong emphasis on the practical relevance of knowledge. The early generation of social workers and social investigators, who began to work in the
slums of large cities during the 1880s, believed that their scientific approaches
to nutrition and hygiene could alleviate the poverty of the newly arrived
immigrants, drawn by the hope of jobs and prosperity to cross the Atlantic.
At the same time, home economics enabled women to assert a gendered
area of skill, while extending its scope. An impressive course in household
arts at Roxbury High School, Boston, in 1905, included the study of planning, building, furnishing, decorating, lighting, heating, plumbing, water
supply, waste disposal and sanitation.[4] By the early years of the twentieth
century the practical application of home economics was being disseminated

evangelically, not only through training schemes and conferences for specialists but through popular advice books and women's magazines such as *Good Housekeeping*. Ironically the new housecraft had a larger impact on a new middle-class constituency keen to improve domesticity, than upon the poor who had been the original targets.

Though home economics would be assimilated into modern housewifery, it also contained a critique of competitive market economics. For both Richards and Campbell, home economics was an integral element of an alternative approach to the economy as a whole which drew on John Ruskin's influential writings. Ruskin's organic concept of the household and his insistence that wealth was life challenged the model of competing atoms intrinsic to free-market capitalism. It gave priority to human needs, and shifted the motive force of production from profit to welfare. Thus responsibility for others became not simply a matter of personal ethics, but the concern of society. Instead of abstracting economics from social existence, Ruskin gave the household a pivotal significance which made it possible to make connections between differing spheres of life. In *Household Economics* (1896), Campbell theorized the economy of the home as comprising 'the link between the physical economics of the individual and the social economics of the state'. The household for Campbell was 'the parent of the state'. Thus the study of home economics, with all its ramifications, investigated the whole 'business of living'.[5] Between 1894 and 1895, when Campbell and Charlotte Perkins Gilman edited the magazine *Impress*, a column initially headed 'Household Economics' expanded into 'The Art of Living', accompanied by a quotation from Ruskin.[6] The Ruskinian concept of a social economy passed into Gilman's writing and had an impact in academia, notably at MIT, at the women's college Wellesley in Boston, at the University of Wisconsin, where the economist Richard Ely was sympathetic to women social reformers, and at the University of Chicago where Marion Talbot and Sophonisba Breckinridge were among the prominent women working in sociology and civics.[7]

The translation of the household into a metaphor for the social economy enabled women to assert a special gendered calling in the reform of life outside the home. The New York Ladies' Health Protective Association announced confidently in 1894:

It is an eminently proper thing for women to interest themselves in the care and destination of garbage, the cleanliness of the streets, the proper killing and handling of meats, the hygienic and sanitary condition of the public schools, the suppression of stable nuisances, the abolishing of the vile practice of expectorating in public conveyances and buildings, the care of milk and Croton water, the public exposure of foods and in fact everything which constitutes the city's housekeeping.[8]

The consequences of 'city housekeeping' were considerable. By 1915 Mary Beard was able to collect an impressive dossier of American women's local municipal zeal in education, health, housing, social services and civic improvement. She described their surveys, voluntary community projects and participation in settlements, their campaigns for public provision, pure food and sanitation, and their lobbying against smoke and noise pollution. Beard stressed how the impetus was not only about drains and dust, but inspired by an aesthetic of the 'city beautiful'.[9]

The political implications of all this reforming enthusiasm were various and extensive. An enlarged notion of housekeeping could bring women to participate in local government, demand action from the state, and strengthen their resolve for the suffrage. It could stimulate questions about the short-term wastefulness which characterized the drive for profit, and could contribute to economic ideas of a social capitalism, capable of taking the long view by conserving and safeguarding resources and establishing the conditions for reproducing healthy citizens. Their ameliorative, evolutionary approach to reform could acquire a sharper radical edge. Middle-class 'city housekeepers' could find themselves in conflict with powerful vested interests over the ownership and use of land, when they declared that decent housing was a right and demanded building regulations and town planning. In Chicago the academic Sophonisba Breckinridge struggled against racial prejudice in housing, while Florence Kelley and Mary Kingsbury Simkhovitch from the Greenwich House Settlement helped produce a newsletter called *Tenants' Weekly*, which aimed to lower rents and reduce taxes on homes. Its slogan was 'The City for the People'.[10]

A social vision of a homely commonwealth could intimate new human relations and a better society. By pushing the idea of 'home' outwards, some reformers subverted existing assumptions about a woman's sphere. 'Home is not contained within four walls of an individual house,' declared social reformer Rheta Childe Dorr in 1910. 'Home is the community.'[11] At the same time, their notions of improvement could be patronizing. Some social housekeepers were inclined to view those they sought to help from a great distance. Mabel Kittredge, who introduced model housekeeping centres in New York to supplement domestic education in schools, recognized that 'Our immigrants must have better homes', and was prepared to support 'Fights for open plumbing, running water in each apartment, decent sinks, more space'. But, she remarked, 'While we rejoice that the Italian and the Russian and the Pole are to realize better home equipment, we forget that these dazed people have no knowledge as to the way to use the improvement.'[12] Patronage could be couched in tones of kindly thoughtlessness. Martha Bensley Bruère and Robert Bruère, two Progressive advocates of education in housecraft, chronicle what happened when girls prepared an all-American luncheon at a Chicago school which included 'well-to-do' as well as poorer Jewish, Polish and Russian children. While the 'brisk little American' girl confidently set the table for the menu of goldenrod eggs on toast; corn-bread cakes; milk; cornstarch pudding and super cookies, the 'little Russian Jewess' was clumsy and unsure of what was 'required' for such a complex feast. The teacher whispered to the investigators, '"Sophie's people practically never sit down to a meal. They are just on the edge of destitution and eat whenever and wherever they can get the food."'[13] American democracy might beckon Sophie, yet in becoming 'Americanized', she would be subtly taught her place – *sotto voce*.

In Britain, working-class women who were the recipients of advice from philanthropists, reformers and radicals often resented the efforts of improvers, being well aware that the middle-class 'experts' were ignorant of the actual circumstances of working-class life. The specialists' knowledge of housecraft was likely to be purely theoretical: middle-class households operated on servants' labour, and reformers who were not married would not even have experience of running a middle-class household themselves.[14] Some of the more radical women did get the point. During World War One, when Clementina Black extolled the virtues of co-operative housekeeping for the middle class, she was careful to stress that working-class women were best equipped to define their own needs.[15]

In the late nineteenth and early twentieth centuries, women within the labour movement were being encouraged to affirm their own understanding of the problems of daily life. 'You would speak eloquently on the agonising discomforts of washing day or the trials of working-class home life under present conditions,' insisted 'Scotia', writing in the *Accrington Labour Journal*'s 'Our Women's Corner'.[16] The Women's Co-operative Guild encouraged its members to apply the system and efficiency of home economics while validating their existing skills. This kind of domestic education was popular because it enabled women to save time as well as money; and instead of being instructed by lofty middle-class lecturers, the women exchanged knowledge on a mutual basis. The household routine of Mrs Bury, a WCG member from Lancashire at the turn of the century, shows how this was done. It also provides an insight into the labour involved in maintaining a home on top of shopping and cooking for the family. Each day was allocated to a specific task. On Monday she tidied and brushed, and put clothes to soak for the Tuesday wash. Wednesday was for starching, ironing, darning and mending. On Thursday she baked bread and cleaned the bedrooms. On Friday the parlour, lobby and staircase along with the living room were cleaned. 'Saturday is left for all outside cleaning – windows and stonework – besides putting all the clean linen on the beds.'[17]

The working-class labour women whose opinions started to appear in socialist papers, on local councils or in women's organizations linked to the co-operative or trade union movement, put forward demands for material changes in everyday living conditions as well as in the routines of housework. 'How can a woman make a comfortable home in a badly-built, ill-drained house?' asked 'Scotia' in the *Accrington Labour Journal* in 1914.[18] Labour women's efforts to improve the home tended to take the existing role of working-class women for granted. As Pat Thane remarks on the outlook of the Labour Party's Women's Labour League: 'They saw the home . . . as potentially a base for the empowerment of women rather than as necessarily the source of their inescapable bondage.'[19]

There were, however, dissenting voices among some politically aware working-class women who had aspirations other than home-making. The socialist feminist Hannah Mitchell, married in 1895, bitterly resented the thrifty but time-consuming 'makeshifts' which were part of respectable working-class family life; a bottle instead of a rolling pin, dishcloths from 'material left over from dressmaking stitched together and hemmed', beds covered with quilts she had to make from 'bundles of cotton prints'. Far from rejoicing in household crafts, she protested: 'I hated them all – and longed to go out and buy something new and pretty. Besides, I grudged the time and labour which might have been spent on books and study.'[20] Ada Nield Chew also rejected the idealization of the homemaker prevalent among socialists as well as conservatives. One of her sketches, published in the *Accrington Observer* in 1913, reflected on the psychological pressure on women to be homemakers. She makes one of her characters declare rebelliously, '"The feminine touch"? . . . Must a woman scour her own doorstep, and wash her own saucepans, in order to have a home? . . . It's not the glueing of the wife to the hearthstone which makes home.'[21] In 1908 Mary Macarthur, the trade union organizer who worked with Chew in the Women's Trade Union League, also criticized people who argued that a woman's true place was in 'the home', saying they really meant 'the cage' because 'they denied women the right to an independent role in the public world'.[22] Like Ada Nield Chew, Mary Macarthur had achieved an independent life as a working-class woman through work and politics outside the home. Another woman who entered politics through trade unionism, Margaret Bondfield, insisted in 1919 that working-class housewives needed time 'to cultivate their minds and plan their lives on large spacious lines'.[23]

Hannah Mitchell (Tameside Local Studies and Archives Centre)

Ambivalence towards the home was expressed by women in the American radical movement as well. Late nineteenth-century Populist women could idealize the life of the rural home as a 'sacred refuge'.

However, Populist women could also be activists in movements like temperance reform, and could express criticism of the assumption that women were naturally suited to housework: 'Some people find it is acutely funny if a woman anywhere is not devotedly attached to making biscuits and darning socks. And yet men have been known who preferred other occupations to ploughing and cleaning sewers, and no one seemed to think they were monstrosities.'[24] Not all working-class women saw themselves as cut out to be housewives. Mary Archibald, the 'square peg in a round hole' from the Seattle Women's Card and Label League, stated in 1918: 'I loved my home, but I hated the everlasting monotony of putting the sugar-bowl on the table and taking it off again three times a day; of wanting something of beauty as well as utility in my surroundings, and never being able to afford it.'[25]

A particularly intense rebellion against the domestic ideal erupted among some American women in free thought circles during the 1890s. In 1893 Lillie D. White challenged the cult of 'Housekeeping' in a series of articles in *Lucifer*, declaring that 'For one thing in my life I am truly grateful. I have never been guilty of being a good housekeeper.'[26] She was scathing about the pressure on women to be homemakers:

> Woman has always been taught that her highest happiness lies in a correct step to the music of pots and kettles, a mastery over the ingredients and process of making palatable bread, butter, pies and pickles, and a general devotion to the loves and duties of home; and my protest is that she has learned the lesson so well.[27]

White maintained that it should not be assumed that women were uniquely suited to washing dishes, scrubbing floors or making beds. She maintained that 'woman's work, her place and sphere so entirely separated from man's special field of action, is a mumbo jumbo that has been revered too long and must be dethroned'.[28] Lillie White's articles caused quite a furore among the anarchist readers of *Lucifer*. Her sister, Lizzie Holmes, returned to the fray three years later in an article on 'The Unwomanly Woman' in *Our New Humanity*. It was wrong, Holmes asserted, to imagine that every woman should become a housewife, whether in isolated homes or in co-operative communities. Giving a gendered twist to the individualist anarchist emphasis on self-determination as the key to human fulfilment, Holmes declared, 'If . . . she tries to conform to an idea not her own, she will not be free and she

will not be a success.'[29] The anarchist Kate Austin, who knew the ardu-
ous nature of housework in rural America, ridiculed the masculine ideal
of the angel at the hearth: 'I've always noticed that the men who talk
that way never feel hurt when the angel chops the wood, milks the cow,
and builds the fire on a cold morning. He is not afraid of that sort of
independence, but only of the kind that might question his authority.'[30]

By the 1900s, while some strands in the socialist movement maintained that capitalism was destroying the home and that socialism would
restore it, Charlotte Perkins Gilman's ideas about transforming home
life were gaining adherents in both America and Britain. Gilman not
only theorized; she proposed imaginative alternatives. 'What Diantha
Did', published in the American *Forerunner* in 1909–10 and in the
British *Daily Herald* in 1912, depicts the heroine Diantha Bell running
a restaurant and food delivery service which takes meals in insulated
containers by gasoline-powered motor van to clients who live in kitchen-
less homes and an apartment hotel, 'a pleasure palace' with swimming
pool, billiard and card rooms, tennis courts, dance halls and landscaped
gardens.[31] Non-domestic women hailed Gilmanism with delight. In the
International Socialist Review in 1911, the American West Coast socialist
Georgia Kotsch agreed 'with Mrs Gilman . . . that a "family unity" which
is only bound together with a tablecloth is of questionable value'.[32]

Gilman's proposals were in tune with a wider search for a new life in
radical circles. In *Women and Economics* (1898), Gilman was careful to tell
her readers: 'No rigid prescription is needed; no dictum as to whether
we shall live in small separate houses, greenly gardened, with closely
connected conveniences for service and for education, for work and
play; or in towering palaces with shaded flower-bright courts and clois-
ters.'[33] The kind of utopia she theorized did not have to be formulaic or
construed as a separate community; it was rather an approach to be acted
out in the here and now. Drawing on Ruskin, Morris and Carpenter,
radicals devised an alternative aesthetic to reshape daily living. Emma
Heller Schumm said of the Whitmanite anarchist Helena Born's room
in Somerville, Massachusetts that it was filled with beautiful 'objects of
daily use', explaining:

> Art was not something to be set apart from life, to be enjoyed only
> occasionally, but it was a living reality always. She therefore gave her
> aesthetic nature its fling, and her home became a poem of artistic
> expression.[34]

From the early 1890s these 'arts and crafts' ideas of simplicity of form and beauty in everyday things exerted an important influence in America, with Boston becoming one of the key centres from which 'arts and crafts' were disseminated. Before becoming a birth control advocate, Mary Ware Dennett was part of a reform milieu who saw arts and crafts as a means to a better way of living. After propagating the new aesthetic through her lectures, she married the architect William Hartley Dennett in 1900, and they worked together on designing their home. But their vision was not a private matter; the Dennetts believed in linking the art of living with social change.[35]

'Simplification' and 'art of living' ideas affected new approaches to architecture and town and city planning. While the architects and planners were male, women reformers played a key role. Settlement organizer Mary Kingsbury Simkhovitch took the chair at the First National Conference on City Planning in New York in 1909. This led to the formation of the first permanent organization for city planning in America.[36] The socialist planner Raymond Unwin may have drawn up the plans for London's Hampstead Garden Suburb, but the initiative came from Henrietta Barnett's experience at the Toynbee Hall social settlement and from housing reformer Octavia Hill. Started in 1907, Hampstead Garden Suburb – with no pubs but lots of grass, tennis courts and bowling greens – was meant to bring all classes together and combine the best of town and country living. Because the central focus of the garden city was everyday life rather than commercial grandeur it was a model that could be adapted easily to the suburb, while the bowling greens reappeared in the early council estates which Unwin later designed – a curious permutation of the utopian faith in nature.[37]

The idea of the arts and crafts Garden City, along with the American City Beautiful movement, stirred Sarah Lees and her friend Mary Higgs to found the 'Beautiful Oldham Society' in 1903. Sarah Lees was a suffragist and Liberal philanthropist who later became the first woman mayor of Oldham. Mary Higgs had been the first woman to take the Natural Science Tripos at Cambridge; married to a Congregational minister, she was a campaigner for provision for the homeless. The Society set about encouraging gardening, tree-planting and flower exhibitions, and campaigned against smoke pollution in the industrial northern town. Patricia Hollis observes wryly how 'the Beautiful Oldham society was met with much local mirth', but Sarah Lees's vision of Oldham 'devoid of black smoke and smuts', without slums, with 'good sanitary conditions',

opportunities for 'healthy recreation and pleasure' and 'fewer tempta-
tions to excessive drinking', delighted an American journalist who, in a
1912 article for the *Designer*, called it 'Mothering a Municipality'.[38] The
woman-inspired city beautiful was big in the US. In 1915 an optimistic
Mary Beard declared: 'There is no doubt that women are the natural
leaders for the realization of the city beautiful – beautiful not with a lot
of expensive cut stone, formidable fences or marble columns, but beautiful with natural parks, with avenues lined with fine trees and with front
yards covered with verdure'.[39]

The radical redesign of the lived environment also received a boost
from the desire of educated middle-class women, both single and
married, to create new forms of domestic life to meet their own specific
needs. Jane Hume Clapperton's idea for a collectivist house in *A Vision of
the Future* (1904) was geared to the needs of a woman writer like herself:

> The bedrooms are furnished on the continental plan with accommo-
> dation for writing, reading, solitary study, or rest by day, and all the
> latest improvements in lighting, heating and ventilation, etc. . . . Two
> eating apartments are placed contiguous to the kitchens and by taking
> advantage of every invention to facilitate cooking and serving, the
> lady-cooks and attendants may place prepared food on the table and sit
> down to partake of it with their friends. One wing of the house is set
> apart for nurseries and nursery training, another for school teaching,
> inclusive of indoor kindergarten; a music-room well deafened enables
> the musical to practice many instruments without jarring the nerves
> of others; a playroom for the young and a recreation-room set apart
> for whist and chess, etc.; a billiard room, and, if desired, a smoking
> room.[40]

Individual privacy was secured by the rules of the house, which prevented
anyone from entering the bedrooms 'uninvited by the inmate'. Nor was
any interruption to reading in the 'library or silent room' permitted.
Clapperton recognized that adults might find it hard to adapt, and, in
order to ensure the rules were kept, rather ominously proposed the 'criticism' sessions adopted by the autocratic John Humphrey Noyes in the
utopian community at Oneida.[41] Nevertheless the cheery Clapperton
maintained that men and women's 'spontaneous impulses are towards
an essentially social life', and believed the reorganization of daily living
would eliminate familial problems.[42]

Clapperton was still thinking within a nineteenth-century associationist framework, but co-operative living gained modern advocates. In 1912 Alice Melvin, a member of the British Society for the Promotion of Co-operative Housekeeping and Household Service, proposed in the *Freewoman* that co-operative housekeeping could take various forms. Either a group could get together and rent adjoining houses, establishing communal kitchens, dining rooms and libraries within them, or garden cities could be built with public services, like Hampstead Garden City. She thought both approaches would particularly benefit mothers and single professional women.[43]

The New York teacher and Greenwich Villager, Henrietta Rodman, who was influenced by Charlotte Perkins Gilman, conceived a plan for a twelve-storey feminist apartment house. Meals were to be produced by staff in the mechanized basement and sent up in lifts to the residents; children were to be cared for in a Montessori nursery, enabling professional women to be mothers and do paid work.[44] In Britain, Clementina Black's wartime project for a co-operative of federated households had single middle-class working women in mind. Again the arrangements were all very modern: the kitchens full of up-to-date technology, food ordered by telephone, goods delivered in motor cars, and a professional staff instead of old-style servants.[45] In 1914 a co-operative housekeeping scheme was devised by the British socialist feminist Sylvia Pankhurst, with working-class as well as middle-class women in mind. She envisaged houses with gardens grouped round a central play area for children, not unlike some council house designs. A 'Socialist Suffragette' offered to start a fund to buy land, but the project did not materialize.[46]

These feminist proposals were marked by a crucial weakness: lack of capital meant they remained pipe dreams. Some women did, however, construct material utopias. Two Letchworth Garden City residents, Ruth I. Pym and S. E. Dewe, established seven cottages with a common dining room and kitchen in 1914; and two more followed in 1916.[47] In New York during the early 1900s, a group of enterprising Finnish immigrant women, who worked as domestic servants, contrived to raise their own capital by being prepared to start small. They pooled their wages to rent an apartment to use on their days off. This grew into the Finnish Women's Co-operative Home – a four-storey building with sleeping accommodation, lounges, club rooms, a library, a restaurant and an employment agency.[48]

Co-operative housekeeping, however, did not necessarily involve capital expenditure. Crystal Eastman cherished happy memories of childhood holidays in the 1890s, when first the mothers, and then the children as they grew older, took turns to organize the cleaning, shopping, gardening and finances of a large group of holidaymakers. The advocate of co-operative housekeeping Ethel Puffer Howes sought to systemize these informal arrangements of mutual aid, arguing after World War One that co-operative home service clubs would enable women to combine motherhood and careers.[49]

One impetus behind the middle-class proposals for communal living, co-operative housekeeping and socialized services was what became known as 'the servant problem'. This was particularly acute in high-waged America; between 1900 and 1920, the number of domestic servants in the US declined by half. The spread of domestic technology had been accompanied by rising standards of cleanliness, leading to an intensification of housework. Hence when the British writer G. K. Chesterton portrayed the home as an oasis of ease in 1927, Crystal Eastman responded irritably that it was not so for 'home-keeping women'.[50] World War One resulted in a temporary panic in Britain about the lack of domestic servants, leading Clementina Black, in a memorandum to the Ministry of Reconstruction's Women's Advisory report on the *Domestic Service Problem* (1919), to suggest that 'the best way of economising domestic service would be for a group of householders to establish a common centre for buying, preparing, and distributing food and for providing central heating and hot water.'[51] But as it turned out, R. Randal Phillips's proposals for highly technologized homes in his book *The Servantless House* (1920) proved to be ahead of their time. British working-class women who had left domestic service for lucrative jobs in munitions would be forced back into service by unemployment during the 1920s.

Working-class women, both urban and rural, had their own problems of time. 'Keeping house' for them meant rising before dawn to light fires and prepare breakfasts, heating water for washing, stoking fires for baking, a ceaseless battle with dust and dirt, mending long into the night. During the 1880s ideas of a right to leisure were developing in the labour movement in both countries, as workers conflicted with employers over issues of time. This encouraged men as well as women to connect the hours of paid work with time spent on unpaid labour in the home. In 1885 the British trade unionist and co-operator Ben Jones advocated 'associated homes', so as to make working-class women's lives easier. Noting the arrival of sewing machines and wringing machines, he observed: 'The fact of so many changes having occurred in domestic life, impels one to ask, Why should there not be others?'[52] Likewise Tom Mann, the socialist 'New Unionist' and advocate of the eight-hour day, argued in 1896 for 'leisure for workmen's wives', in the popular magazine *Halfpenny Short Cuts*. Mann suggested the creation of co-operative groups for shopping, as well as a communal wash house and collective kitchen 'thoroughly fitted with the best appliances', as steps towards 'Associated Homes'.[53]

Hannah Mitchell was sceptical about all this talk, grumbling in *The Hard Way Up* that socialist men still expected their home-made meat pies like their reactionary fellows, and failed to understand 'that meals do not come up through the table cloth'.[54] Despite her disenchantment with housework, she did recognize the implicit forms of co-operation which women developed among themselves, remembering with affection the women of the Midlands mining village of Newhall who imparted to her 'the kind of knowledge one does not get from books . . . pickling, preserving, and making wines'.[55] But Mitchell did not see the creation of co-operative forms of housework as the answer to women's domestic problems. Instead, like many other working-class socialist women, she was in favour of an extension of municipal services which she helped to initiate when she served on Manchester Council's Baths Committees in the 1920s.

In both Britain and the US, socialist women, influenced by the German Marxists August Bebel and Clara Zetkin, imagined that in the socialist future housework tasks would be socialized and domestic labour reduced by technology. By the early 1900s dairying, making soap, candles, weaving, spinning and knitting had all entered the public sphere of manufacturing, while sewing, washing, ironing, nursing the sick, canning, preserving and baking also were becoming paid services or industrial activities. One wing of the socialist movement was inclined to see this as a capitalist invasion of the household, but domestic modernizers regarded the introduction of household technology as domesticity's final knell. They believed the logic of capitalism would abolish housework.

The rebellious Industrial Workers of the World (IWW) organizer, Elizabeth Gurley Flynn, whose wandering lifestyle was hardly conducive to housecraft, put her faith in technology in 1916:

The home of the future will eliminate the odd jobs that reduce it to a cluttered workshop today and electricity free the woman's hand from methods antiquated in an era of machinery. There is no great credit attached to making a pie like mother used to make when a machine tended by five unskilled workers turns out 42,000 perfect pies a day! Cook stoves, washboards, and hand irons are doomed to follow the spinning wheel, candles and butter churns, into the museums, and few tears will be shed at their demise.[56]

In 1927 Sylvia Pankhurst was equally enthusiastic about technology and electricity. She imagined that the hearth-brush and dishcloth would disappear, and meals would be produced from communal kitchens. Clearing up would be made easier by dishwashing machines and paper plates.[57] Unwittingly, the left libertarians Flynn and Pankhurst were heralds of the consumer revolution which would refuel twentieth-century capitalism.

A quite different approach was taken by the American socialist Josephine Conger-Kaneko, who insisted in 1913 that housework was work, and contributed to wealth:

You work ALL HOURS, at BOARD WAGES. That is, you get a part of the food you cook, and live in the house you keep, and you can have a dress occasionally that you make, FOR WORKING ENDLESS HOURS SO THAT YOUR HUSBAND MAY BE AN EFFICIENT WORKER FOR HIS EMPLOYER. . . .

THE UNPAID AND GROSSLY EXPLOITED LABOR OF MARRIED WOMEN IN THEIR HOMES MAKES IT POSSIBLE FOR THE EMPLOYER TO PILE-UP IMMENSE PROFITS OUT OF HIS BUSINESS, WHICH, OF COURSE, IS HIGHLY SATISFACTORY TO HIM.

But is it you, O Woman, who must pay the price?[58]

Her theory that the housewife made an economic contribution to production by maintaining men, and as reproducers of new workers for capitalism, resurfaced in the American Communist Party during the 1930s as a demand for wages for housework.

Changing the sexual division of labour in the home was sporadically mooted. The suffrage movement contributed to an awareness of how gender inequality permeated everyday life in the home. In *Marriage as a Trade* (1912), the British feminist writer Cicely Hamilton stated that she could see 'no reason why it should be the duty of the wife, rather than of the husband, to clean doorsteps, scrub floors, and do the family cooking. Men are just as capable as women of performing all these duties.' Hamilton advocated passive resistance, concluding that the only way 'woman can make herself more valued, and free herself from the necessity of performing duties for which she gets neither thanks nor payment', was to 'do as men have always done in such a situation – shirk the duties.'[59] Eight years on, Crystal Eastman was suggesting: 'Perhaps we must cultivate or simulate a little of that highly prized helplessness ourselves.'[60]

'How can we change the nature of man,' Eastman asked in the left-wing journal the *Liberator* in 1920, 'so that he will honourably share the work and responsibility and thus make the home-making enterprise a song instead of a burden?'[61] She proposed rearing sons to accept house-work – a somewhat uncertain and long-term solution. The weight of cultural expectation was still formidable. Nevertheless, by the 1920s a small group of American women with advanced views were proposing that men should share housework when women worked outside the home. In her article 'Fifty-Fifty Wives', Mary Alden Hopkins observed in 1923 that the problem was the differing attitudes men and women brought to domesticity. Women had to shed a sacrificial mentality.[62] In 1926 Suzanne La Follette complained that whereas work in the home was used as a reason for demanding shorter hours for women in industry, it was never expected that the husband should 'share the wife's tradi-tional burden as she has been forced to share his. I have no doubt that innumerable husbands are doing this, but there is no expectation put upon them to do it, and those who do not are in no wise thought to shirk their duty to their families, as their wives would be thought to do if they neglected to perform the labour of the household.'[63]

Educated middle-class American women who wanted work and married life were the first to experience the double burden which would continue to present modern women with painful choices between jobs and home. They were also the first women of their class to be drawn into the race against time. From the late 1890s, articles began appearing in women's magazines about the terrible feeling of being in a rush which had seized American women. Urged to achieve the 'House Beautiful' yet pulled away from their homes by their clubs and charitable organi-zations, middle-class American women were depicted as being in a

Crystal Eastman, ca 1910–1915, by Arnold Genthe (Schlesinger
Library, Radcliffe Institute, Harvard University)

perpetual state of agitated haste. The middle-class housewife was in a cleft stick, for she was also being rebuked for not concerning herself with wider social issues outside the home. In *Increasing Home Efficiency* (1913), the Bruères upbraided women for 'fluttering about inside four walls under the delusion that these mark the proper sphere of activity'.[64] Their advice was to rationalize housework in order to fulfil social duties in a wider sphere. Variations on the theme were the need to save time on housework in order to be creative outside the home, or to find ways of being creative about housework. Eunice Freeman in the *Colored American Magazine* proposed turning the home into a 'gymnasium' and seeing housework as a way of improving posture. Brooms, bedsteads, dusters and dishes could be transformed into 'the apparatus by means of which the woman can make herself strong, erect, active and graceful'.[65]

A less aerobic approach was outlined by Lillian Gilbreth, in her 1904 *Management in the Home*. She recommended reducing the time spent on the tedious aspects of housework in order to spend more on its creative features and on childcare. This attitude to domestic activity became widespread after World War One. The home must be 'a place in which we can express ourselves', declared Gilbreth in 1927, in *The Home-Maker and Her Job*.[66] Re-making the home was linked to the reorganization of production, which was more advanced in the United States than in Britain. The first three decades of the twentieth century in America saw an intensive acceleration in the drive for even greater productivity. Lillian Gilbreth and her husband Frank were exponents of Frederick Taylor's ideas of scientific management. Trained in industrial psychology, she applied Taylorist ideas of breaking down activities through time and motion studies, and increasing efficiency through ergonomic design. Human-centred domestic ergonomics resulted in kitchens in which everything lay within arm's reach.[67]

Christine Frederick was similarly enthusiastic about bringing the new ideas for increasing workplace productivity into the home. Frederick, who had acquired journalistic skills on the *Ladies' Home Journal*, began her book *The New Housekeeping* (1916) with dramatic brio. 'I was sitting by the library table, mending, while my husband and a business friend were talking, one evening about a year ago. . . . "What are you men talking about?" I interrupted. "I can't help being interested, won't you please tell me what efficiency is, Mr Watson? What were you saying about bricklaying?"'[68] And so, of course, a charmed Mr Watson explains to the enquiring darner how scientific management could be applied in the home to speed up activities which had been governed by age-old customary practices. Frederick told housewives that if they applied scientific management's drive for efficiency to domestic work, they could save not only time and energy, but also natural resources like fuel.

Christine Frederick

If the nineteenth-century efficiency experts had turned the house-wife into an engineer, trained to operate her own modern equipment, and the arts and crafts enthusiasts had promoted her to the status of creative artist, Christine Frederick and Lillian Gilbreth re-designated her as a manager. Frederick's *The New Housekeeping* was subtitled *Efficiency Studies in Home Management*. The housewife was expected to assemble 'Fuel-Savers', 'Time-Savers', 'Labour-Savers', 'Step-Savers' and 'Businesslike Equipment for the Home' such as 'The New Housekeeping Filing Cook Book'.[69] According to Gilbreth, the role of the housewife involved breaking down every necessary domestic operation, along with a knowledge of technology and scientific buying. It required combining an engineer's understanding of how to use resources such as gas and electricity, with a psychologist's skills in judging people. Gilbreth gave the housewife the managerial job of dividing and allocating work in the home, rather than attempting it all herself. She should assess all family members as producers and consumers. 'Father turns in money, the boys cut the lawn, the girls wait on table. Bill plays for the family singing. The baby gives everyone a chance to wait on her and admire her.'[70] The Gilbreth home of twelve children was indeed an efficiency laboratory – and yet they employed a small army of servants, to enable them to pursue their own work! Two of their children wrote a memoir about their curious upbringing, 'Cheaper by the Dozen', which also became a film. The British middle class with their servants restored were slower off the mark; but a variant of time management appeared in *Good Housekeeping* in 1925, when Hazel Hunkins admonished women to 'Keep a Budget', telling them that 'The main thing is the elimination of "hand to mouth" management, and the recovery of control over one's time, energy and money, that we may get out of life those things we really value'.[71]

Household management and housekeepers' control transposed the promise of the good life into individual households. The Taylorist efficiency experts believed that their systems made for less effort. 'Let gravity work for you,' urged Lillian Gilbreth, explaining how dirty washing could be rolled downstairs to save energy in carrying it – apparently forgetting that it had to be picked up.[72] An obvious hitch in all these theories of household management was that time saved in labour was offset by time spent in planning and administering. Likewise, the ideal of shorter hours was thwarted by growing anxieties about germs, along with an elaborated housekeeping which required knowledge of buying as a science, balanced diets and new electrical equipment.

An awkward ideological aspect of the Tayloristic drive to reduce time on housework was that it undermined more traditional ideas of the noble art of housekeeping. One solution was to graft the 'dignity of labour' inherent in the arts and crafts movement onto the new house-keeping. In the midst of her discussion of kitchen utensils, Christine Frederick invoked 'The oft-quoted saying of William Morris that the home should contain nothing that is not at the same time useful and beautiful'.[73] Morris would have been bewildered to find his ideas propagated by household efficiency experts. But there are some intriguing connecting threads. The efficiency experts regarded objects as socially constructed, to be adapted according to either aesthetic or functional requirements, while the relationship of design to functional use had been present in the arts and crafts movement. Thus the kitchen in the early 1900s Hartley-Dennett arts and crafts home had been carefully planned for efficiency, while the popular magazine *House Beautiful* announced itself as 'The Only Magazine in America Devoted to Simplicity, Economy, and Appropriateness in Home Decoration and Furnishing'.[74] Simplification fused aesthetics with improved working conditions for the home-maker. When British women's labour organizations such as the Women's Co-operative Guild and the Women's Labour League sought working-class women's views on the design of housing around World War One, simplification and housework efficiency theories combined. The Women's Labour League sent out a detailed questionnaire canvassing for proposals to improve housing, and the results were discussed at meetings of the organization. Their aim was to eliminate unnecessary work such as climbing up and down stairs, heating water and bringing in coal – a working-class version of Lillian Gilbreth and Christine Frederick.[75]

In the early twentieth century, arts and crafts, which had started on the radical margins, passed into middle-class culture. The social quest for simplification was transposed into an individual assertion of good taste invested with moral qualities. According to the American writer on design, Mabel Tuke Priestman, artistic houses in which 'superfluous ornament and drapery are done away with' were 'conducive to plain living and high thinking'.[76] The arts and crafts conviction that furnishings and design marked the inner personality ramified into new ways of delineating social class by 'lifestyle'. Middle-class reformers, imbued with the moral aesthetic of simplification, disdained immigrant working-class fondness for net curtains and loud clothes. The pejorative association between women and consumption expressed in Thorstein Veblen's influential *Theory of the Leisure Class* (1899) was a recurring trope. In 1902 Mrs Henry Wade Rodgers fretted in *House Beautiful* magazine about whether the aesthetics of simplification were genuine or 'but a pose, a mood of our complex life?' and was anxious lest middle-class women backslide by burying themselves 'under trivial obligations and possessions'.[77] Even after arts and crafts had been overtaken by the post-war enthusiasm for design based on the latest technology, an evangelical anxiety that women might consume the wrong kind of household objects persisted, while any lingering resistance to consumption left over from old aspirations to the simple life was interpreted as requiring more consumer education. Books by writers like Frederick, women's magazines, and the Good Housekeeping Institute all eagerly publicized new products while advocating scientific management in the home.

There was a neat fit between domestic acceleration and the purchase of domestic commodities – the very things that were streaming out along the new assembly lines. Readers of *The New Housekeeping* were informed of the virtues of devices like the 'Speedy Egg-Beater designed on the turbine principle' or a '"Lazy Susan" – The Silent Waitress'.[78] American corporations were quick to pick up on changes in consumer demands, and a two-way relationship developed between household advisers and the world of business. Companies producing household goods, such as Kraft Foods, Sears and Roebuck, and Piggly-Wiggly food stores, appointed home economists to promote their products.[79] In 1914 the African-American reformer Blanche Armwood, a member of the local black elite in Tampa, Florida, persuaded the Tampa Gas Company to assist in forming the Tampa School of Household Arts (THSA), which trained black women to use the new appliances. Nancy Hewitt describes how she persuaded white businesses that black domestics needed training, and convinced the women that it was worthwhile attending the courses: 'Adapting the language of the National Association of Colored Women's Clubs – "Lifting as We Climb" – the TSHA class of 1916 chose for its motto "Lifting Labor from drudgery to attractiveness"'.[80]

By the 1920s the market for household goods in the US had expanded considerably – in contrast to Britain, where the impetus to buy new consumer durables was much weaker, partly for economic reasons, and partly because of domestic service. From the early 1920s US advertising and marketing firms were spending millions of dollars on promoting domesticity and persuading consumers to buy mass-produced goods.[81] This psychological pressure intensified over the course of the decade, carrying with it the promise of a better life. The bohemian impulse towards self-expression and the individualistic ethic of self-help merged to reinvent the home as a key aspect of the American economy. Vacuum cleaners symbolized control, cleaning products meant power, fast foods epitomized speedy convenience.

Charlotte Perkins Gilman had been among the first to theorize the interconnection between apparently isolated homes and the broader society: 'Our houses are threaded like beads on a string.'[82] Gilman had imagined that this would encourage changing the forms of domestic living. In claiming access to social resources, other women dreamers and adventurers had imagined an extension of social provision. Though both aspirations were partially achieved, the home was also reshaped by individual commodities. A new way of life was being initiated which would eventually overtake the utopias of the adventurers. As the Muncie, Indiana Chamber of Commerce put it in the mid-1920s: 'The first responsibility of an American to his country is no longer that of a citizen, but of a consumer. Consumption is a necessity.'[83]

7

Consumer Power

In retrospect the triumph of the Muncie, Indiana Chamber of Commerce might appear to have been preordained, but this was not how it seemed at the time. From the late nineteenth century, the alternative forms of cooking, eating, washing and living arrangements devised by house-keeping reformers, feminists, co-operators, socialists and anarchists, contributed to the reshaping and redefining of both private and social consumption. They also raised the need for new kinds of financial structures. Contests over consumption generated ingenious strategies of resistance, diverse forms of organizing and demands for social provision as well as cash payments from the state.

Food figured largely in schemes to alter consumption. Dolores Hayden relates how the founder of home economics, Ellen Swallow Richards, exhibited a model kitchen at the 1893 World's Columbian Exposition in Chicago. The 'small, white clapboard house' Richards displayed contained a startlingly modern 'scientific laboratory designed to extract the maximum amount of nutrition from food substances and the maximum heat from fuel'.[1] Excited housewives, women reformers and academics teaching the new subject of home economics ate healthy Boston baked beans on brown bread and prepared themselves to pros-elytize for public kitchens on the Richards model.

The kitchens, which aimed to provide good cheap food for the work-ing class and were based on similar philanthropic kitchens in Europe, never proved very popular with the American immigrant poor. But they did inspire similar projects in Britain. 'Distributive kitchens' patronized by the middle class in the early 1900s in London were continuing to thrive in the 1920s, when feminist journalist Evelyn Sharp reported how food in aluminium containers was being delivered by tricycle from a

Bloomsbury basement. The service proved particularly popular among elementary school teachers.[2]

One version of the distributive kitchen which did enjoy a degree of popularity with the working class was the cooked food shop, which pioneered cheap take-away meals. In 1902 Margaret Llewelyn Davies prodded the Sunderland co-operators to back a co-operative cooked food shop, the Women's Co-operative Guild's 'Coffee and Cooked Meat Shop'. Working-class women supported the outlet, queuing for soup, pease pudding, boiled pork and other cooked meats. However, male co-operators were less enthusiastic about the extension of co-operative shopping to reduce women's domestic labour. Communal eating was associated with hardship and distress, and they suspected that the Coffee and Cooked Meat Shop was a charitable soup kitchen in disguise.[3] Co-operative bakeries, however, met with less opposition, and several were established.

A few modern employers were beginning to introduce canteens, and these new commercial forms generated ideas for socially provided services. A speaker at the 1900 Conference of the National Union of Women Workers, urging the need to rationalize housework, pointed to the new works canteens in Colman's factories and argued that municipalities could take on the responsibility for public kitchens.[4]

Running parallel with the beginnings of mass Taylorized catering went a growing minority interest in what was called 'Reform Food'. Alternative businesses sprouted as a result; in the early 1900s the Reformed Food Company in Victoria Street, Westminster, spotting a new niche market, developed a special take-away service for vegetarians.[5] By the early twentieth century vegetarianism was becoming increasingly popular in radical and progressive circles, because of ideas about animal rights and a search for healthier diets. Vegetarian cafés provided women with an acceptable meeting place and were popular among feminists. In 1909 Jane Hume Clapperton hosted a meeting of Charlotte Despard's Women's Freedom League in Edinburgh from the Cafe Vegetaria.[6] Leonora Cohen, a Theosophist and member of the militant Women's Social and Political Union, was also a vegetarian, who in 1914 was running her home in Harrogate as a guest-house. Elizabeth Crawford records how Cohen advertised it in the *Suffragette* as 'Pomona', a 'Reform Food Establishment. Excellent catering by specialist in Reform diets. Late Dinners. Separate Tables.'[7]

Co-operation provided a way of creating socialized services to supplement women's domestic activity. Replacing the back-breaking,

time-consuming family wash day was an obvious starting point: Glasgow
set up a co-operative steam laundry in the late 1890s, and the Women's
Co-operative Guild helped to provide the impetus for others.[8] In
the US, although there was no national organization comparable to
the Women's Co-operative Guild, similar examples of domestic co-
operative services were to be found. In her history of American housework, *Never Done*, Susan Strasser describes how in the early 1900s
women hitched housework to 'HUSBAND-POWER':

> Some Midwestern dairy co-operatives utilized the water supplies and
> steam plants already operating in the creameries to do laundry for
> the co-operating families. At the Milltown Cooperative Creamery
> Company in Wisconsin, fifty families' loads of clothes could be
> washed in forty-five minutes, dried, and ironed with mangles.[9]

Ideas crossed back and forth across the Atlantic. Ethel Puffer Howes,
the American champion of co-operative laundries, kitchens, bakeries
and cafés, along with self-help forms of co-operative housekeeping,
was influenced by the British Fabians and co-operators – who had
in turn been inspired by mid-nineteenth-century US co-operative
housekeeping. Howes, herself a working mother, was able to reach
a wide audience by writing in the *Woman's Home Companion* about
examples of Co-operative Home Services. Her articles publicizing
each new experiment demonstrated that alternatives were possible, and
her sustained efforts shaped co-operative housekeeping as a cohesive
project.[10] Co-operative forms of domestic activity were also initiated
through the labour movement as needs arose among women activists. Seattle women co-operators expanded pragmatically; in 1915
they established a mutual laundry, not only to do their washing but to
provide secure employment for union militants. Labour activist Lola
Lunn established a Women's Co-operative Guild in Seattle on the
British model in 1919, and the following year co-operative women
also created a Women's Exchange which sold or gave away goods
donated by members.[11]

Combining charity with mutual aid, exchanges had been common
systems of direct redistribution and recycling among American women
throughout the nineteenth century. By the early 1890s some had
developed beyond the 'bring-and-buy' stage to act as co-operative
retail outlets. One commentator, Alice Rhine, described how in 1891

low-paid graduates from New York art colleges could take their work to such exchanges and be guaranteed a fair price, instead of earning a pittance from department stores. Kathleen Waters Sander characterizes the exchanges as providing a 'humanistic counter-movement to the industrial workplace'.[12]

There were, however, drawbacks to these co-operative alternatives, for they required effort and time to run and did not always reduce housewives' labour. Charlotte Perkins Gilman, who had acquired a horror of co-operative housekeeping from communal living as a child, preferred private entrepreneurship and commercial services. But, since workers were unlikely to be able to afford these, labour movement women favoured transposing aspects of private domestic activity into social consumption by providing municipally funded services. In the early 1900s the *Clarion* journalist, Julia Dawson, explained in her *Pass On* pamphlet that under socialism 'Experts will come into our homes to do the cleaning as regularly as we get drains flushed by the local authorities now and a good deal oftener.'[13] A similar utopia of housework as a public service resurfaced in a 1923 pamphlet by the Labour MP Herbert Morrison, *Better Times for the Housewife: Labour's Policy for the Homemaker*. This promised a socialist future in which a man or woman employed by the local authority would arrive at one's home on a motorbike with a sidecar full of utensils such as municipal vacuum cleaners and washing machines and, at a low cost, help with the housework. Morrison also envisaged working-class and lower-middle-class housewives sending a postcard overnight to their local council, to order meals which would be freshly cooked and delivered the next day.[14]

While private housework would prove difficult to transfer into social consumption, better progress was made with housing. Social housing schemes were devised by philanthropists, co-operators and the state. Because these required a large capital outlay, they stimulated new kinds of administrative and financial structures. In Britain, when the Ruskinian Octavia Hill persuaded the rich to invest in philanthropic housing ventures she formulated a system of housing management that would be later adopted in council housing. In the US, philanthropic housing associations were established on similar lines to Hill's, and rich women also created model communities. Mary Beard was able to report in 1915 how improved tenements had been built with the help of Mrs W. K. Vanderbilt in New York, while in Los Angeles club women had financed the construction of model cottages with gardens which they hoped would replace the shacks of Mexican immigrant work-ers.[15] In Britain, several kinds of co-operative finance were devised to build housing. Co-partnership schemes in model villages, garden cities and suburbs enabled members to buy a share, sometimes paying in instalments, and end up as joint owners.[16] Another option was for the co-operative movement itself to build houses, using co-operative sources of finance. When in 1908 Oldham council timorously proposed twelve council houses, but failed to act, the resolute Liberal suffragist Sarah Lees formed a co-operative building society among the better-paid mill workers. Within six years they had built a garden suburb of 150 three-bedroom houses, each with a bathroom, offered at rents which were affordable to working-class families.[17] Co-operative capital and labour power were regarded as a means of enabling a co-operative alternative to grow within capitalism.

Liberal and Labour women elected as councillors also agitated for women's basic housing needs, including those of the very poor. The feminist Margaret Ashton campaigned in Manchester for homeless women to be housed, a cause also taken up by Sarah Lees's friend Mary Higgs, who went on the tramp herself to highlight the lack of homes, and in 1910 wrote *Where Shall She Live?* in an effort to secure more women's 'lodging-homes'.[18]

The real impetus for state housing provision came during World War One. Before the war, councils had been given discretionary powers to build, but it was the need to relocate war-workers which provided the incentive for government intervention. The Ministry of Munitions employed Raymond Unwin, who brought his garden city ideas into the design of one of the ministry's projects – a township at Gretna for muni-tions workers.[19] Hence 'council housing' developed as a beleaguered utopia out of the exigencies of the war effort, and the government's apprehensions about industrial and community-based unrest.

In the United States, some innovative financial counter-institutions were developed by African Americans. Largely outside the orbit of white reformers and labour organizers, in a period when racial hostility and prejudice was intensifying, black Americans devised mutual self-help projects to accumulate capital. They used the funds collected to alleviate social needs and create employment. Because access to credit for small loans was so important for poor women, African-American women created myriad small savings societies to help them through hard times, as well as investing in the larger mutual benefit societies which had

Sarah Lees (Oldham Local Studies and Archive Centre)

Oldham garden suburb (Oldham Local Studies and Archive Centre)

grown up within black communities. In Atlanta in 1903, the Working Women's Society sidelined the moneylenders by providing members with interest-free loans, covering their costs by charging weekly dues.[20] Maggie Lena Walker, a former washerwoman from Richmond, Virginia, proved especially inventive. Her aim was to withdraw black spending from white-owned businesses, a species of resistance she called killing 'the lion' by not 'feeding it'.[21] Instead Walker advocated black economic and social alternatives. When she became secretary of a friendly society, the Independent Order of Saint Luke, in 1899, the Order was in decline. Her first step was to gather around her a group of women she could trust, to form a Penny Savings Bank in 1903. Many of the depositors were poor women, but their pennies grew into the large, black-owned Consolidated Bank and Trust Company.

Maggie Lena Walker believed in convincing people about alternative approaches to economic life through lived experience; her motto was 'First by practice and then by precept.'[22] She was a social innovator who linked needs, ideas and money-making projects. In 1898 she founded a female insurance company, and in 1905 a department store to create employment for women and provide good-quality products. The Order of Saint Luke also included a youth section, offered an educational loan fund for young people, and ran a weekly newspaper. Walker encouraged a campaigning approach, advocating both education and the suffrage; what is more, her Order took a strong stand against segregation and lynching, initiating a boycott of streetcars long before the Civil Rights movement of the 1950s and 1960s. Thus in America, black purchasing power was closely linked to black resistance; it could be mobilized to foster alternative kinds of products, shops or financial services and to boycott white businesses.

The tactic of the boycott had deep roots in America's history, from the War of Independence through into the anti-slavery movement, and it was used by many campaigns and movements during the late nineteenth and early twentieth centuries. It featured, for instance, in the Woman's Christian Temperance Union's crusade against drink in the 1870s and 80s. The WCTU's approach combined the external pressure of the boycott with exhortations directed towards drinkers to effect an inward change in consciousness, in order to change their way of life.

Some middle-class social reformers likewise decided that an inner sense of moral responsibility should guide their own consumption

Maggie Lena Walker (Courtesy National Parks Service,
Maggie L. Walker National Historic Site)

patterns. Helen Campbell's work among poor women in the 1880s made her feel that she ought to pare back her own requirements. 'How can I bring more simplicity, less conventionality, more truth and right living into home and every relation of life?'[23] During the mid-1880s, this ethical anxiety materialized into external action when a group of middle-class and working-class women reformers in the New York Working Women's Society, pessimistic about the possibilities of forming effective unions in the clothing factories employing low-paid women, proposed a consumer boycott to improve working conditions. The Working Women's Society, which also campaigned for women factory inspectors, put great faith in personal contact, believing that if women consumers met those who made their garments they would be willing to pay a fair price. Expressing a Ruskinian vision of the economy as an interconnected organism, they declared:

> It is the *democratic demand* for cheapness that keeps alive this sad condition of things. It is *our* needs and our desires that regulate a large part of production. In our eagerness to make our little money go far, are we not careless about the claims of those who make for us, or stand behind the counter which we face? When a neatly made garment is offered to us as a 'cheap', do we stop to ask at whose expense is the cheapness?[24]

The Working Women's Society laid the basis for the New York City Consumers' League, which was formed in 1891. Consumers were encouraged not only to boycott, but to shop ethically. In 1891 the New York League drew up a 'White List' of department stores which met fair standards on wages, hours, physical conditions, management–employee relations and child labour. Middle-class concern about the conditions in which goods were produced united altruism with self-interest. The growing awareness of hygiene and sanitation, and a fear of the spread of infectious diseases, contributed to support for the reform of the low-paid, labour-intensive 'sweated trades'; Josephine Shaw Lowell, the first president of the New York Consumers' League, was also active at a national level on the US Sanitary Commission. The Consumers' Leagues, which began to spread in many cities and towns in the US during the 1890s, varied in their political emphases and in the alliances they made locally. While some League members were moved by ethical feelings of responsibility towards the weak, and others by concerns about public hygiene, those with a more radical perspective pushed for an alliance between consumers and producers. Florence Kelley argued that the Leagues should oppose sweated labour by adopting the idea of a 'trade union label' to prove that unionized labour had been used. She also advocated working alongside the unions. In 1899 Kelley became secretary of the National Consumers' League, which under her leadership evolved into a significant lobby for the state regulation of consumption and production.[25]

Organization around ethical consumption provided a context in which cross-class alliances could operate. When in 1910 the New York Consumers' League set up its own Label Shop on West 28th Street, selling only ethically-produced goods, the International Ladies' Garment Workers' journal – the *Ladies' Garment Worker* – urged working men and women to support the venture. 'Here you will find all kinds of waists and dresses bearing the union label, and the woman wearing a waist with a union label can feel well dressed in a new and larger sense than that term usually implies.'[26] By 1913, however, the journal was noting that consumer power was hitting some unforeseen cultural obstacles; the wives of trade unionists were not automatically committed to trade union goods, while the middle class tended to associate the trade union label with less expensive goods.[27]

Some working-class communities did adopt consumer pressure as an ancillary to trade union action. Members of the Women's Card and Label League in Seattle pledged themselves to buy from stores with the union label. In 1920, when the Seattle Central Labor Council decided to support the American Federation of Labor (AFL) by declaring a boycott of the Bon Marché department store for using non-union labour, the Women's Card and Label League along with the local Women's Trade Union League, the Consumers' League and several other women's groups, resolutely shopped elsewhere.[28] Although the boycott was unsuccessful, the Seattle trade union and co-operative movement acquired a complex understanding of the political economy of consumption. Purchasing power and the boycott were very much part of the culture of American protest and were adopted by black communities, moral and social reformers, and trade unions to affect how things were made and distributed.

In Britain no comparable organization to the National Consumers' League emerged, though spasmodic attempts were made to link producers and consumers. When in 1886 Clementina Black became secretary of the forerunner to the Women's Trade Union League, the Women's Protective and Provident League, she had been so shocked by the bad pay and conditions of women workers that she set up a Consumers' League to complement their action as producers. However, Black quickly turned to the local authorities for backing. In 1890, as a representative of the Women's Trade Union League, she persuaded the Progressives on the London County Council to include women clothing workers within the fair wages ruling that the Council already imposed on its suppliers. Leaving nothing to chance, she proceeded to tell the Council how a 'fair' rate should be determined – 'a rate at which the women employed can live in health and reasonable comfort'. [29] A significant precedent had been set: the local state was being drawn into determining what the pay of workers should be through contract compliance. Though difficult to apply in practice without any system of monitoring or strong trade union organization, in challenging the unrestricted right to profit from cheap labour Black's hybrid of ethical consumption and public buying power gave institutional legitimation to the idea that a 'living wage' was an entitlement.

In the 1900s Black was active in the cross-class grouping which researched and lobbied on behalf of women workers, the Women's Industrial Council, as well as in the Anti-Sweating Campaign which sought to regulate homework and the low-paid trades. Both groupings advocated ethical consumption as a means of complementing legislation. Ethical choice was also promoted by the labour movement through trade union labels and the Co-operative Movements' shops. 'By dealing at our Co-operative Stores, you strike at the great evil of sweating', claimed an advertisement in the *Syndicalist* in 1913.[30] Nevertheless, in her book *The Consumer in Revolt* (c. 1912), the socialist feminist Teresa Billington-Greig argued that the links between labour and consumers needed to be strengthened. She regretted that the attempt to create a Consumers' League on the American model had been 'short-lived', and expressed admiration for the American Consumer Leagues.[31]

By 1912 rising prices were making consumption a pressing issue, and the high cost of living was provoking strikes among many workers who had been outside the organized trade union movement. While one section of the labour movement was preoccupied with parliament, an extra-parliamentary left completely rejected gradual reform through the state. With talk of 'direct action' in the air among networks of dissidents and insurgents, workplace militancy extended into proposals for direct action in the community. Margaretta Hicks started to urge direct action around prices within the Marxist British Socialist Party. Identifying with the approach of the labour wing of US consumer organizing, Hicks saw consumption as integrally linked to production, and regarded consumer pressure as a form of gendered working-class resistance: 'Women have power as consumers. They are pre-eminently *the* purchasers. A strike for better terms is of no utility if the price of bacon and cheese, milk, coal and rent goes up.' Citing a case in the new working-class London suburb of Edmonton, Hicks noted how women had 'struck against the rise in the price of milk, and used condensed until it came down'.[32]

Hicks was excited by the immediate potential for action, stating that resistance over prices could develop into organization to stop the adulteration of food. She proposed 'co-operative clubs' or a 'trade union of housewives' to help women to understand the need to link up with workers to challenge capitalism. In 1914 she described working women organizing around consumption as 'the fellow-half to the trade union movement', adding, 'Each half must support the other to obtain the necessities of life.'[33] In contrast, Teresa Billington-Greig rejected the expectation that consumption was women's particular concern, along with the dichotomies defining the male as worker and the female as consumer. Billington-Greig pointed out that male producers also bought goods, while women worked not only in paid employment but by administering, cleaning, preparing and cooking food in the home. She maintained moreover that it was gender bias to equate 'the status of women' with 'the status of wives'. What about the 'femmes soles' [*sic*] who supported themselves?[34] For Billington-Greig, consumption had to be seen as a significant issue for both sexes.

Both perspectives can be corroborated in the differing forms of consumer action which occurred in practice. In the early years of the twentieth century, consumption would become at once a key arena for a gendered form of class resistance, and an issue which could activate working-class men alongside women. Partly in response to inflation, but also in relation to mass strike action and ideas of economic and social justice, food and rent protests erupted in both North America and Britain. In New York, women's role as consumers was made dramatically visible by a series of collective protests against high prices and rents. Such revolts were characterized by a complicated mix of spontaneous direct action and organization. In 1902, Jewish immigrant women in New York broke into butchers' shops and fought with the police after a rise in kosher meat prices. They also organized a boycott, and set up co-operative stores along with the Ladies' Anti-Beef Trust Association. In 1910 Jewish women in South Providence picketed shops to persuade people not to buy meat until prices fell, and in 1914 Italian immigrant women were in revolt over high prices.

Women's key role as purchasers was a decisive factor in the family economy. What they could buy affected the whole family's standard of living. Consumption was a legitimate sphere of female action, and consequently women saw themselves as taking action on behalf of their families. However, the New York food protests also coincided with militant action in the clothing industry; ideas spilled over from the work-place into the home. As the wife of a cloakmaker, Mrs Levy, declared: 'Now, if *we women* make a strike, then it will be a strike.'[35] Collective action around consumption could thus be seen as a kind of 'women's strike', which combined what women were assumed to do with new ideas of what women might do.

The pre-war politicization of daily life continued during World War One, when rapid inflation provided the stimulus for protests against both food prices and rents. Kosher meat riots broke out in 1917 on the Lower East Side and spread to other areas of New York as well as to Boston, Philadelphia, Baltimore, Chicago, St Louis and Cleveland. The anarchist Marie Ganz has left a graphic account of the 1917 food rebellion, in which a spontaneous female-led type of direct action converged with an awareness of class exploitation: 'At the height of the conflict Mrs Teibel Shimberg, while beating a peddler's head with her shopping bag, caught sight of me. "Look, women," she cried, "here is Marie Ganz. She will show you how to fix the bloodsuckers."'[36] When the socialists 'rushed out' of the Forward Building and tried to lecture the women, they were swept aside. Instead, Marie Ganz proposed appointing a committee and going to City Hall to make 'the city do something to bring us relief and to make possible the purchase of food at prices within our means'.[37] But at City Hall the women were confronted by police on horseback and Marie Ganz, who was known as an anarchist, was arrested. Driven to take desperate action because of prices, the immigrant working-class women who participated expressed a sense of an entitlement to a liveli-hood. They were exercising power previously denied to them in the land of promise.

In Britain during wartime consumers also protested about their standard of living. Though these protests took differing forms from

the upsurges in America, a similar interconnection between spontaneous action, organization and political involvement can be seen. In 1914
the Minute Book of Sylvia Pankhurst's East London Federation of the
Suffragettes details various proposals to meet the acute distress caused by
rising prices. While some members argued for getting members onto
distress committees, a Miss Patterson was in favour of 'shopping for
food at ordinary prices till it is refused, get others to back us and take
the food'.[38] High rents also provoked rebellion. The ELFS paper the
Woman's Dreadnought reported in the same year that women in Leeds
were on strike and 'marching about the streets brandishing pokers, rolling pins and toasting forks, to show that they intend to protect their
homes'.[39] In 1915 a rent strike in Glasgow encouraged resistance on a
wider scale, in which women political activists played a key role. When
Glasgow landlords raised rents, the anger of working-class housewives
was channelled through the Glasgow Women's Housing Association
(GWHA), an organization which included the middle-class socialist
feminist Helen Crawfurd and Agnes Dollan, a former factory worker
and telephone operator. Both were active in the anti-war movement
and in the Independent Labour Party. Dollan was also in the Women's
Co-operative Guild, the Women's Labour League and the Clarion
Scouts. Mary Barbour, who played an important role in the rent strike,
was in both the Housing Association and the Kinning Park Women's
Co-operative Guild; she would go on to be active in the Independent
Labour Party and the peace movement.[40]

Glasgow in this period was an intensely politicized labour city, with
its network of radical Sunday Schools, newspapers, Clarion choirs and
Clarion theatre. Socialists and feminists of differing persuasions, as well
as syndicalists and anarchists, were in contact with one another informally through families and through workplaces. They were, moreover,
able to mobilize less politically minded neighbours and workmates when
grievances became acutely felt. While women took a leading role in the
Glasgow rent strike, Billington-Greig's point that men were consumers
too was borne out by the presence of men on demonstrations. Like the
cost of food, housing was not exclusively a women's issue; it affected the
standard of living of the whole family. Indeed the injustice most bitterly
resented was the threat of eviction to families with men at the front.
The placards photographed in the *Glasgow Herald* stress their patriotism:
'Partick Tenants Strike. Our Husbands, Sons and Brothers fighting the
Prussians of Germany. We are fighting the Prussians of Partick. Only

alternative Municipal Housing' and 'Defence of the Realm. Government Must Protect Our Homes from Germans and Landlords or the People will Protect Themselves'.[41] After six months the government, fearful of civil unrest, did introduce rent restriction. The war encouraged changed expectations of the state and fostered proposals for social control over consumption.

A similar connection was evident in crowd action over wartime food distribution in Glasgow. Again, these rebellions linked men and women; the Parkhead shop stewards supported the women's community-based demonstrations, telling Glasgow Corporation 'that unless food supplies were so regulated that the workers' wives would be saved from the queues, the workers were prepared to get out into the street and stand in the queues'.[42] The militant work-based shop stewards movement which grew up during the war recognized the significance of the relationship between consumption and production; the issue of food prices was taken up by shop stewards in Barrow, Manchester, the Clyde, Birmingham, Coventry and Sheffield in 1917–18. In Coventry and Sheffield (where the leading shop stewards had close links with women campaigning for suffrage), men left the munition works to help their wives in the shopping queues. This was not simply a response to hardship. The more political shop-steward leaders like J. T. Murphy were deliberately trying to connect workplace struggles to those of tenants and women in local neighbourhoods.[43]

Wartime working-class collective direct action around prices and rents was accompanied by pressure to reorganize consumption from very different sources. Both the National Food Economy League and the National Union of Women's Suffrage Societies mobilized around consumption before the state intervened, while the Women's Institute movement was started in 1915 in response to the food crisis. Its original aim was to supplement the work the Women's Land Army was doing to replace men in agriculture, by recruiting married countrywomen to grow vegetables, bottle the fruit from their gardens and keep chickens, pigs and rabbits. The Women's Institutes multiplied rapidly, reaching a membership of 50,000 by 1918; it continued during the post-war years to encourage the production and preservation of home-grown food.[44]

During the war, voluntary efforts were often combined with involvement in the many government committees busily regulating daily life. The Labour Party women's leader Marion Phillips sat on the Consumer Council, while Nellie Cressall, a laundry worker and suffragette from

Sylvia Pankhurst's East London group, served on the Food Control Committee. The Women's Co-operative Guild similarly worked in the War Emergency Workers' National Committee, exerting pressure on the government with regard to prices, food distribution and rents.[45] Margaretta Hicks listed the extraordinarily diverse consumer network which crystallized during wartime: the Fabian Women's Group, the London Kitchen Gardens, the Women's Branch of the Printers, Warehousemen and Cutters Trade Union, the National Aid Corps, the National Food Fund, Childcare Committees, Railway Women's Guilds, Girls Club Dinners, the Food Reform Association and the East London Federation of the Suffragettes.[46] They campaigned for milk depots, cost-price restaurants and school meals, and took up the issue of high prices and food shortages.

The strong wartime pull towards demanding state intervention was accompanied by efforts to ensure women's participation in decision-making. The ELFS maintained its own community services through the clinic at the Mothers' Arms, along with a cost-price restaurant, mixing these self-help projects with calls for government control over the food supply to guarantee equal distribution. The vision which inspired this ad hoc combination of tactics was ambitious: the East London Federation also wanted greater democratic control over pricing. After the Russian Revolution of 1917, Sylvia Pankhurst proposed that Councils of Workers, Soldiers and Housewives should be formed. Pankhurst was extending the idea of a Soviet or workers' council into the community.[47]

The exceptional circumstances of the war, along with the Russian revolution, shifted the parameters of what could be imagined. The American labour journalist Mary Heaton Vorse was caught up in the euphoric re-imagining of the everyday which briefly flared in the British labour movement in 1919:

> Talk flowed up and down England. It swept into the homes of working people through the shop committees and the workers' committees, from the Guild Socialists, to the trade unions, and to the Women's Co-operative Guild, over to the study classes of the Welsh miners. There was everywhere a ferment, everywhere a demand for a new world. . . . England had been one great workshop. New social forms had grown up. New kinds of service had been evolved. New ways of thinking, new ways even of cooking and of distributing food.[48]

These transformatory expectations were not to be realized. Nevertheless, during the post-war years working-class labour activists would continue to make the case for transposing individual consumption into alternative forms of social provision. Women mobilized by war brought changed expectations to peacetime. Among them was trade unionist Margaret Bondfield, who enthused in 1919: 'Already busy women who are fortunate enough to be in reach of a well-managed communal kitchen wonder how they existed without it for so long – for it means not only release from the actual preparation and cooking of food, but also from the growing burden of shopping and the queue-horror.'[49] Bondfield believed that the socialization of cooking would not only save time but be better and more efficient. She predicted less waste and more varied diets. Nonetheless, despite trade union support, the national kitchens and restaurants set up during the war were to decline in the 1920s.

Agitation persisted for working-class women to gain access to municipal resources for washing. Hannah Mitchell, a member of the Manchester Baths Committee during the 1920s, was proud of the 'really up-to-date little wash house' that she managed to get built in her area:

> Housewives could take their washing there and hire a 'stall' as it was called, a deep trough with a boiler behind, plenty of hot water, extractors which left the clothes much drier than the wringing machine at home did, with no expenditure of labour on their part, hot air driers, and ironing tables. A family wash could be done in a couple of hours, and the home kept free of wet clothes and steam.[50]

The municipal wash houses were greatly resented by the commercial laundry owners, especially when machines were installed. From the 1920s they embarked on a prolonged battle against municipal laundries. The gradual demise of the public wash houses was also due to the fact that many working-class women preferred to do washing at home, finding it inconvenient to take washing out while looking after children and cooking.[51]

Housing remained a priority in post-war Britain. Labour women put considerable pressure on the state to continue the public housing schemes initiated in wartime, while asserting women's participation in decision-making.[52] The Women's Housing Sub-Committee (WHSC) had been set up in 1917 within the Ministry of Reconstruction to examine the design of new public housing projects, partly in response to pressure from the Women's Labour League. The WHSC's surveys of women's needs revealed a strong desire for houses with a separate parlour and an indoor bathroom. Witnesses before the Tudor Walters Committee explained that

> the parlour is needed to enable the older members of the family to hold social intercourse with their friends without interruption from the children; that it is required in cases of sickness in the house . . . that it is needed for the youth of the family in order that they may meet their friends; that it is generally required for home lessons by the children of school age, or for similar work of study, serious reading, or writing, on the part of any member of the family; that it is also needed for occasional visitors whom it may not be convenient to interview in the living room.[53]

Labour women also came forward with design proposals which would make houses easier to clean. Many of the WHSC's demands were adroitly sidestepped by the Local Government Board, responsible for building the new municipal housing, but labour women's organizations continued to battle for their housing proposals and for democratic involvement. In 1919, women in Welsh mining villages lobbied for representation on housing committees as well as for pithead baths.[54] In Manchester the local council set up a housing committee of representatives of women's organizations, including Women's Sections of the Labour Party, to scrutinize housing plans.[55] In 1923 the Women's Co-operative Guild Congress 'urged the appointment of a working woman on every housing committee and the minimum requirement of a parlour in addition to a living-room and scullery, three bedrooms, and bathroom with hot and cold water in every home'. They also looked to the state for finance, calling on the government 'to institute schemes enabling local authorities to obtain money at a low rate of interest and to eliminate profiteering'.[56]

The heady ideas of soviets and direct action, along with the shop stewards' networks, disintegrated in the rapidly changing economic and political conditions of the post-war era. Most working-class women activists shifted pragmatically to campaigning through local councils for democratic rights and distributive social justice. In Glasgow, the former rent-strike leader Agnes Dollan became the first female Independent Labour Party councillor in 1919. She continued to campaign for municipal control over housing, transport and public health. In 1921, when Poplar Council, led by the left-wing George Lansbury, refused to impose a rate increase set by the London County Council – on the grounds that richer areas should help to bear the costs of relief in poorer parts of the city – the rebels were imprisoned. Among them were several working-class former East London suffragettes, including Nellie Cressall, pregnant with her sixth child.[57] The struggle for political rights spilled over into ideas of economic and social rights. Over the course of the 1920s, high unemployment forced action around social consumption onto the defensive, though it flared up sporadically in the desperate outbursts of protest against the harsh and humiliating structures of poor relief which accompanied the industrial disputes of the decade, including the 1926 General Strike.

In the US during the 1920s, despite a powerful cultural and political backlash, economic pressures were less harsh. Women were able to achieve reforms at a local level, where the social vision of municipal responsibility survived. In 1926 Bertha K. Landes ran for mayor of Seattle under the banner of 'Our Public Utilities, Our Industrial Future, Our Growing Children, Our City's Good Name', which echoed the politics of pre-war Progressive social reformers.[58] Landes, who had been active in the women's clubs and the Seattle Municipal League, argued that 'City government looks after the welfare of the people, or should. It concerns itself with sanitation and public health, clean and safe streets, protection of the home, education, care of the poor and the sick.' These, she added, were 'all problems which the mothers of the world have had to deal with in their homes and which, when presented on a municipal scale, are quite as much women's as men's problems.'[59] However, Landes did not confine herself to motherly reformation. She made a point of tackling issues like the street railway system and the city's water distribution, as well as dance halls, delinquency, temperance and the milk supply. If women's special concerns were certainly highlighted in her programme, 'citizenship' was presented as gender-neutral. She wanted not simply to add women's issues, but to change how good governance was defined.

Ideas of social and democratic entitlement were also expressed through working-class consumer organizing. In New York rent strikes had become, as Elizabeth Ewen remarks, 'an ongoing form of consumer resistance'.[60] A former trade union militant in the clothing industry, Clara Shavelson (née Lemlich) constructed a continuing organization out of this rebellious mood. The Tenants' Union she helped to create was based partly on the traditional Jewish women's charitable organizations which immigrants had brought over from Eastern Europe, and partly on the recent wartime memory of Community Councils for National Defense formed by the US War Department's agents. By 1919 the militant Tenants' Union was 4,000 strong, leading an outraged judge to describe it as a 'tenants' soviet'.[61]

In the United States wages were higher than in Britain during the 1920s, though by the end of the decade inflation was eating away at the relative prosperity of American workers. Annelise Orleck relates how this erosion of real wages stimulated consumer action: 'former shop workers, wives, sisters, and mothers of union men – began to adapt union strategies like strikes and boycotts to the problems facing them as consumers.'[62] From the late 1920s, Communist women played an important role in this new wave of consumer organizing through the Housewives' Councils. Clara Shavelson was among those arguing forcefully that the economic and political issues behind price rises should be confronted. This more overtly political phase of housewife militancy focused on the power of the meat trusts, and fused direct action with pressure on the government.[63]

Post-war consumer activists were operating amidst rapid changes in mass consumption. In Britain the Co-operative movement was still a mighty force selling everything from food and clothing to furniture, pianos and domestic appliances. Their advertisements proclaimed that their workers were contented, their goods wholesome and reliable and their customers satisfied. They also vaunted their modernity: one 1920s Co-operative Wholesale Society poster for the 'O. K. Wringer' announces 'Modern Ways For Modern Days. Ringing the Changes by Changing the Wringers. The "O. K" Wringer Is A Real Joy Bringer.' Co-operation, moreover, was international in its reach, aspiring to global co-operative trading. However, the Conservatives, having noted how Labour's women-friendly policies had wooed the new female voters, were developing their own politics of consumption. After their defeat in 1924 they began to target working-class women with cheap foodstuffs from the Empire. The connection between the well-being of the family and imperialism was supported by the popular press and, from 1926, through the Conservative Government's Empire Marketing Board.[64] Meanwhile in America, the manufacture and distribution of mass-market products was burgeoning, and home-ownership was being encouraged by the building societies and insurance companies, which were accruing extensive financial power. Advertisers were employing new psychological techniques to promote the modern descendants of the cooked food shops – convenience and fast foods. From the 1920s, the business of engineering public opinion had itself become a sector of the economy. Commenting on the rise of promotional spin, Stuart Ewen observes that 'In a society joined by modern networks of mass communication, the *public sphere* itself was becoming the property of corporate gate-keepers'.[65]

"BUNTY PULLS THE STRINGS."
" The Woman with the Basket" pulls the strings
of the World's Trade,

(National Co-operative Archives)

Control over communications was recognized as vital, not only for governing a democracy but for persuading people to reorient their everyday desires. Advertisers were learning how to market not only things, but intangibles like aspirations and dreams. Advertising and the movies, as Christine Frederick astutely noted in *Selling Mrs Consumer* in 1928, were fostering a yearning for youth, beauty and leisure among a wide stratum of women. Blessing the arrival of the time-saving tin can, Frederick turned her attention to the beauty industry, reporting how worries about 'physical charm' were driving a huge consumer industry.

'Enough lipstick is sold per year now – about two sticks per woman – to reach from New York to Reno.'[66] She also detected a newly emergent trend, 'Selling Health and Naturalness' through 'toilet preparations', predicting that 'We are going to hear more about the health and beauty idea'.[67] Frederick, with her sharp eye for shifts within popular culture, was intrigued that so many American women were refusing to 'give up their youth as their grandmothers did, at 35 or so'. She detected 'flappers of sixty-four' discovering that 'Cosmetics, plus clothes, can do marvels'.[68] Utopia had been given a price tag.

Mrs Consumer, in the kitchen or in front of the mirror, was the good/bad fairy in the new economic scenario. She could spend and keep the world of business happy, or she could wield, in Frederick's words, 'an ominous ruthless power' by refusing to buy, as she had done in the consumer boycotts.[69] In both countries a powerful economic and ideological lobby was pushing for private household services and goods, along with individual home-ownership. This was not simply a matter of filling the cash tills; consumption was the site on which contesting ideologies were being fought out. Symbolically, in 1931 Ethel Puffer Howes's co-operative housekeeping institute collapsed. She was, however, invited to participate in President Hoover's national conference on Home Building and Home Ownership, which Dolores Hayden describes as 'dedicated to a campaign to build single-family houses in the private market as a strategy for promoting greater economic growth in the United States and less industrial strife'.[70]

Post-war radicals and reformers adapted their demands to the changing context with an amalgam of social measures, and efforts to raise the capacity of the working class to consume. In her 1923 study *A Theory of Consumption*, the American economist and labour educator Hazel Kyrk argued for the extension of 'socialized consumption'. Pointing to services which were already accepted as public – from street-cleaning and garbage collection to libraries, parks and swimming pools – she proposed adding further public utilities. Eschewing a 'city housekeeping' approach to social consumption, she linked her civic vision to redistributive policies, favouring a minimum wage over price controls.[71]

Influenced by the under-consumptionist theories of the economist J. A. Hobson, British socialists also put forward various suggestions for increasing workers' spending capacity: minimum wages and 'living' wages, along with state allowances, the endowment of motherhood and, more radically, guaranteed basic incomes. In the early 1920s the

Independent Labour Party related the living wage to the specific needs of women and children; by the end of the decade it would be expressing a general concern for the 'unemployed'.[72] A proposal for a citizens' income was adopted in 1918 by the small revolutionary group, the Socialist Labour Party, which demanded maintenance for all adults, with extra amounts for parents. Like the endowment of motherhood, the demand for a citizens' income was encouraged by the wartime maintenance grants paid to the wives of men in the armed forces, which seemed to link state policy and standard of living.[73] Women reformers continued to bring differing hopes to the endowment of motherhood. While Eleanor Rathbone saw it as a means for women to acquire an independent income, others thought the measure would help to redistribute wealth and boost purchasing power.

The move towards strategies which sought to increase working-class income through state benefits avoided the awkward problems the co-operative housekeepers had confronted in telling others how they should live. On the other hand, it also reduced the possibilities of altering the social organization of domestic activity and daily life. Ethel Puffer Howes's warning that consumer goods could not tackle all aspects of domestic labour went unheeded: 'Quite apart from the fact that millions of us are not able to command them, the washing machine won't collect and sort the laundry, or hang out the clothes, the mangle won't iron complicated articles, the dishwasher won't collect, scrape and stack the dishes; the vacuum cleaner won't mop the floor or clean up and put away'.[74] Also disregarded was the voice of the American 'muckraking' journalist Louise Eberle, writing in *Collier's* magazine in 1910 on the yellow powder 'Eg-o-lene', which substituted for eggs in 'egg custard'. In Eberle's opinion, modern food was 'made to sell and not to eat'. She grimly warned of worse to come: 'Foodless food is not a passing fad, but is the sinister expression of the genius of the present day of the horseless carriage, the birdless wing, and the wireless message. What the human system thinks of it the bodies of the next generation will tell.'[75] With hindsight, this pessimism has taken on a prophetic ring.

8

Labour Problems

'I love you – but I love my work better', a decisive Beatrice told Sidney Webb during their courtship.[1] In 1887 she had already decided to make work, rather than personal relationships, the core of her existence; her aim was to achieve 'the ideal life for work'.[2] Webb would pursue her autonomous course through the dangerous shoals of desire and marriage, determined she was not going to fade, like other intelligent women of her acquaintance, into living only for the work of her husband. Along with the other pioneering women of the 1880s who sought emancipation through work, she was heading into an uncharted future.

Middle-class rebels like Webb were confronted by contradictory attitudes. In aspiring to the public recognition which educational endeavour and intellectual or professional work promised, they were echoing the high value placed on work in Victorian society. They had been shaped by a culture which ascribed virtue to work while delineating a separate female destiny for women through marriage. Work promised a sense of self-worth as a human being which transcended gender; it represented a means of securing a new identity as an individual. Yet, because a feminine identity was so bound up with domesticity and service to kin, the desire to work involved a certain defiance of gender boundaries.

Many of the middle-class dissidents had been reared in families which believed in education and social service, and they brought high ideals to the limited opportunities on offer. Yet the reality of their working lives proved rather more grubby; most of the middle-class women who struggled so hard for higher education and employment were in fact condemned to what Sidney Webb in 1891 called 'routine mental work'.[3] C. Helen Scott, who sought to deepen her education by attending University Extension lectures, urged workers in 1893 to accept

that 'there are toilers in middle-class life too, who leave the study and
the desk, the school and the sick-room, and the social weariness of
the drawing-room, with bodies as tired, with brains more weary, but
with minds and hearts as hungry and eager as those of their, so-called,
humbler brethren . . .'[4]

Not all new women who struck out on their own were from well-
padded upper-middle-class families. Eleanor Marx Aveling, who earned
a living from journalism and translation, was badly paid and faced considerable insecurity. Her childhood friend Clara Collet, who like Beatrice
Webb worked on Charles Booth's social survey, *Life and Labour of the
People* (1889), was the daughter of a principled radical Unitarian who had
scraped together a living from journalism and music teaching. She, in
turn, would find that being a jobbing intellectual curtailed her choices.
Around 1900 she was recording in her diary, 'Gave five lectures on rent
at Toynbee', adding, 'And what I am going to live on next year I don't
in the least know.'[5] In 1902 Collet was drawing on her own experience
when she noted in *Educated Working Women* that the types of employment middle-class women could enter were overstocked and underpaid.
Her advice to the next generation was to become designers, chemists,
foreign correspondents and factory managers.

Whatever problems beset educated working women, those of the
uneducated were far worse. Concerned by the lack of any collective
safeguards for women, and inspired by the organizations formed by
American women craft workers, Emma Paterson, a book-binder, had
started the Women's Protective and Provident League in 1874; this later
became the Women's Trade Union League. The League incorporated the
welfare services provided by workers' friendly societies in a form of social
unionism which gained middle-class support. Its co-operative offshoots
included a Halfpenny Savings Bank, the Women's Labour Exchange, a
workers' restaurant and a swimming club.[6] Like many 'new women', the
Leeds socialist and feminist, Isabella Ford, saw work as a vital form of
self-expression, but recognized such an ideal was remote from the lives of
the Northern working-class women she knew in the textile and clothing
factories of Bradford and Leeds. Their conditions convinced her of the
need for trade unions and women factory inspectors.[7] Along with several
other middle-class 'new women', including Eleanor Marx Aveling, Ford
encouraged women workers to join the militant New Unionism of the
late 1880s and early 1890s. Unlike the craft unions, this democratic trade
unionism was open to the unskilled and to women.

The difficulty of organizing women workers led some of their middle-class supporters to adopt other forms of action to complement union organizing. In 1889 the socialist Annie Besant, who the previous year had helped to publicize a strike by East London match women, persuaded the Tower Hamlets School Board to only tender with firms that did not exploit their workers. Besant and the Women's Trade Union League leader, Emilia Dilke, challenged the firm of Eyre and Spottiswoode which produced cheap bibles, pointing out the irony of women folding bibles for wages that were so low they could be forced into prostitution. The following year the WTUL Secretary, Clementina Black, would extend this precedent by getting the London County Council to determine a fair wage for clothing workers producing its supplies. Not only was this innovatory in proposing that the consumer rather than the employer should decide on pay, she was asserting that women workers were entitled to a living wage.[8]

The women Black was defending were not only non-unionized but working, like many others, in what were loosely termed 'the sweated trades'. High rents discouraged the growth of large factories in the larger cities, so a flexible network of sub-contractors put out the work to small 'sweatshops' or to women working in the home. In London, immigrant Irish and Jewish women were often forced to take on this kind of low-paid and insecure work. Homework was vital for those unable to seek employment outside, such as mothers and the infirm, who would often be helped by children. Though attempts were made to organize home-workers, these scattered and vulnerable workers remained at the very bottom of the labour market. Their predicament defeated the efforts of such resolute new women as Helena Born and Miriam Daniell in Bristol, Eleanor Rathbone in Liverpool and Isabella Ford in Leeds. From the 1890s the WTUL began to adopt a strategy of bolstering organization by lobbying for state intervention.

Labour-intensive 'sweated' work proliferated in American cities as well as in Britain. The radicals and reformers who exposed its existence and investigated its extent were troubled to find not only adults but children working at home and in small workshops. The Illinois Woman's Alliance was formed in 1888 after a journalist's exposure of 'City Slave Girls' in the garment industry. It included social reformers as well as socialists keen to expose child labour along with the low pay, long hours and health hazards associated with women's 'sweated' work. In 1891 two members of the Alliance, Elizabeth Morgan and Corinne Brown, made their way down a dark, narrow passage in Chicago. After lighting matches to see, they reached a basement workroom where ten men, four girls and two little children under ten worked on trousers and cloaks. Morgan reported that 'Lack of air, smell of lamps used by the pressers, and stench of filth and refuse made this a most horrible hole'.[9] It was typical of the small clothing workplaces.

Jane Addams and Florence Kelley's investigations of sweated work at Hull House convinced them of the need to combine organization with legislative protection. In 1893 Kelley was appointed chief factory inspector for the State of Illinois, and drafted a bill to prohibit garment homework and restrict the hours of work for women and children. In making her case Kelley argued that women's biological difference from men required protection. Though she had intended to use the law as a means of shortening the hours of labour for men as well as women, Kelley's position was to provide an excuse for employers to exclude women from occupations which were predominantly male. Kelley's biographer, Kathryn Kish Sklar, points out that she possessed a sophisticated approach to legislation as embodying social relations. Changing the law, Kelley believed, could help to alter people's assumptions.[10] The problem she did not envisage was that the laws could rebound to reinforce and stiffen existing attitudes.

In Britain, the Factory Acts had established a precedent for a degree of state intervention in the workplace. However the role of the state was contentious. Emilia Dilke's husband, the Liberal MP Charles Dilke, tried repeatedly but without success to secure a minimum wages bill.[11] The Dilkes' acceptance of the need for the state put them at odds with more traditional Liberals, and brought them into an alliance with socialists campaigning for shorter hours and legislation to protect women and children. In 1892 Eleanor Marx Aveling lined up with the Women's Trade Union League attempts to extend protective legislation to laundry workers, and denounced the Liberal feminist Millicent Fawcett and the anarchist Edith Lupton because they both opposed state intervention.[12] Poor Edith Lupton's proposal for a Co-operative Association for laundry women was equally scorned by the anarchists then gaining ascendancy in the Socialist League. They told her sternly, 'Nothing but the Social Revolution will raise the mass from the horrible misery from which most working women suffer at the present time'.[13] The problem of course was, what about the meantime?

Working-class women themselves were beginning to assert a claim for leisure time, along with better pay and conditions. When women from Chicago's sewing factories took to the streets for the mass May Day demonstrations which preceded the 1886 Haymarket tragedy, they told the *Chicago Tribune*: 'We want eight hours work with ten hours' pay, which means a fair advance.'[14] Similarly, in Britain it was the agitation for the eight-hour day which prompted Ada Nield Chew to complain in 1894 that the 'under-paid, over-worked "Factory Girl"' was being overlooked. She and her companions were forced to work long hours 'in order to keep ourselves in independence, which self-respecting girls even in our class of life like to do.'[15] Chew went on to say:

> To take what may be considered a good week's wage the work has to be so close and unremitting that we cannot be said to 'live' – we merely exist. We eat, we sleep, we work, endlessly, ceaselessly work, from Monday morning till Saturday night without remission. Cultivation of the mind? How is it possible? Reading? Those of us who are determined to live like human beings and require food for mind as well as body are obliged to take time which is necessary for sleep to gratify this desire. As for recreation and enjoying the beauties of nature, the seasons come and go, and we have barely time to notice whether it is spring or summer . . . 'A living wage!' Ours is a lingering, dying wage. . . . I sometimes wax very warm as I sit stitching and thinking over our wrongs.[16]

Chew was expressing a personal experience, but she was also drawing on a collective culture. By the 1890s women workers in the factory areas of Lancashire had acquired habits of organization through activity in mixed trade unions. They were beginning to take these into labour women's organizations and into the feminist and socialist movements. Awareness of class solidarity was accompanied by a gendered sense of entitlement as working-class women. In 1896 the *Manchester Guardian* reported Mrs Rigby, a Bury member of the Women's Co-operative Guild, as saying at the Guild's conference: 'Those who lived in the textile districts knew the great benefits that had accrued to the workers from a curtailment of the hours of labour. She noticed that many men were going in for even shorter hours, and if it was good for Jack to have shorter hours it was surely good for Jill.'[17] Her intervention was met with 'Hear, hear' and laughter.

Because so many women remained outside the trade unions, attempts were made during the 1890s to involve the unorganized in separate structures. Under the leadership of Emilia Dilke and Clementina Black, the Women's Trade Union League tried to reach laundry workers, rag sorters, and clothing workers.[18] In Manchester, the feminist reformer Margaret Ashton became involved with the Manchester, Salford and District Women's Trade Union Council, which from 1895 supported the unionization of women in the printing trade, linotype workers, rubber workers, box-makers, umbrella makers, typists, midwives, café workers, as well as clothing and textile workers. In a 1937 memorial issue of the *Woman Citizen* dedicated to Ashton, Mary Quaile explained that the growth of separate organizing had been because 'many of the then existing unions' did not prioritize the organization of unskilled or semi-skilled women workers.[19] In the US, women who worked with first the Knights of Labour and then the craft-orientated American Federation of Labor (AFL) encountered very similar problems. The American Women's Trade Union League was formed in 1903 to support the unionization of women who were neglected by the male-dominated institutions.[20]

White reformers and trade unionists alike tended to bypass the conditions under which black American women, mainly confined to domestic and agricultural sectors, laboured. As Anna Julia Cooper observed in *A View From the South* (1892), their toil was hardly seen as 'work':

> One often hears in the North an earnest plea from some lecturer for 'our working girls' (of course this means white working girls) . . . But how many have ever given a thought to the pinched and downtrodden colored women bending over wash-tubs and ironing boards – with children to feed and house rent to pay, wood to buy, soap and starch to furnish – lugging home weekly great baskets of clothes for families who pay them for a month's laundering barely enough to purchase a substantial pair of shoes![21]

Employment options for African Americans were actually narrowing. The late nineteenth century saw an intensification of racial prejudice marked by the 'Jim Crow' segregation laws in the Southern states, which were supported by white people determined to reverse the gains made since slavery and drive African Americans out of better-paid jobs. From 1885 schools were segregated, along with railway carriages, streetcars, hotels, restaurants, parks, playgrounds, theatres and meeting places.

Segregation was accompanied by the economic decline of industries, such as tobacco, in which African Americans had worked. 'How many occupations have Negro women?' asked Maggie Lena Walker. 'Let us count them: Negro women are domestic menials, teachers and church builders.'[22]

African-American women reformers like Maggie Lena Walker were inclined to accept that women needed to work, and in order to provide more attractive forms of employment they set up their own co-operatives and businesses. They also played a leading role in creating the mix of self-help services which helped shape black communities in the South, as well as in the newly settled poor neighbourhoods in the North.[23] While stressing economic independence and self-help, black American culture also put a high value on co-operation and sacrifice. Sharon Harley observes how mothers' paid employment was justified by a strong belief that parents should put aside 'their own needs and wants for the advancement of their children and kin'.[24]

In the textile areas of Lancashire where women workers were part of a labour force with traditions of unionization, there existed a similar prag-matic acceptance that women went out to work even when they were married and had children. The attitudes of Ada Nield Chew's husband George were shaped by his background in a Lancashire weaving family where it was customary for women to work, as well as by the new ideas of women's independence discussed in the Independent Labour Party for which he worked as an organizer. He accepted that his wife should work and contribute to the family income, but he also assumed that their daughter Doris's welfare was her responsibility. This separation of functions meant that Ada exercised control over the ultimate decisions in Doris's upbringing – but she was also taking on the greater part of the work in the home.

The most acute tension for Ada Nield Chew was in how to recon-cile her work and her close emotional bond with her daughter. When Doris was two, her mother went off to do her organizing work for the Women's Trade Union League, leaving Doris with her father. Doris recalled how 'my mother was so stricken by the look on my face and the unbelieving exclamation of "Mamma" when I was brought to the station to meet her on her return, that she decided then and there that she would never leave me behind again.'[25] So, from 1900 until 1905 when she went to school, Doris travelled with her mother. Motherhood was a knot, not only ideologically or politically, but personally.

Women with children who were involved in social and political work faced painful choices if their relationship disintegrated. In 1888, aged twenty-two, the anarchist Voltairine de Cleyre formed a free union with an older free thinker, a carpenter called James B. Elliott. By the time she fell pregnant the following year, she already knew they were incompatible. Elliott wanted a conventional domestic woman; she needed a wider life. De Cleyre left her son Harry with her former partner, though she paid for his education. Harry, who became a house painter, loved her nonetheless and was proud of her life and work.[26] The working-class Polish immigrant Anzia Yezierska found marriage and domestic life were undermining her desperate desire to 'make herself for a person'. She also left her husband and young child, teaching herself English so she could write down her experiences.[27]

Middle-class women with children had to make distressing decisions too. Charlotte Perkins Gilman's daughter Katharine was brought up by her first husband and his second wife, Grace Channing. Gilman missed her daughter and regarded her life as a failure after the collapse of her marriage, but Katharine felt her mother had abandoned her. 'I suppose you were hurt in many ways I never knew,' Gilman wrote to her daughter in 1933.[28] When her marriage broke down, Florence Kelley made her home at Hull House, campaigning through the settlement on employment and housing. However, she felt conditions in the slums of Chicago were too dangerous for her children, who were cared for by friends. 'I miss the chicks with a perennial heartache,' she told her mother in 1892.[29] The debates around women's employment were shadowed by many such wrenching personal dilemmas.

Middle-class adventurers were prepared to sacrifice much for their own right to work; indeed a few were arguing that women should be able to combine careers with motherhood. Nevertheless, their knowledge of working-class women's conditions convinced many of them that married working-class women should not be in the labour force. Concern about the unhealthy and dangerous circumstances of labour also led some to advocate legislation restricting the hours and regulating the types of work women could do. In America, attempts at state regulation faced particularly daunting resistance, not simply from employers but from the judicial system, which was inclined to reject any interference in the wage contract.[30] In 1908 two members of the National Consumers' League, Louis Brandeis and his sister-in-law, Josephine Goldmark, followed Florence Kelley's tactic in making the case for Oregon's ten-hour law on the grounds of women's physical weakness and the importance of their reproductive role in maintaining the 'strength and vigour of the race'.[31] The result of the Brandeis brief would be a Supreme Court ruling that treated women workers as a special case. By implication all women were mothers, and women were cast as victims. Protection was thus boxed in by a restrictive definition of absolute gender differences. Trade union attitudes compounded the difficulties of extending workplace protection more generally. Alice Kessler-Harris observes how the AFL 'resisted efforts to legislate on behalf of men and acquiesced reluctantly and ambivalently to efforts to legislate for women'.[32] Between 1909 and 1917, laws restricting women's hours were to be introduced in nineteen states. This contrasted with the slow progress made in the legal protection of wage rates: as late as 1927, campaigners for a minimum wage law had only achieved success in nine states.

During the 1890s the British Women's Trade Union League complemented organizing with legislative pressure for the minimum wage. Some campaigners, like Clementina Black, argued for the more generous 'living wage' which acknowledged livelihood needs. But the question of how best to tackle the problem of low pay remained. In the early twentieth century the chances of organizing women were looking somewhat better. In 1906 the WTUL was replaced by the National Federation of Women Workers. A new generation of leaders took over: the Scottish draper's daughter, Mary Macarthur, became Secretary, and Gertrude Tuckwell, a niece of Emilia Dilke, was President. Women were gaining a stronger profile in the labour movement, and Macarthur and Tuckwell, both socialists, were able to lobby on their behalf. Nevertheless the problems were daunting: 'Women are unorganized because they are badly paid and poorly paid because they are unorganized', Macarthur told the House of Commons Select Committee on Home Work in 1907.[33]

This Gordian knot led Macarthur and Tuckwell into the broad alliance agitating for state intervention to regulate sweated work, which coalesced in Britain during the 1900s. In the nineteenth century some male and female outworkers had been part of the trade union movement, but by the early twentieth century, inner-city homeworkers were increasingly regarded as belonging to an unorganizable under-class. In 1906, Tuckwell declared that homeworking 'pressed . . . into service' a labour force of the unfit, 'the aged and infirm, the crippled and the half-witted'. It forced children to 'toil early and late' and perpetuated the

Keir Hardie with Mary Macarthur (Press Association)

reproduction of unhealthy, badly educated, casualized workers. Tuckwell enquired rhetorically: 'How shall we put hearts and energy into citizens reared under such conditions?'[34]

The Anti-Sweating League did not take the homeworkers' need to earn a livelihood into account. Homework was simply seen as a system of production which should be eradicated, and Gertrude Tuckwell did not think married women should work at all. The campaign gained momentum from anxieties about social cohesion, a political need to counter the vociferous lobby for immigration control, and the eugenic panic about physical degeneration. Fears that disease could be passed on from producers to consumers, and a conviction that dependence on cheap labour held back the development of the economy, also played a part.

Importantly, though, the Anti-Sweating League made homework visible, through conventional means of communication such as reports, pamphlets and meetings, as well as by more dramatic methods. In 1906 it mounted an 'Exhibition of the Sweated Industries' in London, in association with the Liberal *Daily News* and the wealthy Quaker manufacturer,

George Cadbury. Women workers appeared in person making cigarettes, jewel-cases, matchboxes, stockings, tennis balls, brushes, furniture and innumerable other everyday items. Fashionable London society learned that the women making the cheap goods they bought worked between twelve and sixteen hours a day, to earn five to seven shillings a week.[35]

The anti-sweating campaigners also helped to legitimate state intervention around wages. Instead of either a minimum wage or the licensing of homework customary in the US, the Trades Boards in low-paid industries, introduced in 1909, were based on the Australian model. The Boards regulated pay in industries such as laundry work and clothing, where many of the workers were women. While they established a degree of state intervention in the rate of pay, employers were quick to exploit loop-holes. The effectiveness of the Boards depended on workers complementing regulation through organization. In 1910 the women chain-makers at Cradley Heath resisted successfully when some employers and middlemen tried to evade the rates set by the Trades Board. Mary Macarthur's campaign on their behalf resulted in sympathetic press coverage and an early Pathé newsreel.[36] However, as Sylvia Pankhurst pointed out in 1912, employers would quickly devise a way round the minimum rates by giving an extra load of work out and expecting it to be finished in the same time.[37]

Other measures to counter women's poverty were being debated in the early twentieth century. During the 1900s members of the Fabian Women's Group argued for equal pay, married women's right to work and the endowment of motherhood. However, equal pay caused some dissension. Beatrice Webb favoured the minimum rates set by the Trades Boards because she feared women would not be employed if they gained equal pay. Eleanor Rathbone was also opposed to equal pay, which she believed would result in even worse job segregation between the sexes.[38]

A mix of organizing and pressure for legislation also existed in the United States. Along with the Consumers' League, the Women's Trade Union League lobbied for women workers and pressed for protective legislation at work. The League gathered support from settlement workers, socialists and feminists, and also gained a base among women clothing workers in the early twentieth century. Though the American industrial system was modernizing rapidly in the 1900s, the use of women's cheap labour persisted in the clothing sector, and from 1909 defiant immigrant women were radicalized in a series of insurgent strikes against low pay and lack of safety in the factories. In 1911, a fire at the

Triangle Shirtwaist Company in New York killed 146 young women and injured many more. New Yorkers watched in horror as the terrified garment workers jumped to their deaths. A bolted lock was produced at the inquiry; but the jury, asked to decide whether the employers knew the door was locked, found them 'not guilty'. One of the survivors, Rose Safran, who had been involved in an earlier strike at Triangle, reflected after the fire: 'If the union had won we would have been safe. Two of our demands were for adequate fire escapes and for open doors from the factories to the street. But the bosses defeated us and we didn't get the open doors or the better fire escapes. So our friends are dead.'[39] The workers and their middle-class allies knew that the Triangle factory was typical of other work places. The tragedy brought home the flagrant human cost of America's economic growth.

Despite the exploitative circumstances of work, the crowded tenement neighbourhoods near the factory districts generated a vigorous radical culture. Young militant working women were educated and politicized by the debates and ideas which circulated within their communities and beyond. They hungrily searched out books and ideas. Clara Shavelson stitched shirts for twelve hours and then went to the New York Public Library, to read works by Russian writers. Pauline Newman joined the Socialist Literary Society and read George Eliot, Thomas Hardy and Shakespeare, listening to Jack London and Charlotte Perkins Gilman when they came to give talks. Rose Schneiderman borrowed books from other workers, and read the serialization of Emile Zola's *J'Accuse* in the Yiddish evening paper *Abendblatt*, commenting later, 'I devoured everything I could get my hands on.'[40]

Although all three women would remain politically active throughout their lives, they knew from their own experience and observation that most women workers had an equivocal relationship to their work. In 1912 Clara Shavelson described the young immigrant workforce in New York: 'In the beginning they are full of hope and courage. Almost all of them think that some day they will be able to get out of the factory and work up, but continuing to work under long hours and miserable conditions they lose their hopes. Their only way to leave the factory is marriage.'[41] The nature of working-class women's employment undermined the association of work with individual fulfilment which prevailed in middle-class circles. Because they laboured for low pay in grim, damaging surroundings over which they exerted little control, self-actualization implied escaping from work, not gaining entry. Moreover

Rose Schneiderman (Tamiment Library)

they brought gendered expectations of a woman's identity into the factories. These in turn were reinforced by their situation as workers; young
working women, whose wages rarely extended to the pleasures of city
life, relied on men friends to 'treat' them when they went out. Women
trade union organizers such as Clara Shavelson and Rose Schneiderman
knew that this desire to escape into romance and marriage made unionization more difficult, but they could not and did not condemn young
women for it.

Such ambivalence did, however, trouble a new wave of idealistic
college students, inspired by feminist ideas of independence to support
women's trade union organizing. To one Detroit trade union organizer
they seemed patronizing. In 1908 Kate Ryrie criticized well-off students
who looked down on the working-class young women's desire to find a
husband 'as vulgar and silly'. Ryrie asserted:

> Let them change places with her in reality and not as a few days'
> slumming experience, and I'll guarantee that they'll be as anxious to
> get out of the factory by the marriage route as they were to shake off

its dirt and get back to the shelter of their luxurious homes after their week's experience. They would then know the importance of the lover question with the average working girl.[42]

The Women's Trade Union League responded by trying to develop a union culture which could reach out to their members as women and as workers. Education was the key element in the League's social unionism; indeed, many recruits arrived by way of union-oriented English language classes. For a small payment the League also offered health care, along with advice on 'sex hygiene'. Lectures and classes covered not only industrial questions but the pros and cons of marriage and romance, domestic labour, even Lester Frank Ward's ideas about women's crucial role in early societies. A great pool of thwarted talent was released through these adult education projects. Intellectually minded League women went off to study at the University of Chicago; in 1916 Julia O'Connor, a telephone operator and organizer, sailed through a course called 'Trade Unionism and Labor Problems' with higher grades than the college students. Women's colleges such as Vassar, Wellesley, Barnard and Bryn Mawr similarly developed close links with the Women's Trade Union League. Boston telephone operators went on outings to Wellesley College and attended lectures given by Vida Scudder and other academic labour sympathizers, while Hazel Kyrk was one of a group of women economists who taught on the Bryn Mawr trade union courses.[43]

Regardless of all this ingenuity and innovation, the American Women's Trade Union League, like its British counterpart, encountered considerable obstacles in organizing women workers and began to incline towards campaigning for legislation. This caused division within the League. Differing conceptions of the role and structure of trade unions emerged, as well as conflicts over legislation and the state. One organizer, Helen Marot, left the WTUL partly because she disagreed with the reliance on protective legislation, but also because she contested the League's approach to ethnicity. Marot thought they should focus on uptown, mainly American-born women who stood more chance of organizing themselves, rather than working with immigrant women on the Jewish East Side. Rose Schneiderman and Pauline Newman, both from immigrant backgrounds, were deeply committed to the ghetto and resentful of Marot's attitude, which they saw as prejudiced and elitist.[44]

However, the WTUL aimed at bringing women into the American

Federation of Labor, which had a strong tradition of autonomous union-ism, and this is echoed in Marot's argument in *American Labor Unions* (1914) that trade unions created workers' sense of their own power, and that a vital aspect of consciousness was undermined by reliance on the state. Recognizing that women were less likely than men to organ-ize, she attributed this partly to their work being unskilled, and to their responsibility for the home. Placing a strong emphasis on consciousness, Marot believed that cultural assumptions towards women and women's 'attitude toward themselves' held them back as workers.[45]

The anarcho-syndicalist Industrial Workers of the World groups also stressed the development of workers' power, scorning reformist trade unionists that turned to the state. The IWW leader Elizabeth Gurley Flynn saw unions as demonstrating 'education in action', and her outlook was global. In 1909 she wrote in the IWW's *Industrial Worker* that capi-tal had organized the productive process 'according to the commodity produced, from the source of the raw material straight through the distribution of the finished product'. By retaliating with 'one big union', the IWW provided an object lesson in resistance. 'You find that straight line of capitalist industry sliced across by the union, just a little slice here and there.' The extension of workers' power required the creation of 'an international union' while overcoming prejudices within the US itself. Flynn believed it was futile to erect barriers against other workers, because capital could go anywhere in search of its 'cheap labour'.[46] In contrast to Marot, Flynn insisted that the making of the American work-ing class meant overcoming divisions of skill, gender, ethnicity, race and nationality.

When in 1912 immigrant textile workers rebelled in Lawrence, Massachusetts, Flynn and the IWW struggled to organize 30,000 work-ers of around forty nationalities. Flynn was inspired by the solidarity of the unskilled immigrant strikers. She envisaged a unionism without boundaries in which 'the Polack and the Jew and the Turk . . . forgot their religious and national differences . . . and felt that an injury to one is an injury to all'. She recounted an incident at Lawrence when a young woman was stopped on the picket line by an Italian boy of about sixteen. 'You go to work? No! Nice girls no go to works. Nice girl go ahome and sleeps'.[47]

Flynn was conscious of the need to reach women in the home, and community support proved extremely important in the Lawrence strike. The IWW was able to build on networks which already existed among

Elizabeth Gurley Flynn (Tamiment Library)

women, thus linking the dispute with discontent in the community. The strikers themselves noted the lived connection between producers and consumers.[48] Community participation also served to broaden the impact of the strike. Middle-class supporters such as the socialist Mary Heaton Vorse were moved not only by the refusal of the strikers to be provoked into violence, and by the solidarity between ethnic groups, but also by this activism within the community which involved women and children.[49] When Margaret Sanger was forcibly stopped by railroad authorities at the station with a group of children who were to be cared for temporarily by well-wishers, the Lawrence strikers' cause became a humanitarian issue.[50] Lawrence acquired a symbolic significance, epitomizing a stark clash of opinion about how America was to define itself as a society in the early twentieth century.

Community involvement and the appeal to public opinion became a broadly accepted strategy against the intransigence of employers and the violence of the police. The American working-class movement would be particularly creative in bridging the gap between workplace and neighbourhood, and women played a vital role in developing these links, especially in close-knit mining areas. During the 1913–14 miners' strike in Colorado, co-ordinated by the veteran organizer 'Mother Jones', then in her eight-ies, families as well as workers confronted the coal company. Women emerged out of this bitter strike and lockout with a class consciousness which was marked by their specifically female experiences.[51]

The outbreak of World War One changed the whole context of organizing, straining long-standing loyalties and friendships among campaigners. Reformers, socialists, anarchists and feminists divided among themselves on the war, which became the overriding political issue. Repression against those who opposed the war was particularly harsh in the United States: thousands of IWW members received long jail sentences, and Emma Goldman was deported. Yet, para-doxically, the upheaval the war caused in daily living meant that ideas of equality, previously seen as utopian, came to seem credible. In both countries, as women found themselves doing work which was comparable to men's, they questioned gender inequality and trade union resistance to their entry into 'male' jobs. Equal pay was no longer a wild wish; it appeared decisively on the agenda of women's demands. It was supported by members of the American Women's Trade Union League, and was one of Sylvia Pankhurst's campaign issues in East London. By 1918 it was being claimed as a right in Britain by striking women transport workers, who told passengers they wanted the same money as men for doing the same job.[52] The need for women's labour during the war had fostered a new confi-dence and brought equal pay out on to the streets.

Male trade union opposition was somewhat muted by wartime exigencies, but when the war ended conflict erupted because the soldiers were returning. Immediately after the war the WTUL joined with suffrage women in America to protest the block on women trans-port workers becoming conductors. In 1919 the women's supporters made their case both in terms of equal rights and through a concept of social reciprocity in relation to the state. 'A government that demands universal service from its citizens in time of war should provide universal employment at a living wage for its citizens in time of peace.'[53] The war years had encouraged not only ideas of gender equality, but a tacit social contract between individuals and the state which transcended the right to profit.

The wartime extension of the state into wider aspects of daily life meant that women reformers and investigators had gained experience serving on committees, surveying women's working conditions, or introducing welfare provision for women workers. These top-down interventions connected women's position at work with life outside work, but they did so in an authoritarian fashion. In response British labour women created a coalition which attempted to negotiate a greater degree of democratic control. The Federation of Women Workers, along with the Women's Co-operative Guild, the Women's Labour League and the Railway Women's Guild, combined to form the Standing Joint Committee of Industrial Women's Organizations (SJCIWO). In 1917 it called a conference which examined the impact of welfare supervision in industry. While in favour of an increase in women factory inspectors, the women who attended were wary of the employers' welfare workers, protesting against 'any extension of control over the private lives of workers' and insisting that 'the welfare – social and physical – of the workers is best looked after by themselves'.[54] The SJCIWO argued instead for trade union committees to negotiate not simply over wages and conditions at work but also around workers' wider social needs, proposing hostels which would be funded by local authorities and jointly controlled by them and by the trade unions. The interconnection of areas of life in wartime led to ideas of how democratic organization could extend beyond the workplace. This was accompanied by a rudimentary critique of the terms on which individuals could access state resources, which in turn suggested the need to rebalance the inequitable power relations between state and society.

Commentators were struck by the new-found confidence of well-paid women munitions workers. During the war, hitherto unorganizable groups of workers also discovered that they enjoyed a new bargaining power; a domestic workers' union in Birmingham was able to secure minimum wage rates for servants at the age of twenty-four, paid holidays and comfortable working and living conditions.[55] Moreover in both Britain and America the numbers of women in trade unions increased dramatically. In her pioneering history *Women in Trade Unions* (1920), an optimistic Barbara Drake would argue that the war politicized many working women by bringing them into the trade union movement.

However, the post-war move out of well-organized male jobs and the tendency for women to return to unorganized sectors soon reduced the impact of the wartime growth in union membership and the capacity of marginal groups to resist.[56] Mounting unemployment in Britain and

a series of labour defeats enabled employers to push down the minimum rates in low-paid industries. Once again women were frequently
presented with domestic service as the sole alternative to unemployment. Complaints about being pushed towards service were heard in
1922 when the shop workers' leader, Margaret Bondfield, chaired a
Trades Union Congress conference of unemployed women. Yet the
bold interconnecting vision acquired in the war years persisted. The
women at the conference wanted all workers – including homeworkers,
cleaners and domestic servants – to be covered by the Unemployment
Insurance Act.[57] Awareness of women's specific needs and of gender
inequality also proved resilient. In the early 1920s Lily Webb, who
came from a Lancashire textile family, was active in the newly formed
Communist Party and in the National Unemployed Workers' Union,
advising women activists on unemployment. Though the Communist
Party put the stress on women's exploitation as workers, Webb, at the
grass-roots, was aware of women's need for social provision such as
food centres, clinics and maternity hospitals. In her reports from the
Manchester region in the paper *Out of Work*, she was sharply critical of
the men's tendency to ignore these issues.[58]

Women clerks looking for work (Working Class Movement Library)

One labour market shift did survive the war. Growing numbers of women in both Britain and the US were entering 'white-collar jobs' as clerical and sales workers, while the more highly educated were moving not only into teaching but into the civil service, academia and the professions. The numbers of women graduates were particularly striking in the US, where in 1920, 7.6 per cent of women attended college. A few even penetrated the male bastions of finance. The American Augusta Bratton, having achieved success in banking, argued that there was 'room in the business world for both masculine and feminine brains'. She was not sure, however, whether women unlike herself were motivated to cope in a man's world: 'They are still taking advantage of their sex to usurp privileges which would never occur to men to take'. The tough-minded Bratton considered that women must stop giving in to 'trivial ailments when it is not absolutely necessary'.[59] She warned women that if they wanted equal pay, they must prove themselves. How women were to relate to the competitive market place was to be an issue which refused to go away.

Post-war women workers in the United States were expressing an equally confident sense of their ability to fight their own battles. With America booming and unemployment relatively low, some working women were assuming rights rather than defining themselves in relation to men. Dana Frank records how in a 1919 Seattle debate about whether a 'family wage' earned by the man should be the goal, 'Feminist Unionists argued that women had the right to work both as independent individuals and out of need to support their families'.[60] While African-American working-class women were largely excluded from better-paid jobs, the sociologist Elise Johnson McDougald noted an informal assertiveness among them, even outside the organized sectors. In her essay 'The Double Task: The Struggle of Negro Women for Sex and Race Emancipation' (1925), she wrote that 'The Negro woman . . . is revolting against residential domestic service. It is a last stand in her fight to maintain a semblance of family life. For this reason, principally the number of day or casual workers is on the increase . . . how else can her children, loose all afternoon, be gathered together at night-fall.'[61]

A strong emphasis on women's independence was also evident in the demand by the egalitarian American feminist Alice Paul, and the powerful National Woman's Party, for an Equal Rights Amendment to the Constitution to establish women's equal economic rights during the early 1920s. To the egalitarians, the claims of Florence Kelley from the Consumers' League, and Mary Dreier from the Women's Trade Union League, for special laws for women workers around maximum hours, minimum wages and the prohibition of night work, seemed to be stuck in the past. Moreover the old problem for those who sought regulation in the workplace remained: the only way of upholding federal intervention against the freedom of contract was by making a case that women were naturally, rather than socially or economically, incapable of defending themselves at work. This was anathema to the liberal egalitarians, who defended women's unrestricted freedom to have fulfilling careers or do skilled jobs.

Some American women tried to combine claims for equality with protection. The socialist feminist Harriot Stanton Blatch rejected the tactic of classing women with children, contending that special protection would exclude women from skilled work. Instead, Blatch argued, protection had to be for both sexes.[62] But of course this approach was in conflict not only with employers' profits but with widely held convictions about the freedom of the market. Women trade union activists, who initially had supported legislation because unionization among women was so hard, became increasingly exasperated by the egalitarians' disregard of the actual circumstances of women workers. WTUL member Pauline Newman pointed out that the freedom and equality most working-class women had enjoyed before any restriction on time was merely the freedom to work long hours for low wages, or to 'leave the job and starve'.[63] Over the course of the decade the battle lines polarized.[64]

Similar disputes occurred in Britain, even though the economic and political context was quite different. Unemployment was high and the Labour Party accepted the regulation of industry. Concerned to halt the downward slide of women's wage levels, the Standing Joint Committee of Industrial Women's Organizations pushed for the unionization of women and state protection. In 1924, when the Labour Party was in power, their efforts resulted in a new Factory Act restricting the hours of women and young workers to a forty-eight-hour week.[65] Feminists in the National Union of Societies for Equal Citizenship opposed the Act, but this conflict did not assume the rigid and hostile form which emerged in America. NUSEC eventually dropped its position of outright opposition towards protection, in favour of a policy committed to consulting the needs of women in specific industries. Though in 1927 a group of egalitarian feminists left NUSEC in a dispute over protective legislation, there was a range of views and demands among both feminists and labour women. Women in both groups could support equality and protection; Dora Russell, for instance, argued for protective legislation for all workers and special measures for women around maternity.[66]

Behind the conflicts over women as workers lay dissimilar views about how women should be and live. A woman's individual right to work was regarded by feminists who stressed equality as the touchstone of emancipation. Work for them not only brought economic independence, it constituted a vital means of expressing one's abilities. In their view, appeals for protection fell into the old traps which presented women as essentially different and inferior to men. This was an elitist and abstract point, according to the reformers and socialists who focused on protection. They stressed the unfulfilling nature of most work within present conditions, and thought in terms of women's basic well-being. Instead of regarding women workers as autonomous units, they took into account familial and kinship networks. The socialists among them argued for the need to curb capital's power through state laws; the regulation of the working hours and conditions of women and children was assumed to be simply a first step.

Women's labour problems were clear-cut and material: lack of options, low pay, and inequality at work and in the unions. However, efforts to solve them turned out be difficult, divisive and tactically messy. The conflicting remedies proposed included a free labour market, making demands for state intervention, encouraging contract compliance, consumer pressure, mutual self-help projects, social and community trade unionism, or combining community and workplace rebellions. The disagreements which arose in the course of agitation were not only about tactics; they reflected divergent approaches to gender, to the individual's relation to society and indeed to work. Yet despite the failure to agree on common policies, these debates over what should be done about women's work led some of the adventurers towards a wider process of rethinking which encompassed the scope of labour, what work might mean, how mass production might change, and how the economy could be structured.

9

Reworking Work

The intrepid middle-class women of the 1880s and 1890s had claimed access to careers regardless of personal sacrifice; 'modern' young women in the early twentieth century were convinced that paid employment would be one element in a life of self-realization and self-expression. For Emma Goldman, who doubted that work within the present system, even for supposedly privileged women, could be either fulfilling or emancipatory, this enthusiasm to enter the labour market was a delusion on the part of middle-class feminists. In 1914 she claimed that the extension of women's education in the US was producing, not freedom and self-determination, but a multitude of genteel proletarians:

> Every year our schools and colleges turn out thousands of competitors in the intellectual market, and everywhere the supply is greater than the demand. In order to exist, they must cringe and crawl and beg for a position. Professional women crowd the offices, sit around for hours, grow weary and faint with the search for employment, and yet deceive themselves with the delusion that they are superior to the working girl or that they are economically independent.[1]

In the same year, the British anarchist Lily Gair Wilkinson similarly criticized 'women of the privileged class' for struggling to gain entry into the professions and 'all those tortuous paths of life which men have cut out for themselves.' Instead of wanting to become 'lawyers, doctors, parsons, stockbrokers' or even factory workers, Wilkinson believed that women should instead seek 'freedom in communal life'.[2]

Olive Schreiner's influential *Woman and Labour* had adopted a quite different slant in 1911. '*We take all labour for our province!*' asserted the

South African writer, endorsing feminists' demands to enter male-defined employment with the declaration: 'From the judge's seat to the legislator's chair; from the statesman's closet to the merchant's office; from the chemist's laboratory to the astronomer's tower, there is no post or form of toil for which it is not our intention to attempt to fit ourselves.'[3] Schreiner explained in her introduction that the book had occupied a large part of her life. She brought to *Woman and Labour* her own desperate longings for an individual identity, as well as her experience in wider social movements. The book enabled her to unravel a cluster of tangled strands around gender and work which she had encountered since the Ibsenite rebellions of the 1880s.

Cronwright and Olive Schreiner, 1894 (Carpenter Collection, Sheffield Archives)

Woman and Labour bridged the chasm which divided the new women's assertion of individual autonomy from socialist theories of 'the Woman Problem', which stressed the class exploitation of women as workers or the social contribution of women as mothers. Examining the interactions between reproductive and productive activity, Schreiner observed that 'modern social conditions' were reducing the tendency for women to bear children as well as the numbers in each family, and therefore mothering was now less likely to fill 'the entire circle of female life'. As a result, the argument 'that the main and continuous occupation of all women from puberty to age is the bearing and suckling of children' was being undermined, along with the assumption 'that this occupation must fully satisfy all her needs for social labour and activity.' Such a perspective had become 'an antiquated and unmitigated misstatement'; for Schreiner, it followed that a pattern of living must be devised so that women could be both mothers and workers.[4]

Schreiner argued that the scope of women's economic contribution had narrowed with the development of capitalism, reducing many women to 'parasitism'. This contraction, she maintained, had been the motive force for what she called 'the Woman's Labour Movement', which had arisen 'among women of the more cultured and wealthy classes' who were demanding that 'professional, political and highly skilled labour [should be] thrown open to them'.[5] Cutting through the disputes over whether women should work or not, Schreiner demonstrated that they already did. She poked fun at the 'lofty theorist' who stood 'before the drawing-room fire in spotless shirt-front and perfectly fitting clothes', declaiming 'upon the amplitude of woman's work in life as child-bearer'.[6] The personification of the gender and class prejudices which determined how labour was seen and evaluated, he was oblivious to the sweated women workers and domestic servants who enabled him to philosophize in style, yet outraged by the thought of women doctors, legislators and professors. 'It is not the labour, or the amount of labour, so much as the amount of reward that interferes with his ideal of the eternal womanly.'[7]

The invisibility of poor women's work was not an original idea. Anna Julia Cooper had made the same point in 1892 in *A View from the South*, in relation to black women's work.[8] In the late 1890s the American anarchist Kate Austin, who was familiar with women's work on farms, had noted how a double standard was applied to differing types of work:

Isn't it queer that women can do the hardest kind of manual labor . . . and not a protest is heard. Should she take it into her head to study medicine, practise law, lecture or write on women's rights . . . the whole masculine world is convulsed, wise old fossils write . . . ponderous papers on the subject, the home is in danger, woman is unsexing herself, getting coarse and masculine.[9]

Schreiner's broad view of labour as reproductive activity as well as production for wages, and the connections she made between paid and unpaid activity, were also not entirely new.[10] Housework had been acknowledged as work by the British feminist Ada Heather-Bigg in an 1894 article in the *Economic Journal*. Heather-Bigg argued that women's employment had simply become visible through wage-earning: when men opposed women's work, 'what they object to is the wage-earning not the *work* of wives'.[11] The domestic labour of working-class women had also been noted by Schreiner's friend Edward Carpenter, in his *Love's Coming of Age* (1896).[12]

While elements within *Woman and Labour* were already in circulation, the compound was Schreiner's. She presented a challenge to the manner in which women's paid and unpaid economic and social activities were undervalued. The book struck a profound chord among socialist and feminist women struggling to rethink work in relation to child-bearing, domestic life and consumption. Among them was the economic historian Alice Clark, who described *Woman and Labour* as 'epoch-making' in the Preface to her 1919 *Working Life of Women in the Seventeenth Century*. For Clark the crux of Schreiner's book was her insight into 'the difference between reality and the commonly received generalisations as to women's productive capacity'.[13]

Clark belonged to an impressive network in the Fabian Women's Group who were exploring how the daily lives of women had been excluded from the historical record. Based at the London School of Economics founded by Beatrice and Sidney Webb, this new generation of Fabian women combined an interest in history and social theory with an awareness of modern women's dilemmas in balancing work with marriage and a family. Among them was the former student of Beatrice Webb, Bessie Leigh Hutchins, who, along with Mabel Atkinson, introduced Schreiner's *Woman and Labour* to the Fabian Women's Group. Hutchins, a member of the research group the Women's Industrial Council, wrote in both mainstream economic journals and in the feminist *Englishwoman* on women's work, and in 1915 was the author of a pioneering study, *Women in Modern Industry*.[14] Clark and Hutchins, along with Barbara Drake, were able to draw on the social and economic history pioneered by the Webbs, and, like the Webbs', their interest in the present raised questions about the past. From this little group of Fabian women came the demand for work and motherhood.

Clark's historical research documented how women's productive activity had contracted with the shift from domestic industry. Her perspective moved the focus away from a purely political or legal definition of rights, undermining the nineteenth-century liberal view that women had steadily progressed towards emancipation. Clark believed historians and sociologists should not only look at politics, but consider economic and social development as a whole, including 'the conditions under which the obscure mass of women live and fulfil their duties as human beings'.[15] This integrated approach conceptualized labour in terms of gaining a livelihood, rather than as paid employment alone. Clark adopted a mode of analysis which implicitly subverted existing ways of seeing gender relations and economic life.

While women like Schreiner and Clark theorized women's labour in relation to social existence, others were imagining how work might be. The influence of Ruskin and Morris contributed to an interrogation about how work was done and what was produced, which ran in counterpoint to practical efforts to improve women's work in the here and now. Morris's conviction that work should be both fulfilling in the doing, and worth doing because it resulted in goods which were useful and beautiful, inspired the arts and crafts revival. Though the movement was led initially by men, women took up crafts such as embroidery, metalwork and stained glass. A few became designers and promoters of arts and crafts ideas. Julia Dawson, who set up the Clarion Guild of Handicraft in 1902, took her human-centred approach to technology from Morris, stressing that machines should be used to enhance the dignity of labour, rather than to de-skill the worker.[16]

In America Mary Ware Dennett, who in 1894 became head of the new Department of Design and Decoration at Philadelphia's Drexel Institute of Art, emphasized personal fulfilment through arts and crafts, telling her students that 'Beauty, and art, which is the expression of beauty, should be a part of everyone's life.' She wanted art not 'for art's sake but for everybody's sake', believing that 'All great art of the world has been the art of the people, and the trouble with our time is, that what art we have is confined to a very small class of people.' While critical of the uniformity of machine-made goods, she did not dismiss machinery. Instead, Ware Dennett followed Morris in insisting that 'machinery should be a servant to man, not make man its slave and attendant'.[17] Ethical aesthetics with a social edge drew her into reform circles during the 1900s, when she joined the Boston Consumers' League and became active in the women's movement. She would later gain notoriety as a birth control campaigner.

Ellen Gates Starr, who helped Jane Addams to establish Hull House in Chicago, was an art bookbinder, and the two women enthusiastically incorporated arts and crafts into the work of the settlement. Both women had close links with Britain; Ruskin and Morris were key influences at Hull House, and Addams would later be in contact with the British arts and crafts designer Charles Ashbee, whose Guild and School of Handicraft sought to bring a new social meaning to labour. Addams demonstrated ingenuity in adapting arts and crafts to fit the needs of the Chicago poor; she regarded craftwork as a means of restoring self-respect among the older immigrants, dislocated in the strange foreign city.[18] She also hoped that enabling children who were being Americanized to appreciate their parents' skills might help to overcome tensions in immigrant families, bringing respect for women as well as men. When the Hull House Labor Museum opened in 1900 displaying the diverse craft skills of Chicago's immigrants, Addams remarked with pride: 'The women of various nationalities enjoy the work and the recognition which it very properly brings them as mistresses of an old and honored craft.'[19]

Addams saw the process of making as a means of remembering, reflecting how 'the whirl of wheels recalls many a reminiscence and story of the old country, the telling of which makes a rural interlude in the busy town life'.[20] She felt sure that the dignity endowed by the recognition of skill could enable the immigrant poor to step with confidence into American society. The practical Addams wanted to help them relate to the new world, while retaining valued aspects of their earlier lives. Nevertheless, she also imagined them contributing towards the possibility of another kind of America. In Eileen Boris's words, 'The Labor Museum consolidated the past with the present to emphasize a co-operative vision of the future'.[21] Addams hoped that maintaining craft skills might humanize the conditions of machine production.

Ellen Gates Starr, however, was fiercely critical of machine-led production. Writing in *Hull House Maps and Papers* (1895), she noted that Ruskin and Morris had shown:

The product of a machine may be useful, and serve some purpose of information, but can never be artistic. As soon as a machine intervenes between the mind and its product, a hard, impassable barrier – a non-

Ellen Gates Starr with Peter Verburg at the Hull House
bindery (Sophia Smith Collection, Smith College)

conductor of thought and emotion – is raised between the speaking
and listening mind. If a man is made a machine, if his part is merely
that of reproducing with mechanical exactness the design of some-
body else, the effect is the same.[22]

Starr's romantic rejection of the machine landed her in the central
contradiction of arts and crafts – the high costs which excluded the poor
as consumers and producers. When she tried to teach her bookbinding
skills at Hull House, the expensive materials proved well beyond the
reach of local working-class women. Starr transposed her hostility to
machine-based labour into a more general support for working-class
resistance during the militant strike wave, which occurred between
1912–17.

The American social reformer Vida Scudder had discovered Ruskin
when she studied at Oxford. After her return from Britain to the US, she
helped to set up the College Settlements' Association in 1889, and taught
for the American University Extension movement in Boston's Denison

House Settlement. Like many other middle-class settlement workers and reformers, she sought to overcome class divisions through closer human fellowship. Believing that this involved both social and personal changes, she interpreted Ruskin's legacy as 'the extension of the moral consciousness through all relations of production and consumption; the simplification of life, and the abandonment of luxury at least during the present crisis; the active devotion to some form of social service.'[23]

Vida Dutton Scudder, 1884 (Sophia Smith Collection, Smith College)

Scudder's ethical commitment led her to question the existing class structure which distorted relations between people in differing classes. Asserting a Whitmanite desire for individual fulfilment through democratic communion, she argued that the problem was how to realize the 'craving' for more 'contact' and 'for full expression and reception of personality . . . in all the rich relations of actual life by the constant extension of fellowship'.[24] Practical engagement moved her leftwards; contact with labour struggles at Denison House was followed in 1903 by her work as an organizer in the Women's Trade Union League. In 1912 she joined the Socialist Party, and inspired by the solidarity and fraternity of the Lawrence workers, became a trade union educator.

The rapidity of change in production methods and their impact on the labour process in the early years of the twentieth century encouraged some radical dreamers to engage in a total critique of the existing structures and purposes of work. In 1910 the anarchist Voltairine de Cleyre wrote in *Mother Earth*:

> The Great idea of our age . . . is the *Much Making* of Things; not the joy of spending living energy in creative work; rather the shameless, merciless driving and over driving, wasting and draining of the last bit of energy, only to produce heaps and heaps of things – things ugly, things harmful, things useless and at the best largely unnecessary.[25]

For de Cleyre, production, consumption and ways of living were integrally linked. Emma Goldman's perspective was similarly interrelated. She was scornful not simply of the kind of objects made under the capitalist system of production, but of the impact of exploitation and competition on human well-being and culture. 'Real wealth consists in things of utility and beauty, in things that help to create strong beautiful bodies and surroundings inspiring to live in.' Existing work resulted only in 'gray and hideous things, reflecting a dull and hideous existence'.[26] Worst of all, modern production methods were reducing workers to 'brainless automations'.[27]

De Cleyre and Goldman's loathing of the mass production methods which were taking hold in America was echoed in Britain. The British anarchist Lily Gair Wilkinson protested at the repressive consequences of the acute awareness of time which governed offices as well as factories. Writing in Margaret Sanger's *Woman Rebel*, she described graphically the impact of a time-controlled consciousness:

> As you stand listening to the menace of the clock and wondering whether you will break free or trudge back to the office, you have a sudden revelation. You realize that while there are men and women who hold from others the means of life – the rich surface of the earth and the means of cultivating that richness – so long there will be no freedom for the others who possess none at all. For possession by a few gives power to the few to control the lives of the millions who are dispossessed, and to bring them into life-long bondage.[28]

In her pamphlet *Woman's Freedom* (1914), Wilkinson echoed Edward Carpenter in calling for a return to a 'simpler life', which she believed would be more 'wholesome'.[29] Wilkinson favoured handicrafts produced at home along with agriculture. She imagined men as well as women living together and working together at home.

The bohemians of Greenwich Village borrowed some elements of arts and crafts stress on creativity in labour, as well as the anarchist rejection of the clear-cut demarcation between work and leisure. Art, labour, politics, creativity and sex were at one in the inchoate milieu of bohemia. Mabel Dodge Luhan's restless search for experience epitomized the rejection of boundaries, while the writer Susan Glaspell insisted that in the Village, 'Life was all of a piece, work not separated from play'.[30] Although political and social change formed part of the bohemian agenda, the emphasis was on personally living against the grain, prefiguring fusion amidst fragmentation.

Despite their multiple outlooks, adventurers influenced by Ruskin, Morris and arts and crafts sought to integrate work and life, conceiving a human-centred technology, an everyday aesthetic of use and pleasure, and new kinds of democracy in daily encounters. Asking questions about work led them to examine received ideas about the body and human relationships, the environment and culture. Some of the more radical dreamers also rejected the contemporary drive for greater productivity. At this point, however, they faltered; for their absolute renunciation offered no way in which they could engage with the transformation which was rapidly overtaking them.

Some American women reformers, in contrast, embraced Taylorist production methods as an advance on the arbitrary coercion which marked relations between workers and employers in factories and sweat-shops. Lillian Gilbreth believed that scientific management offered a far preferable form of industrial organization, because it could recognize workers' level of productivity fairly and reward them accordingly. She also saw the regulation of input as a means of preventing fatigue. Working with husband Frank as an industrial consultant, Gilbreth pioneered the human relations aspects of scientific management in her studies of the engineering industry, and in her later work on the clerical, retail and laundry sectors.[31]

Her 1914 study *The Psychology of Management: The Function of the Mind in Determining, Teaching and Installing Methods of Least Waste* merged an interest in psychology with her own theories of home-making. Gilbreth argued that close observation of the physical expenditure of energy had to be complemented by management taking into account the interconnection between the worker's mind and body. This focus on the needs of individual workers led her to advocate rest breaks. She also pioneered the ergonomic study of how to improve lighting and chair design, devising better working positions in order to minimize fatigue and backache. Gilbreth set out to persuade both workers and employers that ergonomics could be beneficial in human terms, while also raising productivity.[32]

Employers were apt to take on those aspects of Taylorism which enabled them to increase output and minimize workers' control, sooner than measures aiming to enhance the welfare of workers. However, under attack during the early twentieth century from vigorous 'muck-raking' journalists who denounced corporate greed, some big employers perceived that the old, blatant 'tooth and claw' style of capitalism required a new look. They became prepared to incorporate some of their crit-ics' proposals, so long as there were benefits for their companies. In 1902, when Ida Tarbell was engaged on research into the Standard Oil Company, the charismatic and charming boss of Standard Oil, Henry Rogers – 'tall, muscular, lithe as an Indian' – met with her secretly. Rogers worked hard to win her support for company policy, graphically evoking the Iowa hills where she had lived as a child and where he had laid the basis for his fortune in oil.[33] Tarbell commented in her autobiog-raphy, *All in a Day's Work*: 'Mr Rogers may be regarded, I think, as the first public relations counsel of the Standard Oil Company.' She was 'the first subject on which the new policy was tried'.[34] Rogers had softened her critique of the corporate elite.

However, Tarbell found herself isolated in her efforts to spin a more ethical capitalism. To her 'chagrin' she was dismissed as a 'muckraker' by President Roosevelt, who believed her exposure of capitalism's flaws might entice people towards socialism, while her reformer friends wanted clear-cut denunciations of capital and did not feel her criticisms went far enough.[35] Tarbell's friendship with Lillian and Frank Gilbreth led her to see Taylorism as a means of reforming industry. In *New Ideals in Business* (1917), she proposed that scientific management constituted an alternative to corrupt monopolies. In 1917 Tarbell served on the Woman's Committee of the Council of National Defense. This experi-ence convinced Tarbell, who opposed the political enfranchisement of women, of the need for economic and social planning. Wartime welfare measures appeared to confirm the optimistic approach she and Lillian Gilbreth took to scientific management.[36]

Both women were convinced of the liberating potential of machine production. Lillian Gilbreth believed that the harmonious merging of the worker with the machine was necessarily beneficial, while the expansion of production would mean higher wages and more affordable mass-produced commodities. To Gilbreth, the 'Machine Age' in home and factory meant a better life for all. Tarbell shared this sanguinity about technology. She recalled in her autobiography:

> Machines were not devils to me as they were to some of my reform-ing friends, particularly that splendid old warrior Florence Kelley, then in the thick of her fight for 'ethical gains through legislation'. To me machines freed from heavy labor, created abundance . . . I was able to understand what the enemy of the machine rarely admits: that men and women who have arrived at the dignity of steady workers not only respect, but frequently take pride in, their machines.[37]

Kelley's colleague from the Consumers' League, Josephine Goldmark, who had helped to formulate the Brandeis brief on protective legislation, took a more sceptical attitude towards modern industry and technol-ogy in her impressive study *Fatigue and Efficiency* in 1912. Drawing on Ruskin and Morris as well as contemporary studies of psychology and labour relations, Goldmark examined conditions in industries which ranged from canneries to textiles and criticized the stress, monotony and fatigue experienced by workers. She saw labour relations and produc-tivity as integrally connected. Describing the stress experienced by 'telephone girls' as a result of overloading, shift work and overtime, Goldmark linked the operators' point of breakdown to a breakdown in efficiency.[38] In contrast to Gilbreth, she also remarked how the 'fixed and mechanical' nature of the rhythm of machinery was at variance with 'the individual's natural swing or rhythmic tendency'.[39] Observation of modern production methods led Goldmark to conclude: 'The injury of highly speeded machine work lies . . . in this, that the mechanical, rapid rhythm of machinery dominates the human agent, whatever be his natu-ral rate or rhythmic tendency. The machine sets the tempo; the worker must keep to it.'[40]

Goldmark documented how American capitalism in recent decades had been able to ignore the consequences of pressing 'all workers to their physical limits, and to dismiss them as soon as efficiency shows signs of failing'.[41] The endless flow of young immigrant workers provided a

renewable source of labour. She feared that this remorseless exploitation would have negative consequences in the long run, inasmuch as
it would affect reproduction. Goldmark was making a case for a more
social form of capitalism designed to perpetuate itself effectively. More
immediately, her findings that shorter hours of work resulted in higher
productivity would strengthen arguments for reducing the time spent at
work.

An unintended consequence of Taylorism's preoccupation with
measuring time would be a stronger sense of entitlement to 'time off'.
This was expressed not only in terms of political demands, but also
became part of the cultural assumptions of young American factory
workers, shop workers, clerks and 'typewriters' in the early twentieth
century. As Kathy Peiss shows, they were beginning to regard leisure as
'a separate sphere of life to be consciously protected'.[42] Similar attitudes
were appearing among some university graduates. Elizabeth Hawes had
learned about Ruskin, the Fabians and social housekeeping from her
teachers at college, but joining the post-war bohemian exodus to Paris
where she worked for a couturier, she and her fellow Americans raced
against time: 'We got our jobs so boiled down that we never had to work
more than half a day, sometimes not even that. . . . The idea was not
like the French, that life is leisurely and work may be done slowly. We
did our work with utmost speed so that in one day we could easily do
three days' tasks.'[43] This new generation did not believe people should
live only to work; they wanted to work less and spend more, rather than
celebrate the dignity of labour. To their elders, reared on the merits of
thrift and denial, they appeared frivolous – but theirs was a negotiation
with a productive system they had no hope of reshaping. Instead they
sought ways of evading its reach.

In the post-war era, several women theorists did engage critically with
the new circumstances of work while retaining transformatory hopes.
In Britain Barbara Drake struggled, in *Women in Trade Unions* (1920), to
combine the ideals of labour as craft with the reality of mass production
stimulated by wartime industry. Contesting the assumption that scientific
management necessarily had to reduce the 'mechanic . . . to a common
measure with the machine', Drake remained nonetheless concerned
with a transition to a society that was not geared to profit: 'As control
of industry passes eventually from the hands of an autocratic employer
into those of a workers' democracy, indeed, these methods, from being
mechanical, may become co-operative; and they may express, if not the

passion of the artist, at least the human instinct to share in the common service of humanity.'[44]

The American Mary Parker Follett moved from community work to writing about the workplace. Her interest in the dynamics of groups had its origins in her experience of doing vocational guidance work in Boston, and serving in 1912 on the Boards which fixed minimum wage rates in Massachusetts. Contact with forward-looking capitalists, such as the store owner Edward Filene and the manufacturer Henry Dennison, introduced her to Taylorism; then, during the war, she observed the operation of the War Labor Boards. In the 1920s she adapted her knowledge of organizing small neighbourhood groups to the world of business, becoming a lecturer on personnel administration.[45] In her influential book *Creative Experience* (1924), Follett advocated self-governing teams in the workplace. Though she stressed the human factor in production, she believed in the need for leadership as well as participatory teams.[46] Her innovatory insight was that instead of trying to iron out conflict, management should see it as potentially useful. In her 1925 *Constructive Conflict*, Follett put forward the idea that personnel administrators should embrace conflict and 'set it to work for us'.[47] Conflict in psychological terms could be seen as the 'interacting of desires'.[48] Follett, who had a critical interest in Guild Socialism, lived in Britain from 1928 until 1933 with her partner Katherine Furst. Forgotten in the US during the 1930s, she was taken up by the 1980s advocates of 'new' management, who were interested in her work teams as a means of identifying potential problems in the production process. Those who wanted to tap into individual workers' attitudes in order to alter the culture of organizations also drew on Follett. It was a curious mutation to emerge from late nineteenth-century social housekeeping.

In a book with the fashionably Bergsonian title, *The Creative Impulse in Industry* (1918), socialist Helen Marot wrestled more directly with devising an approach to production which was neither Taylorist or state-led, and yet avoided the anarchists' absolute rejection of the state. Influenced by the Fabians, Marot was familiar both with the discussions on industrial democracy taking place in the British Labour Party, and with anarcho-syndicalist ideas of direct action. Whereas Follett was a reformer tinged with participatory democracy, Marot was shaped by the eclectic and dynamic currents of libertarian social thought swirling through progressive circles between 1912 and 1920. After working with the Women's Trade Union League, she edited the magazine *The Dial* with John Dewey and Thorstein Veblen, absorbing Dewey's connection of democracy to 'self-realization' and Veblen's social critique of industrial capitalism. Like the future writer on technology and cities, Lewis Mumford, who also worked on *The Dial*, Marot was influenced by the British planner Patrick Geddes's appreciation of the need to take account of lived experience in sustainable social planning.[49]

Marot's criticism of scientific management focused on its preoccupation with measuring workers' energy in order to harness human capacity. She argued with extraordinary prescience that the Taylorists failed to grasp that 'the real incentive to production was . . . a realization on the part of the worker of its social value and his appreciation of its creative content'.[50] In Marot's view, 'the economic organization of modern society, though built on the common people's productive energy, has discounted their *creative potential*.'[51] Marot also foresaw that while scientific management would initially bring industrial stability, it would lay a new basis for longer-term conflict; an insight which would be borne out by the clashes of the 1930s led by the Congress of Industrial Organizations (CIO).[52] She discerned too that while a state-led socialism might 'curb' exploitation, it did not automatically follow that it would 'of itself induce creative effort'. Simply securing 'sufficient leisure and food for general consumption' did not enable 'the creative impulse' to 'operate'. Marot predicted: 'The signs are that a socialist state would lean exclusively on the consumption desire for production results, just as the present system of business now does.'[53]

By 1919, Marot was aware that the reliance of social reformers on 'state machinery' during the war had left them without an effective strategy for post-war circumstances. With the government withdrawing, the attempts at legislative reform were in peril, their roots 'too tender to penetrate beyond the surface of our political and industrial institutions'.[54] But her efforts to present an alternative perspective fell on stony ground. Marot herself was targeted in the post-war paranoia about a spider's web of subversion extending from the extreme left to social reformers. By the end of 1919 she had abandoned her attempts to graft a deeper form of democracy and creative self-actualization onto modern industry and machine production. She developed instead an interest in psychology, but was not able to find a new career as an industrial pundit.[55] Nonetheless she had pinpointed a key weakness in Taylorist theories of production.

Radicals and reformers of the 1920s focused on improving conditions within existing structures, rather than transforming how work was done and what was made. Utopian dreamers who opposed mass production were apt to appear somewhat cranky, elitist and out of touch. Enthusiasm for craft persisted, bringing many women into design and encouraging handicrafts in schools. But these developed on the margins; they did not constitute a critique of the economy as a whole, and mainstream opinion on the left continued to assume that increased production could potentially offer workers a better life.

A broader approach to the economy did, however, linger on. Hazel Kyrk's *A Theory of Consumption* (1923) accepted that mass production brought benefits, but argued that the unequal distribution of wealth created a distortion in the deployment of human energy, by concentrating on the production of commodities desired by the rich. She thought that a greater degree of equality would increase demand for differing types of goods and also benefit the economy as a whole.[56] Questioning whether the 'material means of life and culture' should be left simply to 'the distribution of purchasing power', Kyrk argued that people on lower incomes should be able to enjoy commodities and services.[57] She also attempted a fundamental rethinking of what constituted 'the economy', by taking into consideration consumption, standards of living, housing and household labour as well as production. Ironically this attempt to integrate social and economic existence eventually resulted in a subtle demotion. Instead of reinventing economics, the study of consumption and domestic labour would be redefined as 'home economics'.[58] Not only was this assigned a lower status as an academic field, it tended to be corralled into cookery instead of mounting an assault on capital.

During the 1920s, critiques of work were more likely to appear within culture than in politics. A minority of artists and writers recoiled from standardization, which they regarded not only as an economic phenomenon but as a takeover of human consciousness, entering deep into institutions and the psyche. Rebellion against Taylorist fragmentation and standardization inflected the search for new ways of imagining which preoccupied the international avant-garde. In Nella Larsen's critique of a black educational institution she called 'Naxos' in her 1928 novel *Quicksand*, scientific management served as a metaphor for internalized subordination to white power in social relationships and cultural conformity:[59]

> [Naxos] had grown into a machine. It was now a show place in the
> black belt, exemplification of the white man's magnanimity, refutation

of the black man's inefficiency. Life had died out of it. It was . . .
only a big knife . . . cutting all to a pattern, the white man's pattern.
Teachers as well as students were subjected to the paring process, for
it tolerated no innovations, no individualisms.[60]

By the late 1920s social, economic and political factors had converged
to raise doubts about the cluster of assumptions which had fuelled the
efforts to change how everyday life was lived. Nevertheless, the dreamers
and adventurers who from the 1880s had questioned so many aspects of
women's destiny had also raised fundamental questions about the economy as a whole. Implicit within their condemnation of relationships of
inequality were challenges to the organization of economic and social
existence. They were prepared to interrogate the labour process, the
domination of machine technology, a prosperity based on the expanding
consumption of individual commodities. Some desired an entirely new
way of producing and consuming; others a more humane capitalism.
Some wanted labour to be recreated as art, others to minimize labour
time to allow for more leisure. Some demanded more state; others less.

En route, they controverted accepted ways of seeing, demolishing
the demarcations imposed upon thought. Paid labour connected to
livelihood; production expanded into life; creative humanity defied the
machine; the personal stress of the 'telephone girl' illuminated the flaws
of an economic system. Divided they might be; pusillanimous they were
not.

10

Democratizing Daily Life: Redesigning Democracy

In 1913, the recently founded *New Statesman* magazine produced a special supplement on 'The Awakening of Women', the title echoing that of Kate Chopin's 1899 'new woman' novel. Charlotte Perkins Gilman was one of the contributors, and Beatrice Webb wrote the Introduction. The 'awakening', insisted Webb, had to be seen in much broader terms than simply the political struggle for the vote, or even feminism. A wider women's movement existed which, she believed, was related to the international movement of labour and 'unrest among subject peoples'. Webb recognized that women in this wider movement were challenging not only gender but other relations of subordination. Struggling to express how awareness had emerged through participation in social movements, she suggested that theoretical 'schemes of reform' had combined with 'heroic outbursts of impatient revolt' to generate the 'cross-currents of method and immediate aim'.[1]

The British working-class socialist and feminist Hannah Mitchell describes just such a moment of epiphany in her autobiography, *The Hard Way Up*. One day in the mid-1890s, while listening to a 'callow youth' in a Methodist chapel debate hold forth on how Adam, Saint Paul and Milton had all agreed that women should not take part in politics, bottled-up resentment had caused her to spring to her feet in fury. Congratulating 'our "young friend" on his intimate knowledge of the Almighty's intentions regarding the status of women', she suggested that he broaden his reading to include 'more democratic poets'. Mitchell 'then flung at him and the meeting a chunk of my recently acquired Tennyson. "The woman's cause is man's; they rise or fall together"'. As she sat down in some confusion there was 'applause from the women

Beatrice Webb, ca 1900 (Passfield Collection, Library
of the London School of Economics)

present', and the 'sex prejudice' contingent 'lost much of its self-assur-ance'.[2] Across the Atlantic, Anna Julia Cooper quoted exactly the same line from Tennyson in *A View from the South* (1892), when testifying to the cross-currents of personal experience which brought black women into social action.[3] Both Mitchell and Cooper knew about oppression from their own lives and both had to struggle against the silence which was expected of them. The books they loved helped them to counter bigotry.

The tensions women faced around the prevailing demarcations of public and personal activity galvanized resistance. If they were alerted to wider ideas and other forms of subordination, this subjective rebel-lion could extend outwards. Women who had experience of organizing within a range of social movements came to see relationships between diverse causes. Frances Ellen Harper, who had been active in the anti-slavery movement, women's suffrage and the Woman's Christian Temperance Union, told the National Council of Women in 1891 that racial subordination in the United States was akin to anti-Semitism. She went on to challenge imperialism and the class system: 'Among English-speaking races we have weaker races victimized, a discontented Ireland and a darkest England.'[4] This empathetic understanding of interconnect-ing injustices, combined with women's own efforts to break through the cultural barriers they encountered, could foster a holistic approach to social citizenship which extended into all aspects of existence. In Britain a delegate to the 1915 Co-operative Congress, Guildswoman Mrs Wimhurst of Woolwich, summed up how one thing led to another: 'Social reform consisted of things that merged together; it could not be chopped into sections'.[5]

Such awareness did not, however, do away with inequalities, divi-sions and prejudices which remained within the movements for change. These presented tremendous obstacles for women who sought to stake out their own rights as citizens while democratizing daily life and rela-tionships. Faced by a white suffrage movement concerned to mollify white Southerners and a male-dominated black movement, Anna Julia Cooper retaliated with a cultural concept of African-American female power: 'Only the BLACK WOMAN can say "when and where I enter, in the quiet, undisputed dignity of my womanhood, without violence and without suing or special patronage, then and there the whole *Negro race enters with me*."'[6] Cooper ingeniously adapted an idea of women as harbingers of a new social order present within early nineteenth-century radical thought, giving it a political edge which challenged not only the complacency and prejudice in white women's organizations but also the chauvinism of some male black leaders. In 1898 Mary Church Terrell, speaking at the National American Woman Suffrage Association, took a slightly different tack, presenting black women as playing a special redemptive role: 'With tireless energy and eager zeal, colored women have, since their emancipation, been continuously prosecuting the work of educating and elevating their race as though upon themselves alone devolved the accomplishment of this great task.'[7]

Anna Julia Cooper (Oberlin College Archives, Oberlin)

Nevertheless, in practice the defining of entry points proved to be a daunting and often divisive Catch-22 for both white and black women. Mrs Wimhurst might state proudly that for members of the Women's Co-operative Guild, co-operation and citizenship were indivisible, but radicals and reformers alike kept coming up against a frustrating dilemma.[8] If they stressed that they had a specific contribution to make as women, they could be enclosed within restrictive and externally defined limits; but when they sought to transcend the gender divide by laying claim to universal human rights, their particular demands could be passed over. Dreamers in very different situations discovered that their efforts to democratize daily life required a parallel project of redesigning democracy.

A determined attempt was made to combine the universal and the particular in a gendered redefinition of social citizenship. This was not simply an abstract affair: it involved confronting the issues through practice. The first paid organizer for the Women's Co-operative Guild, Sarah Reddish, who had begun her working life aged eleven as an outworker winding silk, stood as a candidate for Bolton Town Council in 1907 on the grounds that 'Work on town councils was human work, and why should work for humanity be confined to one sex?'[9] In 1894 Reddish mustered her experience as a politically active working-class woman in a concerted challenge to the assumed divisions of who did what and who belonged where:

> We are told by some that women are wives and mothers, and that the duties therein involved are enough for them. We reply that men are husbands and fathers, and that they, as such, have duties not to be neglected, but we join in the general opinion that men should also be interested in the science of government, taking a share in the larger family of the store, the municipality and the State. The WCG has done much towards impressing the fact that women as citizens should take their share in this work also.[10]

Reddish cut through the domestic/female – public/male divides head-on by raising men's role in the home alongside women's position in the social and political sphere. She also rejected the argument that women's familial duties debarred them from asserting individual claims.

The need to affirm women's autonomy by creating a woman-friendly form of social citizenship brought a gendered slant to contemporary debates pitting individualism against collectivism. In 1899 Enid Stacy, who had followed Helena Born and Miriam Daniell in organizing women workers in Bristol, attempted a synthesis of individual and social claims in her essay on 'A Century of Women's Rights'. She looked forward to the time when 'Women's Rights' would be replaced by the broader human aim of securing 'to each human being such conditions as will conduce to full development as an individual and a useful life of service to the community'. Stacy tried to balance individual and personal rights with public, political rights and duties. This is how she detailed them:

1. As individual women. The right to their own persons, and the power of deciding whether they will be mothers or not. . . .
2. As wives. Perfect equality and reciprocity between husband and wife. This necessitates legal changes, notably as regards the Law of Divorce; e.g., whether the law be made laxer or more stringent it must affect both sexes alike.
3. As mothers. Guardianship of their children on the same terms as in the case of fathers . . .[11]

Stacy's fourth claim was for full political citizenship and her fifth for women as workers. This final category caused a certain difficulty for her. She asserted that the ultimate aim was 'a co-operative commonwealth', ensuring 'to each citizen, irrespective of sex, a choice of employment indicated by the results of education and only limited by individual capacity.'[12] More immediately, within the capitalist system of production, she believed it was the duty of the state to protect motherhood for the future. Though legislation at work would cover men as well as women, specific measures should take into account the needs of 'women as mothers prospective and actual'.[13]

From the 1890s onward, the collectivist assumption that the state had a duty to protect women's reproductive capacity would be associated with demands for social resources to enable mothers to mother better. Such claims converged from dissimilar sources: eugenicists, imperialists, social-purity campaigners and philanthropic reformers could be aligned with liberal and socialist women. Motherhood campaigners agitating for social citizenship brought with them differing conceptions of the state. The divisions between reformers and radicals were never completely hard and fast; broadly, however, reformers were inclined to regard the existing state as morally improving or as embodying modernizing efficiency, while those radicals who wanted state intervention on behalf of mothers held that the rights of mothers as citizens constituted an extension of democracy, and so implied a critique of the existing state.

Though authoritarian forms of social maternalism stressed regulation, radical social motherhood advocates emphasized the democratic implications of including the mother within the terms of citizenship. In *The Economic Foundations of the Women's Movement* (1914), the British Fabian and Schreiner enthusiast Mabel Atkinson argued that 'No act of citizenship is more fundamental than the act of bringing into the world and protecting in his helpless infancy a new citizen.'[14] This specifically gendered approach to citizenship could be broadened into a claim on social resources which involved rethinking the economy, and the value of human activities in society. The entitlement of mothers to resources could consequently be expanded into a far-reaching case for a truly social democracy. The British socialist Dorothy Jewson adapted an idea put forward by Charlotte Perkins Gilman, writing 'We believe women and children have a right to A SHARE OF THEIR OWN in the wealth of the country'.[15] She observed, 'Other services are concerned with the making of THINGS, but motherhood with the making of human beings.'[16] Writing in the left-wing socialist paper the *Daily Herald* in 1912 on the need for the franchise, Mabel Harding also echoed Gilman's vision of mothering as a potential for a social alternative to a male-defined, competitive capitalism. For Harding, 'Motherhood in its wide sense' implied being responsible for life beyond the immediate family:

> Pure food, a municipal milk supply, healthy schools, the raising of the school leaving age, sound moral training without any squeamish holding back knowledge of the facts of life that boys and girls should know, the abolition of sweated labour, and a host of other subjects, are all woman's concerns and part of her social motherhood.[17]

Ideas of the citizen-mother were not only expressed in terms of a state-led collectivism. They could also constitute an attempt to regenerate democracy by extending the reach of the household into the community and hence into the public realm of politics. Commenting on Margaretta Hicks's advocacy of consumer organizing, June Hannam and Karen Hunt remark: 'For a fragile moment some socialist women had started to imagine one way in which the border between the "domestic" and the "political" could be dissolved so that a socialist strategy could be forged which no longer privileged production over consumption.'[18] Contesting the barriers which separated daily activities involved the adventurers in battles around the boundaries which marked out the domestic and intimate sphere as exclusively female, and the world of work and public politics as male. As a consequence of these conflicts, many women came to challenge the scope of politics and reimagine daily life and relationships.

Whether they sought to emphasize shared human rights or foreground the existing activities and needs of women, the women who dreamed of a new day were met with prejudice when they tried to put into practice even the most moderate aspects of their larger visions. Democratic social citizenship proved a circuitous affair, and stratagems had to be renegotiated, over and over again. Like many other women, Margaret Ashton saw the franchise as a way of achieving wider social changes for women. But in the meantime she also wanted to contribute actively by becoming a local councillor. Patricia Hollis chronicles how in 1907 Ashton stood as an Independent in St George's ward for a place on Manchester Town Council, on the basis of her knowledge of building. She was not successful. 'The following year she stood in Withington ward. . . . No talk of her expertise in drains and ventilation this time, but about the need of women and children for homes, schools, clean water, baths and wash houses, adequate street lighting and safe trams.'[19]

A pragmatic Ashton cannily threw in women's special need for well-built and properly drained houses along with paved courts and alleys. She proceeded tactfully, promising male voters that 'if she were returned there would be no necessity for her to encroach upon the men's work'.[20] As Hollis wryly remarks, it was not 'entirely clear what she had left them to do'.[21] Ashton's modus operandi was to stretch 'women's' concerns and assure men that 'Matters of great importance to women had been overlooked, not because men desired to neglect them, but because they never thought of them'.[22]

The Women's Co-operative Guild's membership card graphically depicts the organization's aspiration to expand women's workaday consciousness. A woman in an apron stands in the foreground, clutching her basket, with the tall chimneys of an industrial city below her in the valley; she is looking beyond them, gazing upwards and shielding her eyes against the sun. Yet the cool Bloomsbury eye of Virginia Woolf, scrutinizing members of the Women's Co-operative Guild at their conference in 1914, detected only the pull of a culture which kept them earthbound: 'Their lips never expressed the lighter and detached emotions that come into play when the mind is perfectly at ease about the present. No, they were not in the least detached and easy and cosmopolitan. They were indigenous and rooted to one spot.'[23] To Woolf the women seemed so embedded that the exploratory intellectual enquiry so vital to her as an individual appeared impossible.

Nonetheless co-operative women did want the chance to live a better life as individuals, and their participation in the Guild was a means of gaining confidence and acquiring a broader culture. They theorized on the basis of what they knew and the Guild encouraged them to look outwards, far beyond the basket and the chimneys. An alternative social order, self-realization and democratic citizenship nestle in the expansive ideal future outlined by Florence Farrow, a working-class member of the Derby Women's Co-operative Guild, in 1919. Every mother should receive a pension for each child born to her. Women should not accept babies being deprived of milk because of high prices, but should demand municipal control of milk. There should be municipal baths, better housing, heating and lighting, and greater democratic control over energy supplies. Teachers should be better paid as a step towards improving the education of working-class children. Municipal cinemas should be set up where children could be shown 'pictures which would bring out the best of them and give them a love of things beautiful'.[24]

'The Woman with the Basket' (National Co-operative Archive)

Here the vision of a better life for individuals is presented in social and relational terms. In imagining her motherly utopia, Farrow was typical of the women that American labour journalist Mary Heaton Vorse met on her visit to post-war England. Shaken by the bleak poverty she encountered, but inspired by the 'enormous ferment' of debate among working-class women, Vorse recalled:

I felt that an immense power would be unleashed if one would organize, not only the clubwomen of leisure but the working women and the housewives of workers. If they could be organized in England, why not in America? I wrote an article prophesying that 'Ma' would come out into the world as she had in England, for the stir among working women seemed to me the real feminist movement.[25]

The working-class women Vorse encountered were engaged in collective agitation over their social rights in relation to their families and communities. Ideas of women's emancipation were articulated around shared needs as a class, and it was assumed that better conditions for women and children would also be beneficial to working-class men as husbands and fathers. However, a minority of women within the trade union movement were beginning to raise issues of equality vis-à-vis men. Varying concepts of rights and entitlements were thus emerging from the women's labour movement. Like other elements in Webb's wider women's movement, they, too, were far from being homogenous.

Different concepts of citizenship had been able to coexist amidst the fluidity of the movement for enfranchisement, but as the momentum diminished after World War One, conflicts over priorities, strategies and policy crystallized. Disagreement among feminists, social reformers and women trade unionists over whether to claim citizenship on the basis of equal rights or of women's specific needs, became polarized over the issue of protective legislation at work; however, this was really only the tip of a deeper contention around identity, nature and culture. These were not only theoretical disputes; they affected how the democratization of social and economic existence was envisaged.

In the post-war era, feminists in both countries were at odds about how femininity was to be conceived and valued. In her response to testimonies by modern women published in the *Nation* between 1926 and 1927, the American Jungian, Beatrice M. Hinkle, alluded to a dismissal among feminists of 'their woman's nature'.[26] In both America and Britain a 'new feminism' emerged which focused on women's needs around biological reproduction. In recognizing women's dissimilarities from men, they went on to propose that these made alternative perspectives possible. Though some 'new feminists' thought the distinct values they envisaged arose from women's particular position in society historically, rather than from a timeless 'nature', to their opponents , the egalitarians, any assertion of women's difference tended to be regarded as a trap.

Writing in the 1924 symposium *Our Changing Morality*, the American Isobel Leavenworth complained that it was 'most unfortunate that the majority of people hope to improve matters through an extension of the feminine ideals of the past.'[27] She and other egalitarian feminists considered existing 'femininity' to be as distorted as the existing forms of 'masculinity'.

Though these disputes were often bitter and painful, locally women continued to argue pragmatically for an amalgam of equality and special needs, simply because they could see that women required both. Even among women who ostensibly belonged to opposing camps the differences were nuanced, and there continued to be overlapping areas of agreement. The American Crystal Eastman, attached to the egalitarian wing of the feminist movement, attended the National Conference of Labour Women in Britain in 1925, and noted favourably a resolution to deal stringently with any representative of the Labour Party who did 'not support sex equality, economically, educationally and politically'.[28] Impressed by the range of debate, Eastman recorded how the women demanded a National Wheat Board to secure cheap bread, a trained nurse in every secondary and primary school, the extension of the suffrage to women under thirty, and birth control in health centres. The egalitarian Eastman conceded a '"women's emphasis"' in the political outlook of the women at the conference. By this she meant the weight given to 'the supreme importance of human well-being, especially the well-being of children'. She concluded that 'It is not so much that women have a different point of view in politics as that they give a different emphasis.'[29]

In contrast Eva Hubback, who had taken part in the British suffrage movement, did believe most firmly that women brought a different point of view to politics. She belonged to the 'new feminist' camp in the National Union of Societies for Equal Citizenship, which saw the egalitarians' approach as outdated. In 1926 she was arguing that as legislative equality 'was undoubtedly in sight', the time had come to move on. As a 'new feminist' she believed 'that the whole structure and movement of society shall reflect in a proportionate degree the experience, the needs and the aspirations of women'. For Hubback this meant recognizing that demands for family allowances and birth control were at the very 'core' of feminism, because maternity, childcare and housekeeping were what chiefly occupied the daily lives of most women.[30] In 1929 Hubback aligned herself with Labour Party women in demanding special legislative protection for women.

In America Suzanne La Follette had come to precisely the opposite conclusion. The elevation of motherhood was merely 'sentimentalism'.[31] Instead of a woman-inspired future, she argued in *Concerning Women* (1926) that economic freedom was the next question to tackle. She did not think that women's emancipation could 'proceed much farther as an independent issue.' Instead La Follette believed the time had come to 'merge the feminist in the humanist'.[32] She was, however, in agreement with Hubback on the need for wider social change: 'every phase of the question of freedom for women is bound up with the larger question of human freedom'.[33]

The dilemma of whether to stress women's similarities with men or to assert their differing needs as women also presented itself within the trade union movement. The secretary of the National Federation of Women Workers, Mary Macarthur, acknowledged differences in women's relationship to paid employment, but insisted that there was 'no inherent sex incapacity' in the recognition of the need to unionize.[34] However, while Macarthur was an adroit operator within the trade unions, their bureaucratic structures were daunting and alien to many women; nor were male trade unionists necessarily woman-friendly.[35] On the other hand, by the 1920s separate women's trade unions did not seem to be the answer because they could not adequately defend vulnerable women workers.

Radical British women in the immediate post-war era, encouraged by the increase in unionization during the war, approached women's position in the workplace with a new resolve. Workplace organizing was regarded as a key arena for democratic engagement, a space for exercising social and economic power which could be expanded even further. When Barbara Drake wrote her path-breaking *Women in Trade Unions* (1920) she acknowledged both male hostility and the structural and cultural obstacles holding women back. However, she was hopeful that the Standing Joint Committee of Industrial Women's Organizations, which had already brought women co-operators into combination with women trade unionists, might extend to include professional women's organizations. Drake wanted to break down the social gulf between consumers and workers, as well as the class distinctions between workers of hand and brain, in a broader movement of labour:

> The forward attack by labour on capital, which aims at giving a new and nobler direction to industry, will almost certainly be led by men,

but the less dramatic yet equally vital movement whose object is to secure a full share of wealth, not only to the poorest of the workers, but to the least of all citizens, may not improbably find its leaders amongst women.[36]

Drake's thinking on industrial democracy, redistributive justice and a broader trade unionism was, however, shaped by the structure of the labour market; men predominated in heavy industry. The new labour citizenship was to be equal but complementary.

Drake was influenced not only by Fabianism, but by the industrial militancy of the pre-war years, when she had come into contact with Guild Socialist ideas of workers' control. William Morris was one of the inspirations for Guild Socialism, and the movement seemed to present a way of activating participatory democracy around economic and social needs without strengthening the centralized power of the state. Drake wanted to transform both the possibilities for organizing and the labour process itself. In *Women in Trade Unions* she asserted that the 'democratic control of industry' would give rise to 'such a new respect for human labour' that the worker would become 'a "directing intelligence"'.[37] Though ostensibly discussing 'Woman's Place in Industry', she switched to using 'he' when she predicted this broadening of democracy at work – a revealing indication of how concepts of the dignity of labour and workers' control were implicitly perceived around a gender-blind, male model. Feminizing the theorizing of democracy in the workplace proved as sticky as changing habits of labour organizing.

In the United States, women who had gained experience of labour issues by participating in radical and reforming projects before and during the war were similarly grappling with the dramatic changes in industry. Several moved from a focus on women's issues to the industrial question as a whole, and sought to redefine the terms of industrial democracy. Nelson Lichtenstein comments: 'World War I and the social turmoil of its immediate aftermath briefly tripled the size of the union movement and generated a wave of institutional experimentation that included government arbitration, works councils, employer representation plans, producer co-operatives, and nationalization schemes for industry.'[38] Lichtenstein suggests that for women reformers 'industrial democracy' was a more palatable formulation than 'workers' control', which was linked not only to the syndicalist left, but closely associated with skilled male workers' defence of privilege.[39]

The writer Lewis Mumford, Helen Marot's colleague at the *Dial*, has recorded how at the end of World War One hope flared in America for 'reconstruction' through 'shop committees, industrial councils and democratic participation; perhaps national guilds to control the major industries and ultimately their government ownership'.[40] He recalled Marot's enthusiasm for the soviets in Russia and for British Guild Socialism in 1918.[41] In her 1914 book *American Labor Unions*, Marot had expressed respect for the anarcho-syndicalist Industrial Workers of the World's recognition of workers' initiative. She believed in self-determination, learning through doing and human agency, echoing the syndicalists when she asserted: 'whenever labor attacks the evils which beset it, *new power is created*'.[42]

But, though Marot had been impressed by the anarchists' and anarcho-syndicalists' role in the Lawrence textile strike and shared the libertarian left's suspicion of statist solutions, in her 1918 book *The Creative Impulse in Industry* she rejected workers' direct action, saying that British shop stewards and the IWW were simply 'protecting the workers' share in the possession of wealth'. They 'did not *develop* the idea of industry as an adventure in creative enterprise'.[43] Lewis Mumford comments that her intention was 'to appraise the productive process, not just in terms of profits, wages and the physical output of goods, but in terms of the kind of human being it nourished'.[44] Marot was acutely aware of the tensions between the self-expression of the individual and a wider social group. She also retained elements of the utopianism of earlier radical dreamers, who had been prepared to imagine new forms of human relationships. Both personal fulfilment and co-operative transformation were integral to her ideas about how to democratize life at work.

Marot applied John Dewey's educational ideas to production. Work should be about the self-actualization of the worker: a process of realizing the capacities of every individual. She was not, however, an individualist. She theorized in relational terms, fusing the Bergsonian creative impulse with a Ruskinian critique of the social purposes of economic activity. Echoing Helen Campbell and Charlotte Perkins Gilman's phrase, the 'art of living', Marot stated: 'Art in living together is possible where the intensive interest of individuals in their personal affairs and attainments in their social group, in their vocation, in their political state is deeply tempered by a wide interest and sympathetic regard for the life of other groups and people.'[45] Despite her reservations about mass production, like Barbara Drake she put her faith in the associative possibilities which modern industry opened up for 'relationships which are socially creative'.[46]

The American social reformer Mary Parker Follett was also interested in the debates within the British Labour Party on increasing the democratic participation of workers in industry. She was aware, too, of the ideas of left-wing shop stewards like J. T. Murphy as well as the Guild Socialists, but feared their approach would foster 'group selfishness'.[47] In her book *The New State: Group Organization The Solution of Popular Government* (1918), she argued the state should 'Include industry without on the one hand abdicating to industry or controlling industry bureaucratically'.[48] However, in this work her vision of group organization centred not on industry but on democratic engagement within neighbourhoods. Follett was articulating what other women adventurers had struggled towards in practice, through those myriad attempts to create forms of social provision which met human needs.

Follett's new state was rooted in Idealism. It combined the social liberal T. H. Green's organic Neo-Hegelianism with social housekeeping, and a dash of John Dewey's learning through doing. Follett defined the 'essential political problem' as 'how to be the state'.[49] She believed the answer was genuine community action which could overcome the divide between individual and state: 'If we want milk and baby hygiene organized, our own local doctors should in proper co-operation with experts on the one hand and the mothers on the other organize this branch of social service.'[50] Active participation would ensure needs were met, save time, and integrate further investigation into the actual predicament of the neighbourhood. She insisted that 'The community itself must grip its own problems, must fill its own needs, must make effective its aspirations,' and criticized 'reform associations' which substituted themselves for action from the community, along with municipal services which she saw as robbing people of their 'responsibilities'.[51]

Along with her wariness of state provision, Follett retained her social-housekeeping suspicion of Tammany Hall-style intrigue and thought that as society organized itself, politics would simply dissolve. 'The platitudes and insincerities of the party meeting will give way to the homely realities of the neighbourhood meeting'.[52] The neighbourhood groups were to act as the means of translating needs from civil society to the sphere of power. They were the key to a citizenship which was 'active', 'responsible' and 'creative',[53] based not on 'individual self-expression but community self-expression'.[54] A sanguine Follett believed this participation process would enable 'local, intimate and personal concerns' to be expressed.[55] By dissolving the spatial boundaries between home and city, as well as the conceptual divide between private and public, she sought an internalized sense of democracy. She wanted politics to cease being 'external'; instead, people themselves were 'to be politics'.[56]

Follett's mistrust of purely external remedies was characteristic of social reformers and radicals influenced by organic Idealist approaches to state and society. Fostered by Protestantism, this rejection of 'externalism' had been a feature of nineteenth-century charitable endeavours. It had transmuted during the late nineteenth century into an ethical concern to link inner transformation with political and social democracy, shifting somewhat in the early twentieth century when differing forms of consciousness and an interest in irrational influences on politics were being theorized. While Follett tried to connect internal consciousness with external action for change, Elaine Showalter shows how during the 1920s an avant-garde among American feminists were reassessing their preoccupation with public action.[57] For some, the supposedly heroic political and social struggles of their youth were beginning to look like a terrible waste of energy. Ideals had withered. Others wanted to explore desires which could not be bundled neatly into demands, and to express doubts which did not fit into campaigns – even campaigns around personal issues, such as birth control. 'I have traded my sense of exhilarating defiance (shall we call it feminism?) for an assurance of free and unimpeded self-expression (or shall we call that feminism?). In other words, I have grown up', declared Ruth Pickering, a former member of the Heterodoxy Club.[58]

Striking a personal note could signal retreat from involvement in external causes; but it could equally be a means of simply reflecting on unresolved emotions. Earlier generations of activists had also tussled with intimate feelings which they could not square with their political views. Emma Goldman, filled with tempestuous passions aroused by her unfaithful and bumptious lover Ben Reitman, was troubled by the contradictions she saw in herself. She was publicly advocating free love in her lectures, yet felt bruised and humiliated by his infidelity. She said, 'I have no right to speak of Freedom when I myself have become an abject slave in my love.'[59] Looking back on her youthful bohemian experimenting, Mary Heaton Vorse dissected the collapse of her first long-term relationship:

I had . . . insensibly altered our relations over a period of years, and did it without realizing it. . . . The more I worked, the less he did. What did my success do to him? It dimmed life in some way. It sapped some vital force in him. There he was, suddenly no longer needed. . . . And his sickness with himself reacted on me.[60]

While an awareness of a rift between politics and the personal was not unique to the 1920s, the psychological validation of the subjective voice certainly enabled women to express personal perceptions which disturbed their political beliefs, and permitted a greater degree of self-consciousness about any discordance between public political stances and private feelings. Psychological confessions flowed into a popular idiom of women's writing. In an article for *Cosmopolitan* on 'Why I have failed as a mother', Vorse observed that men and women continued to have very different attitudes to work. Hence women who tried to combine love and work were likely to experience a 'double failure'.[61] Though the confessional style was less prevalent in buttoned-up Britain, in 1928 Leonora Eyles ruminated frankly on her divorce in *Good Housekeeping*. She had crushed her 'overmastering desire for love-making and romance', because she distrusted expressing longing for her former husband. She had been too 'proud – or it may be too mean-spirited – to let a man see how much he is needed'.[62]

In the 1920s, modern women's uncertainties about how to balance new gender identities with personal relations led them to grapple with the unconscious, theoretically as well as subjectively. In 1927 Dora Russell argued that women were held back not only by external political, social and economic obstacles, but by unconscious psychological 'stops and inhibitions planted in childhood'. She related these individual psychological restraints to the broader male-defined culture. 'It is as if a pianist were trying to perform in gloves or an actor to give an intimate and delicate performance in a mask. Our whole view of woman is still a mask between her and reality.'[63]

The hegemonic power of male culture had likewise troubled earlier generations of adventurers. If women were to become active citizens, transforming social relationships in the personal and public spheres and redesigning democracy en route, it was evident that cultural and psychological changes were needed. The problem was that adventurers were unable to decide quite how alternative forms of culture and a new consciousness would come about. One view held that an unperceived female culture was immanent in the everyday. In 1886 the writer Emma Brooke, a friend of Olive Schreiner and Eleanor Marx, defied Karl Pearson in the Men and Women's Club with an assertion of women's tacit awareness. Brooke told the logical Pearson that there were different forms of knowing; one was experiential, 'founded on stored-up observations . . . and incessant watchfulness'. He needed to learn from women themselves. 'You must listen to their words, observe their faces in the unconscious moments when nature and feeling speak for themselves'.[64]

For Brooke, female ways of perceiving were flickering and implicit. However, powerful archetypes crystallized women's difference as a positive cultural alternative to a male realm of reason and 'objectivity': women were invested with qualities of spirituality, of expressive emotion or of psychic insight into the unknown. The woman seer could allegorically show the way, like that 'radiant creature' in Winifred Harper Cooley's 1902 utopian novel, *A Dream of the Twenty-First Century*. A medium-like receptivity also appealed. 'I am the mirror', wrote Mabel Dodge Luhan, inspired by Greenwich Village's elevation of sensibility.[65] Marie Stopes would achieve popular success by cleverly spinning her persona as an authoritative woman of science into the visionary purveyor of sensuous dreams.

Alongside attempts to recover alternative sources of woman-power went a contrary conviction that an entirely new culture must be created. For the American anarchist Lizzie Holmes in 1896, this iconoclastic counter-culture was a matter of individual will: 'We need earnest women; women who feel so deep in their souls the suffering of humanity, so great a desire to speak and work for liberty and justice as to forget completely the false lines, the false modesty, the false ignorance once marked out for us.'[66] Emma Goldman also believed that making a new culture for women, and indeed for men, involved direct action in personal life as well as politics.

Living differently was a common theme among a wide cross-section of adventurers and dreamers who saw it both in terms of gender and as a means of envisaging alternative futures. When in 1907 Mary Heaton Vorse joined sixteen other young bohemians, including her husband, in a co-operative housing venture near Washington Square in Greenwich Village, she was bursting with optimism. It seemed as if 'this business of women's co-operating in wage-earning was the solution to domestic life' and that 'all the things the feminists had promised with the cry of economic independence had come true'.[67]

Settlement life presented a less extreme means of prefiguring new forms of social relations through personal contact. Jane Addams objected to Hull House being called a 'sociological laboratory', asserting it was 'much more human and spontaneous than such a phrase connotes'.[68] At their most democratic, the settlements enabled a cultural exchange between people with very dissimilar backgrounds. Mary Kingsbury Simkhovitch, having moved from wealthy New England to work with poor tenants in New York's Lower East Side, was excited and stimulated by settlement life:

> It was a new kind of university with the lessons hot from the griddle . . . The East Side raised a thousand questions. It demanded study, understanding, friendship, action. It meant a rapid plunge – first, to learn to read and speak Yiddish, to go to the theaters and restaurants, to participate in the social and political life of the community. In the long period of my education this was the most exciting chapter for here everything was tested.[69]

She experienced an empathetic cultural immersion. 'Before any help can be given the situation must be felt, realised and understood at first hand. Only that which is lived can be understood and translated to others.'[70] In 1898, the British socialist and feminist Isabella Ford stressed the need for a similar openness: 'Unless you have lived among oppression and injustice it is most difficult to realise how full of it is our own industrial system, particularly when it touches women.'[71]

While such reformers and radicals sought empathy and learning through doing, a contrary assumption also marked many philanthropic ventures of the late nineteenth century, which simply took the superiority of middle-class know-how about diet, housework, childcare or the right to paid employment for granted. A certain tension existed too between activists and academics. Jane Addams and Florence Kelley, themselves committed to systematic enquiry into conditions, were inclined to be sceptical of the emerging social science at the University of Chicago. Despite close contact with Marion Talbot and Sophonisba Breckinridge, they felt that even sympathetic academics were too removed in their studies of social problems. They believed in learning through practice and a reciprocal exchange with the people they served.[72] However, in the early twentieth century, as a new generation of women graduates acquired professional qualifications as sanitary inspectors or social workers, their new-found expertise tended to reinforce the view that enlightened, modern attitudes, associated with formal education and academic skills, were necessarily to be preferred. Working-class women were frequently regarded as too enmeshed amidst pots, pans and the proverbial 'old wives' tales' to understand their own interests.

Adventurers were deeply divided over methods of knowing. Some championed reason, the intellect and professional expertise; others endorsed understandings based on observation, lived experience and tacit knowledge. The anarchist Helena Born regretted that most people took their knowledge at second or third hand, rather than using their own eyes: 'The nature-lover desires his knowledge direct from the source.'[73] In 1913 the American reformer, Clara Cahill Park, invoked the tacit knowledge of 'the plain mother' against a male member of the New York Charity Organization Society, who maintained mothers' pensions would undermine women's self-respect. 'You see,' Park explained, 'mothers, in spite of the sociologists, feel themselves, for once, on their own ground in this matter; and . . . will continue to think that, as far as children are concerned, not they, but the learned doctors, are in the amateur class.'[74]

Distrust of removed, intellectual knowing was bound up with an awareness of how it was frequently associated with the powerful and used to stereotype the subordinate. In 1892 Anna Julia Cooper poured scorn on white male writers' ignorant depiction of black people, ridiculing them for coming up 'with dissertations on racial traits of the Negro' based on 'a few psychological experiments on their cooks and coachmen.'[75] Isabella Ford firmly opposed middle-class women determining working-class women's needs and interests, insisting in her pamphlet *Industrial Women and How to Help Them* (1901) that 'The industrial woman must work out her freedom for herself. We cannot, we have no right to do it for her. We cannot possibly know her needs so well as she herself can.'[76] Such efforts to democratize ways of understanding, perceiving and acting presented a radical critique of cultural dominance.

Yet over the years it would become apparent that there were drawbacks in both approaches to knowledge. Those who backed professional expertises could be insensitive, autocratic and incapable of learning from the received understandings of other groups and cultures; conversely the exponents of experiential knowing could cultivate a complacent anti-intellectualism. The experience of just being the intuitive, expressive one, or just being a mother, could confine rather than liberate. Implicit understanding was liable to get stuck in complaint or erupt in momentary protest, rather than redesign alternatives. Moreover it could sentimentalize the oppressed, ignoring unpalatable actualities.[77]

It was evident to some dreamers of a new day that more than immediate experience was required to devise new values and put new strategies into practice. For if ready-made alternative vistas were already there, smouldering in the culture of the present, society would be far quicker to change. Charlotte Perkins Gilman saw how tacit and habitual assumptions contributed to women's subordination. In *Women and Economics* (1898), she comments on the way living conditions become familiar through use, and how the 'common sense' which solidifies around them perpetuates the status quo. She grasped the difficulty of how to make the shift from what was to what might be conceivable.[78] Instead of positing an absolute alternative which had to be willed into being, Gilman's rooted utopias marked out a space in which she could counter the prevailing forms of common sense by transposing existing desires into a new habitat. One of the reasons for the influence she exerted is that she wrestled with that most intractable of questions: how to set store by the existing ways of being a woman, while opening up possibilities for individuals to venture beyond these and come to relate with others differently. In her utopia, *Herland* (1918), motherliness becomes a metaphor for a broader vision of mutuality. It embodies values of nurture, love and co-operation which offer the potential for a new culture.[79] Gilman translated the older utopian tradition, in which woman redeems through love, into a concept of how a transitional culture might be conceived.

Tremendous difficulties remained nevertheless unresolved. Even Gilman's dynamic rendition assumed that all women were, or wanted to be, mothers. Mothering as a metaphor could constrict as well as expand the parameters of social citizenship. The dreamers who sought to make women, as a group, the catalyst for change continually stumbled against the problem of how to devise alternative perspectives without restricting women's options for autonomous diversity. Again and again, in proposing ways in which women could cohere around their specific interests, dreamers slid into yet more restricting demarcations. Stella Browne made a valiant attempt to introduce a concept of collective agency by making reproductive control for women the equivalent of workers' control for men. This rephrasing of anarcho-syndicalism in relation to the body did offer a dynamic fusion between the individual and a wider social context; unfortunately it also introduced a theoretical categorization which implicitly excluded women from the workforce and men from sexual reproduction. What is more, the dreamers found themselves at odds with one another. Awakened they might be; in agreement they were not. The sacrificial redeemer present in both social purity and social mothering jarred with aspirations for assertive cultural transgression and power. The supporters of protective legislation wanted to regulate women's work; the egalitarians wanted unrestricted equality.

Theoretical and strategic disputes around women's efforts to democratize everyday life and culture tended to recur with each decade, presenting themselves each time in somewhat differing forms. The translation of the personal into politics, difference and equality, the individual and the social, all caused conflict; so did the role of the state and the manner in which a new culture and consciousness might be created. These circular returns could become discouraging over time, causing even the most enthusiastic dreamers to wonder about their optimistic faith in women as the agents of change. When hopes flagged Gilman, along with other women adventurers, fell back on the reassuring prognosis that change was structurally evolving.

Such an oscillation was not, in fact, peculiar to women. It was equally evident in the wider debates around agency and structure occurring in the same period. Evolutionary ideas and a teleological belief in progress permeated all branches of nineteenth-century progressive thought. Liberals, anarchists, socialists and Marxists were ever on the look-out for signs of a new world growing within the old – especially when prospects for change dimmed. Even the anarchist Lizzie Holmes, who put such an emphasis on willing alternatives, invoked evolutionary change. In 1887, calling for associations to set up 'labour exchanges' as a means of swapping goods and services and creating alternative mutual systems of credit, she ruminated, 'It may be possible that after all a new construction of society may grow up and flourish underneath the old corrupt shell, until when the time comes the old systems will fall away decayed and useless, without commotion or violence.'[80]

If trust in the structural evolution of a better society was reassuring, notions of agency and mission were more psychologically compelling, and even the most scientifically minded adventurers could share with the utopians a chiliastic sense of a dawn of redemption. Sweeping aside all the awkward disagreements about redefining democracy and democratizing daily life, Beatrice Webb perceived the wider movement of women, the labour movement and the rebellion of the colonized as 'swinging eventually in the same direction . . . the transformation of the ideas, customs and laws accepted by the bulk of apathetic and preoccupied humans'.[81]

'The Tree of Life' (National Co-operative Archive)

Not surprisingly, the last thing the adventurers could agree on was what this point of arrival would look like. Some imagined a better regulated, socially minded capitalism; others, following Edward Bellamy's *Looking Backward*, a state-led socialism; yet others yearned for a free communal life close to nature. For temperance reformers, utopia was dry; for bohemians it positively brimmed with stimulating sensations; for maternalists it was fecund; and for the independent types, dynamic and free-wheeling. Mary Parker Follett's City Beautiful was urban living domesticated. She insisted the 'endeavour' should not simply be municipal cleanliness, but 'a true home for the people', where they could experience 'recreation, enjoyment, happiness'.[82] In contrast, for the sophisticated and modern Elsie Clews Parsons the attraction of the city lay in its anonymity: 'In very large communities there is an ignorance of the personal relation to others, an inevitable ignoring which contributes unconsciously to tolerance toward experiment and variation in sex relations.'[83] Nor was it only a matter of differing concepts of the ideal polis; dissension appeared over whether to opt for a new urbanism or for the countryside. The dreamer par excellence, Voltairine de Cleyre, true to her Mid-Western roots, favoured 'small, independent, self-resourceful, freely co-operating communing'. Her 'ideal' was 'a condition in which all natural resources would be forever free to all and the worker individually able to produce for himself sufficient for all his vital needs'.[84]

For Voltairine de Cleyre, it was really the quest that mattered. Her anarchism was dynamic and fluid:

> It is not an economic system; it does not come to you with detailed plans of how the workers are to conduct industry; nor systemized methods of exchange; nor careful paper organizations of the 'administration of things'. It simply calls upon the spirit of individuality to rise up from its abasement, and hold itself paramount in no matter what economic reorganization shall come about.[85]

Her aspirations for the future were transcendent: 'Aim at the stars, and you may hit the top of the gatepost; but aim at the ground, and you will hit the ground.'[86] Others might appear less individualistic and more circumspect, but they, too, caught glimpses of new relationships in the everyday. Deeply moved by the 'fraternity' of the Lawrence strikers in 1912, Vida Scudder imagined a just society in which every man and woman received a ' "fair reward" for their labour' and 'those of differing races, shall, indeed, be of one heart, one mind, one soul'.[87]

The adventurous innovators of the late nineteenth and early twentieth centuries cannot be characterized as sharing a coherent politics. They evade even the loose definition of a wider 'movement' proposed by Beatrice Webb, for they go off in a myriad of directions. Yet the extraordinary 'awakening' of women constituted an incontestably creative force for change. A vigorous impulse to reform, and transform, touched every aspect of daily life, from baby clothes to global trade. Jiggling the demarcations between the personal and the public, and upsetting received opinions concerning gender, the dreamers of a new day stimulated far-reaching questions about politics, citizenship, democracy, work, culture and social existence. They might have been at loggerheads over the delineation of policies and utopias, but about the big thing they could agree; life was never to be the same again.

Conclusion

As the years went by, women who had dreamed of a new day were inclined to become a little grumbly. Change proved not to be linear; instead it was patchy and seemed painfully slow. By the early 1930s the British feminist Ray Strachey complained of a hostility among young women to 'feminism'. She thought this was because they were ignorant 'of what life was like before the war'.[1] Even when the American New Deal began to initiate long-awaited social reforms and bring former adventurers in to run them, some veterans remained dissatisfied because radical women in the new generation were apt to focus pragmatically on poverty and unemployment. The progressive reformer Mary Beard and the socialist feminist Harriot Stanton Blatch had held conflicting views on equal rights as a feminist strategy, but both were critical of the New Deal reformers around Eleanor Roosevelt. 'They believe in seeing and acting on "one thing at a time"', Beard complained to Blatch in 1933. The adventurous dreamers had been about seeing change in manifold dimensions, envisaging new kinds of human beings and new kinds of social relationships.[2] They had assumed that one thing would lead to another, gradually or rapidly, depending on their political perspective. By the depression years of the 1930s circumstances and attitudes had shifted profoundly.

On the other hand, connections appeared in new contexts. In their study of the American suburbs, *Picture Windows* (2000), Rosalyn Baxandall and Elizabeth Ewen record how Catherine Wurster Bauer, the executive director of the AFL's Housing Committee, initiated a community housing project with playgrounds, laundries, tennis courts and swimming pools in Philadelphia, sponsored by the American Federation of Hosiery Workers. They also show how the idea that housing should be an area of

democratic decision-making persisted in the co-operative community of
Greenbelt, where individual housing combined with co-operative enter-
prises. In 1937 an excited resident, Mary E. Van Cleves, was reported
in the local newspaper, the *Greenbelt Co-operator*, expressing a sentiment
nineteenth-century utopians would have recognized: 'We are pioneers
of a new way of living'.[3]

The 1930s also saw new expressions of communal consciousness
among both black and white women. Darlene Clark Hine records how
the Housewives' League of Detroit backed black business as part of their
effort to 'Stabilize the economic status of the Negro through directed
spending'.[4] During the mid-1930s a wave of 'mass strikes', in which
community action connected with workplace rebellions, provided an
extended context for what the *Nation* dubbed 'consumer consciousness'.
In 1936 the *New Republic*, remarking on how 'the roles of producer and
consumer are intimately related', described the housewives' action as
stretching the theoretical ideas of the labour movement.[5] These links
between work and community found institutional expression in the
new industrial unionism of the Congress of Industrial Organizations
(CIO). From the mid 1930s, the CIO, which included Communists
and Trotskyists, was encouraging alliances between workers and the
community through the 'women's auxiliaries', leading Mary Heaton
Vorse in *Labor's New Millions* (1938) to hail a unionism that did 'not stop
at the formal lodge meeting' but 'saw the union as a way of life'.[6]

Though the Communist Party leadership was critical of a Party activist in California, Mary Inman, who insisted that housework was as much
part of the productive economy as work for wages, she and other women
including Elizabeth Gurley Flynn and the Trinidadian Claudia Jones did
influence the CP's attitudes towards women's cultural subordination.[7]
Moreover, protest about housework extended beyond the left. In an
article entitled 'Occupation: Housewife', the popular journalist Dorothy
Thompson related in the *Ladies' Home Journal* in the late 1930s how a
woman of her acquaintance had been annoyed to find herself classed as
a 'housewife'.

> 'The trouble with you', I said, 'is that you have to find one word to
> cover a dozen occupations, all of which you follow expertly and more
> or less simultaneously. You might write: "Business manager, cook,
> nurse, chauffeur, dress maker, interior decorator, accountant, caterer,
> teacher, private secretary" – or just put down "philanthropist"'.[8]

In Britain labour women and social reformers struggled, regardless of the depression, to assert a humane economics based on the needs of women and children. Some of the policies they devised would come into effect during World War Two and influence the post-war welfare state. In the 1930s, many of the dilemmas confronted by the pioneering adventurers in linking the personal to the public world remained. It was still difficult for women to speak about sex in a public context. Stella Browne was quite extraordinary in admitting that she had had an abortion while giving evidence to the Birkett Committee on maternal mortality in 1937.[9] Though Browne continued her efforts to extend the scope of democratic control, she and other women sexual radicals were constrained by the prioritizing of production on the left and the conviction that sex and reproduction were peripheral to politics.

Nevertheless, 1930s women were searching for new cultural forms of examining sexual feelings. In 1934, the British novelist Naomi Mitchison argued in *The Home and a Changing Civilisation* that while it was important to work for policies such as Family Endowment, just patching things up through the accretion of reforms was not enough. Arguing that the core of sexual power relations had to be addressed, she pondered the implications of the 'shadow of ownership' in sexual relationships. Mitchison observed that 'intelligent women' were so determined not to be 'owned socially' that they were refusing to be 'owned personally', even though it 'hurts them', while other middle-class women acquiesced in being owned socially but were grabbing back as much as they could from men in return. Eschewing these options, Mitchison proposed that being owned personally had to be extracted from being owned socially; 'modern' women's quest was for sexual experience, premised on mutual possession.[10]

Nor did women give up on imagining new kinds of femininity and masculinity. Influenced by the women social economists she encountered at university as well as by 1920s Parisian haute couture, Elizabeth Hawes set out to combine elegance and ease in the women's clothes she designed for mass production, and suggested to men that formal suits might be discarded. What about the sensuous comfort of flowing sheikh-style robes, she asked in her 1939 alternative fashion manifesto, *Men Can Take It*.[11] The robes proved a step too far. Nevertheless, by imagining what might be and living differently the dreamers had indeed helped to shape alternative personal possibilities for women. Free love, openly lived lesbian relationships, new kinds of families, new approaches to bringing up children, new theories of education, new attitudes to diet and to the body came out of that extraordinary ferment.

They also insinuated their new day by leaving little social utopias scattered in their wake: nurseries, maternity welfare centres, birth control clinics, housing for homeless women, garden cities and council houses with bathrooms and indoor lavatories, electricity and gas. These in turn stimulated other proposals. The socialized municipal wash house gave rise to a more individual utopia – the Women's Co-operative Guild's demand in 1946 for a municipally funded washing machine in every council house.[12]

The dreamers' social inventiveness crystallized into opposing ideas which lingered obstinately on: that all women of every race and class should have equal rights; that responsibility for welfare and well-being should be shared by the whole society; and that individuals were not entirely to blame for their misfortunes. These modest-sounding proposals contained far-reaching implications, as did the practical 'schemes of reform' Beatrice Webb noted in 1913. The very existence of forms of social consumption within the texture of everyday living embodied a critique of the market as the best means of meeting all wants, hinting at a subversive economics structured around human needs. The dreamers' heroic outbursts, and the values which inspired them, faded from memory; but much of what they achieved persisted within unremarked aspects of modern living.

Yet it is also true that as the innovations came to be absorbed into the realm of 'the obvious', some of the radical social meanings invested in them fell away. How could all those new women self-consciously wearing advanced dress and riding their bicycles imagine that trousers would be donned and bicycles mounted without a thought? The simplifiers and nature enthusiasts of the 1880s and 1890s could not have conceived that their arts and crafts enthusiasms would produce the standardized bungalows of the twentieth century, or result in several generations of primary-school children doing raffia work. The allegorical dreamers could hardly have foreseen that their interest in fictional utopias would give such a boost to the advertising industry, nor could the enthusiastic inhabitants of garden cities have comprehended that their alternative businesses, catering for radical tastes, would pioneer niche markets. 'Advanced living' metamorphosed into a series of post-war 'lifestyles' with its detritus of formica-topped kitchens, hippy beads, legwarmers and torn jeans. The inventors of daily life in the twentieth century could not control outcomes.

Writing on the *Problems of Everyday Life* in 1924, Leon Trotsky had observed: 'In order to change the conditions of life we must learn to see them through the eyes of women'. Trotsky's insight into 'masculine egotism in ordinary life' would be eclipsed in the left-wing theorization of the everyday which followed.[13] Between the wars the Surrealists wanted to transfigure everyday existence by seeking the wondrous through the transgressive revelations of dreams and desires; they were less enthused by mundane propositions for change, or, indeed, for seeing through the eyes of women.[14] Because Marxists gave priority to the workplace, other aspects of daily living tended to be regarded as, at best, of secondary significance; at worst as the preserve of capitalist mass consumption. In post-war France, the Marxist theorist Henri Lefebvre recognized that daily life was shaped by history, and stressed the significance of consumption. His *Everyday Life in the Modern World* (1968) notes in passing how women were 'consigned' to the everyday and mentions their 'incessant protests', but it presents them as targets of consumer capitalism, not as historical agents in a sustained struggle to alter the circumstances of social and sexual reproduction.[15] Women were inscribed, for Lefebvre, into the semiology of advertising.[16] It was as if the adventurous and inventive women dreamers had never been. All those battles around personal and social existence, all those passionate debates about daily life, seemed to have been deleted from the record.

But then, in the late 1960s, the women's liberation movement surfaced and within a few years feminists in many countries were endeavouring once again to bridge the personal and the political, production and community, society and the state. The new movement contributed to a revived interest in the history of experiments in free love, same-sex relationships, communal living, community action and a wider scope for trade unions. Moreover the adventurers' efforts to reconfigure social citizenship and social rights have been revisited by the wider women's movements which developed alongside feminism. Globally, working-class women have agitated for equality in trade unions and taken action in communities in support of men on strike. Poor women have devised new forms of association to defend their livelihoods. They have also campaigned for access to resources, from water to housing, from sanitation to land, and have risen against the destruction of the environment by large corporations. Ideas of ethical consumption as a means of improving workers' conditions are again on the agenda, along with those of a living wage and citizen's income. The rebellions mounted in recent decades by women worldwide for rights and entitlements have contributed to an assertion of the need to extend democracy into every aspect of everyday life. The boundaries between inner and outer change and differing ways of knowing are being reimagined and reinvented; clear-cut dichotomies are being resisted in favour of fluidity. This new 'awakening' of women throws the efforts of the dreamers and adventurers of the late nineteenth and early twentieth centuries into new relief.

In seeking to translate personal experiences and desires into the public sphere of politics, while attempting to balance autonomy with loving relationships, caring for others with self-realization, modern feminists have come up against many of the dilemmas which puzzled the adventurous dreamers of an earlier era. Moreover, in many parts of the world, women have wrestled with powerful economic and political interests in their efforts to claim resources from the state while retaining democratic control over how they are used. Radical and ingenious stratagems have been devised to enable women participating in community and local politics to affect the centres of power. Like the dreamers before them, women in contemporary movements over the last few decades have been forced to realize that the changes sought have to be regarded as a continuing quest. Indeed, each gain reveals unexpected problems which have to be tackled anew.[17] There is no automatic accretion of improvement. The initial imprint of action can be erased and lost to view, just like the visions of the late nineteenth and early twentieth-century dreamers.

Those women who invented so much have been partially forgotten because they were not at the centre of power, nor were they engaged in heroic acts or glitzed with glamour. But societies are recreated in more ways than meet the eye. The mundane, the intimate, the individual moment of anger, the sense of association: all contribute to the fabric of daily life. The rediscovery of their lost heritage is revelatory, and not only because these energetic innovators dreamed up so much that we take for granted in the world. They also staked out a remarkably rich terrain of debate around questions which are equally vital today. How to renew the body politic; how to take account of specificities while maintaining a wider cohesion; how to allow for individuality while finding connection through relationships and social movements; how to combine inner perceptions with outer change; how to respect the insights and experience of the subordinated and still move from what is to something better; all these are as germane as they ever were. Nor was the awakening of the late nineteenth and early twentieth centuries simply a matter of the intellect; it involved the spirit too. The utopianism of our adventurous foremothers intimated new ways of being and relating: together they effected what Linda Gordon has called a 'transformation of hopes'.[18] Perhaps this faith in possibility is their most precious legacy. Across the decades the voice of the redoubtable Lois Waisbrooker rings with the dreamers' zeal and energy, rallying the faint-hearted among the new wave of 'everyday makers': 'The first step . . . is to believe that it *can* be done; the next that it *will* be done, and lastly to determine to do it *ourselves*'.[19]

Acknowledgements

The inspiration for *Dreamers of a New Day* was Dolores Hayden's *The Grand Domestic Revolution: A History of Feminist Designs for American Homes, Neighborhoods, and Cities* (1981). Hayden's fascinating account of women reshaping everyday life struck powerful chords with my own observations of women's activism in trade unions and community politics, my work in the early 1980s at the Popular Planning Unit as part of the Greater London Council's Industrial Strategy, and then for the United Nations University's economics institute, WIDER, where I began to learn of the global networks being formed by poor women. My knowledge would be deepened by the commitment of women organizing around homework in Britain and internationally.

It has been my good fortune to write in a period when a historical culture informed by feminism has not only 'brought women in', but questioned who and what can be seen. *Dreamers of a New Day* rests on the extraordinary growth of interest in women's and gender history which has occurred since the emergence of the women's movement in the late 1960s. To assert the inventiveness of women is not to deny men's role as historical agents; instead, women's history as I see it seeks to rebalance the frame of reference. Rather than creating a new separate sphere, the aim is to alter the bias in perspectives in which women have been either absent or added as appendages.

My mother used to joke that my father had big ears because he was a farmer's boy, used to listening to the earth. In looking back at the 'everyday makers', I have drawn on the historical equivalent of putting your ear to the ground – an approach I learned from Richard Cobb and E. P. and Dorothy Thompson. Ideas most certainly come from those who write books, articles, pamphlets, reports, but they are also generated through action and lived experience, recorded in passing and snatched up by many people about whom little is known. I have consequently sought out obscure 'dreamers' who questioned prevailing assumptions, along with the figures who left more extensive traces. It is an orientation which is appropriate not simply for women but for all those who are excluded from dominant versions of what has been.

I owe a profound debt to Rosalyn Baxandall, who suggested books and articles and read early drafts of the manuscript, making detailed comments and criticisms; and to my agent, Faith Evans, whose editing skills, insights and knowledge of the period were invaluable in helping me to rewrite chapters. The enthusiasm and expertise of my publishers at Verso have been crucial in enabling me to complete a project which has been long in the making. Tom Penn's meticulous editorial suggestions and criticisms helped me to express concepts with greater clarity, and his empathetic interest inspired me. Lorna Scott Fox's copy-editing not only spotted errors but cleverly improved my phrasing. Big thanks are due to Sonia Lane and Anne Morrow, my RSI rescuers, who typed the manuscript and gave greatly appreciated support. I am also grateful to Logie Barrow, Susan Porter Benson, Lucy Bland, Myrna Breitbart, Stella Capes, Lee Diggings, Carina Galustian, Linda Gordon, Temma Kaplan, Ruth Milkman, Alison Ravetz, Linda Walker, Colin Ward, Harriet Ward, and Barbara Winslow who provided help with written and visual sources. Particular thanks are due to Candace Falk, Barry Pateman and Jessica Moran at the Emma Goldman Papers Project at the University of California at Berkeley, who not only guided me to references but dug up material even after I had returned to Britain. Thank you as well for the encouragement of Stephanie Barrientos, Huw Beynon, Diane Elson, Swasti Mitter, Lynne Segal and Hilary Wainwright who saw the relevance of this history to contemporary movements and policies relating to gender, class and race.

For permission to quote I am grateful to the following: Tamiment Library/Robert F. Wagner Labor Archives, New York (Helena Born Papers); Sophia Smith Collection, Smith College, Northampton, Mass. (Ellen Gates Starr Papers); Sheffield Archives (Carpenter Collection). For permission to reproduce images and help in finding pictures I am grateful to all the institutions credited and to the members of staff who dealt with my requests. Special thanks to Derek Clarke for his patience and forbearance in helping me make contact online.

Notes

Introduction

1 Winifred Harper Cooley, 'A Dream of the Twenty-First Century', in ed. Carol Farley Kessler, *Daring to Dream: Utopian Stories by United States Women 1836–1919*, Pandora Press, Boston and London, 1984, p. 207. See also Winifred Harper Cooley in *Woman's Who's Who of America 1914–15*, p. 203. See also cutting in Women's Rights Papers Biographies; Box 3 Series 2, Sophia Smith Collection, Smith's College Northampton, Mass.

2 Ada Nield Chew, 'Mother-Interest and Child-Training', in ed. Doris Nield Chew, *Ada Nield Chew: The Life and Writings of a Working Woman*, Virago, London, 1982, p. 249.

3 Clementina Black, *Woman's Signal*, 29 August 1895, quoted in David Rubinstein, *Before the Suffragettes: Women's Emancipation in the 1890s*, The Harvester Press, Brighton, Sussex, 1985, p. 217.

4 *Punch*, 26 May 1894, quoted in Rubinstein, *Before the Suffragettes*, p. 17; Christine Stansell, *American Moderns: Bohemian New York and the Creation of a New Century*, Metropolitan Books, Henry Holt and Co., New York, 2000, pp. 26–34.

5 Mary Ritter Beard, 'Mothercraft', in ed. Ann J. Lane, *Mary Ritter Beard: A Sourcebook*, Schocken Books, New York, 1977, p. 79.

6 On the social and economic background, see Neville Kirk, *Labour and Society in Britain and the USA*, Vol. 2, Scolar Press, Aldershot, Hants, 1994; Joshua Freeman et al., *Who Built America? Working People and the Nation's Economy, Politics, Culture and Society*, Pantheon Books, New York, 1992; John Whiteclay Chambers II, *The Tyranny of Change: America in the Progressive Era, 1890–1920*, Rutgers University Press New Brunswick, New Jersey, 2001.

7 Eds Peter Gordon and David Doughan, *Dictionary of Women's Organisations, 1825–1960*, Woburn Press, London, 2001, pp. 174–5. See also Patricia Hollis, *Ladies Elect: Women in English Local Government, 1865–1914*, Oxford University Press, Oxford, 1987, pp. 27, 307–36, 358–9.

8 Pamela M. Graves, *Labour Women: Women in British Working-Class Politics, 1918–1939*, Cambridge University Press, Cambridge, 1994, p. 175.

9 Deborah McDonald, *Clara Collet, 1860–1948: An Educated Working Woman*, Woburn Press, London 2004, pp. 45–7; Jean Bethke Elshtain, *Jane Addams and the Dream of American Democracy*, Basic Books, New York, 2002, pp. 74–5.

10 Patricia Madoo Lengermann and Jill Niebrugge-Brantley, *The Women Founders: Sociology and Social Theory 1830–1930*, McGraw-Hill, Boston, 1998, pp. 229–75.

11 Johanna Alberti, *Eleanor Rathbone*, Sage Publications, London, 1996, pp. 21–9, 68–75.

12 Sally Alexander, 'The Fabian Women's Group 1908–52' in ed. Sally Alexander, *Becoming a Woman and other Essays in 19th and 20th Century Feminist History*, Virago, London, 1994, pp. 149–58.

13 National Woman's Alliance, 'Declaration of Purposes', quoted in Mari Jo Buhle, *Women and American Socialism 1870–1920*, University of Illinois Press, Urbana, 1983, p. 88.

14 Buhle, *Women and American Socialism*, pp. 89–103.

15 Clementina Black, quoted in ed. Ellen Mappen, *Helping Women at Work: The Women's Industrial Council 1889–1914*, Hutchinson and Co., London, 1985, p. 61.

16 See Barbara Winslow, *Sylvia Pankhurst: Sexual Politics and Political Activism*, St. Martin's Press, New York, 1996.

17 Chambers II, *The Tyranny of Change*, pp. 167–8.

18 See Ellen H. Richards and S. Maria Elliott, *The Chemistry of Cooking and Cleaning: A Manual for Housekeepers*, Home Science Publishing, Boston 1897, pp. 81–3,137; Dolores Hayden, *The Grand Domestic Revolution: A History of Feminist Designs for American Homes, Neighborhoods and Cities*, MIT Press, Cambridge, Massachusetts, 1982, pp. 151–3, 186–7; Kathryn Kish Sklar, *Florence Kelley and the Nation's Work: The Rise of Women's Political Culture, 1830–1900*, Yale University Press, New Haven, Connecticut, 1995, pp. 141–5, 306–11; Sarah Deutsch, *Women and the City: Gender, Space and Power in Boston, 1870–1940*, Oxford University Press, Oxford, 2000, pp. 182–3.

19 Stephanie J. Shaw, 'Black Club Women and the Creation of the National Association of Colored Women' and Linda Gordon, 'Black and White Visions of Welfare: Women's Welfare Activism, 1890–1945', in eds Darlene Clark Hine, Wilma King, Linda Reed, '*We Specialize in the Wholly Impossible': A Reader in Black Women's History*, Carlson Publishing, New York, 1995, pp. 433–47, 449–85; Dorothy Sterling, *Black Foremothers: Three Lives*, The Feminist Press, New York, 1988, pp. 83–140.

20 Frances Ellen Harper quoted in Hazel Carby, *Reconstructing Womanhood: The Emergence of the Afro-American Woman Novelist*, Oxford University Press, New York, 1987, p. 70.

21 Polly Wynn Allen, *Building Domestic Liberty: Charlotte Perkins Gilman's Architectural Feminism*, The University of Massachusetts Press, Amherst, 1988, pp. 41–5, 86–121; Ann J. Lane, *To Herland and Beyond: The Life and Work of Charlotte Perkins Gilman*, Pantheon, New York, 1990, pp. 160–4, 297–299; eds Mary Ann Dimand, Robert W. Dimand, Evelyn L. G. Forget, *Women*

of Value: Feminist Essays on the History of Women in Economics, Edward Elgar, Aldershot,1995, p. 55.

22 Martin Henry Blatt, *Free Love and Anarchism: The Biography of Ezra Heywood*, University of Illinois Press, Urbana, 1989, p. 152. See also Hal D. Sears, *The Sex Radicals: Free Love in High Victorian America*, Regents Press of Kansas, Lawrence, 1977, pp. 111, 204–19.

23 Lucy Bland, *Banishing the Beast: English Feminism and Sexual Morality, 1885– 1914*, Penguin Books, London, 1995, pp. 159–61.

24 Pauline Elizabeth Hopkins, quoted in Carby, *Reconstructing Womanhood*, pp. 121–8.

25 Lucy Delap, *The Feminist Avant-Garde: Transatlantic Encounters of the Early Twentieth Century*, Cambridge University Press, Cambridge, 2007, pp. 22–8, 45–6.

26 Delap, *The Feminist Avant-Garde*, pp. 29–34, 49–52.

27 Storm Jameson, *Journey From the North*, Vol. 1, Virago, London, 1984, p. 65.

28 Adeline Champney, *The Woman Question*, Comrade Co-operative Company, New York, 1903, p. 20.

29 Mary Parker Follett, *The New State: Group Organization, The Solution of Popular Government*, Peter Smith, Gloucester, Massachusetts, 1965, p. 189.

1 Adventures in the Everyday

1 See Howard S. Miller, 'Kate Austin: A Feminist-Anarchist on the Farmer's Last Frontier, *Nature, Society, and Thought*, Vol. 9, No. 2, April 1996, pp. 195–8.

2 Lizzie M. Holmes (née Swank), quoted in Meredith Tax, *The Rising of the Women: Feminist Solidarity and Class Conflict, 1880–1917*, Monthly Review Press, New York, 1980, p. 41.

3 *Chicago Tribune*, 3 May 1886, quoted in Tax, *The Rising of the Women*, p. 50.

4 Lizzie M. Holmes (née Swank), 'Our Memorial Day', *The Alarm*, 16 June 1888, Vol. 1, No. 14, p. 1.

5 Lengermann and Niebrugge-Brantley, *The Women Founders*, p. 230.

6 See Chew, *Ada Nield Chew*, pp. 75–134.

7 Quoted in G. R. Searle, *A New England? Peace and War, 1886–1918*, Clarendon Press, Oxford, 2004, p. 71.

8 Frances E. Willard, 'Women and Organization', Address to the Woman's National Council of the United States, First Triennial Meeting, 1891, Library of Congress, available online: http://www.history.ohio-state.edu/ projects/prohibition/willard/willard.htm (accessed 27/05/02).

9 Mary Church Terrell, 'The Progress of Colored Women', Address before the National American Women's Suffrage Association, 1898, available online: http://www.gos.sbc.edu/t/terrellmary.htm (accessed 21/05/02).

10 Shaw, 'Black Club Women and the Creation of the National Association of Colored Women', in eds Hine, King, Reed, '*We Specialize in the Wholly Impossible*', pp. 436–7; Tera W. Hunter, *To 'Joy My Freedom: Southern Black Women's Lives and Labors After the Civil War*, Harvard University Press, Cambridge, Massachusetts, 1997, pp. 136–7.

11 Louisa Twining, 'Workhouse Cruelties', *The Nineteenth Century*, Vol. XX, July–Dec., 1886, p. 709.

12 Kate Richards O'Hare, quoted in eds Philip S. Foner and Sally M. Miller, *Kate Richards O'Hare: Selected Writings and Speeches*, Louisiana State University Press, Baton Rouge, 1982, p. 200.

13 Vida D. Scudder, *Social Ideals in English Letters*, Houghton, Mifflin and Co., 1898, p. 300.

14 Emily Ford, 'Reminiscences' 1880–1910, Ford Family Papers, Mss. 371/3, p. 3, Brotherton Library, University of Leeds.

15 Ellen Gates Starr to Mary Blaisdell, 23 February ,1889 (?) , Correspondence, Series 2, Box 8, Ellen Gates Starr Papers, Sophia Smith Collection, Smith's College, Northampton, Mass; Jane Addams, *Twenty Years at Hull House*, Macmillan, New York, 1938, pp. 115–17.

16 Carol Dyhouse, *No Distinction of Sex? Women in British Universities, 1870–1939*, UCL Press, London, 1995, p. 193.

17 Mrs Havelock Ellis (née Edith Lees), 'Olive Schreiner and her Relation to the Woman Movement', mss Havelock Ellis Papers; British Library.

18 Lizzie Holmes, 'The "Unwomanly" Woman', *Our New Humanity*, Vol. 1, No. 3, March 1896, p. 13.

19 *Commonweal,* 16 August 1890; 13 September 1890.

20 Beatrice Webb (née Potter), August 1885, quoted in Carole Seymour-Jones, *Beatrice Webb: Woman of Conflict*, Pandora, London, 1993, p. 128.

21 Anzia Yezierska quoted in Annelise Orleck, *Common Sense and a Little Fire: Women and Working Class Politics in the United States, 1900–1965*, The University of North Carolina Press, Chapel Hill, 1995, p. 39; on Yezierska see Elaine Showalter, *A Jury of Her Peers: American Women Writers from Anne Bradstreet to Annie Proulx*, Virago, London, 2009, pp. 313–21.

22 Anna Julia Cooper quoted in Mary Helen Washington, Introduction, *Anna Julia Cooper, A Voice from the South*, Oxford University Press, New York, 1988, p. xivii.

23 Jane Edna Hunter quoted in Shaw, 'Black Club Women', p. 438.

24 Florence Kelley to Friedrich Engels, 1887, quoted in Sklar, *Florence Kelley and the Nation's Work*, p. 143. See Helen Campbell, *The Problem of the Poor: A Record of Quiet Work in Unquiet Places*, Fords, Howard and Hulbert, New York, 1882.

25 Beatrice Webb, quoted in Seymour-Jones, *Beatrice Webb*, p. 78.

26 Virginia Woolf, Introduction, in ed. Margaret Llewelyn Davies, *Life As We Have Known It*, Hogarth Press, London, 1931, p. xxxvi.

27 Jane Hume Clapperton, *Scientific Meliorism and the Evolution of Happiness*, Kegan Paul Trench and Co., London, 1885, p. 286.

28 Terrell, 'The Progress of Colored Women'. Available online: http://gos. sbc.edu/t/terrellmary.html (accessed 27/05/02).

29 Catherine Webb quoted in Alistair Thomson, '"Domestic Drudgery will be a Thing of the Past": Co-operative Women and the Reform of Housework', in ed. Stephen Yeo, *New Views of Co-operation*, Routledge, London, 1988, p. 123.

30 Charlotte M. Wilson, 'What Socialism Is', Fabian Society, Tract No. 4, June 1886, in ed. Nicolas Walter, *Charlotte Wilson: Anarchist Essays*, Freedom Press, London, 2000, p. 53.

31 See Sheila Rowbotham, *Edward Carpenter: A Life of Liberty and Love*, Verso, London, 2008.

32 Helena Born to William Bailie, 1 May 1898, Born Papers, The Tamiment Library and Robert F. Wagner Labor Archives.

33 Charlotte Perkins Stetson (Gilman) Diary, 28 September 1896 and Charlotte Perkins Stetson (Gilman) to Houghton Gilman, 4 June 1897, Charlotte Perkins Gilman Papers, Schlesinger Library, Radcliffe Institute, Harvard University.

34 Mary Gawthorpe, *Up Hill to Holloway*, Traversity Press, Penobscot, Maine, 1962, p. 121.

35 Alison Ravetz, *Council Housing and Culture: The History of a Social Experiment*, Routledge, London, 2001, pp. 29–32; Carolyn Steedman, *Childhood, Culture and Classic Britain: Margaret McMillan, 1860–1921*, Rutgers University Press, New Brunswick, New Jersuey, 1990, pp. 47–8; Jill Liddington, *The Life and Times of a Respectable Rebel: Selina Cooper, 1864–1946*, Virago, London, 1984, p. 68; Mary A. Hill, *Charlotte Perkins Gilman: The Making of a Radical Feminist, 1860–1896*, Temple University Press, Philadelphia, 1980, p. 242.

36 Scudder, *Social Ideals in English Letters*, p. 219.

37 Constance M. Chen, *'The Sex Side of Life': Mary Ware Dennett's Pioneering Battle for Birth Control and Sex Education*, The New Press, New York, 1996, p. 22.

38 Hill, *Charlotte Perkins Gilman*, pp. 264–72.

39 Lengermann, Niebrugge-Brantley, *The Women Founders*, pp. 75, 242; Sklar, *Florence Kelley*, pp. 100–105; Karen Hunt, *Equivocal Feminists: The Social Democratic Federation and the Woman Question, 1884–1911*, Cambridge University Press, Cambridge, 1996, pp. 81–117.

40 Lengermann, Niebrugge-Brantley, *The Women Founders*, p. 298.

41 Delap, *The Feminist Avant-Garde*, p. 205.

42 Maurine Weiner Greenwald, 'Working-Class Feminism and the Family Wage Ideal: The Seattle Debate on Married Women's Right to Work, 1914–1920', *Journal of American History*, Vol. 76, No. 1, June 1989, p. 135.

43 Sterling, *Black Foremothers*, pp. 90–92. On the Pioneer Club, see Erika Diane Rappaport, *Shopping for Pleasure: Women in the Making of London's West End*, Princeton University Press, Princeton, 2000, p. 96.

44 Phyllis Grosskurth, *Havelock Ellis: A Biography*, New York University Press, New York, 1985, p. 191; Sheila Rowbotham, *Women in Movement: Feminism and Social Action*, Routledge, New York, 1992, pp. 158–61.

45 Ellen Carol DuBois, *Harriot Stanton Blatch and the Winning of Woman Suffrage*, Yale University Press, New Haven, Connecticut, 1997, pp. 60–85; Lane, *Mary Ritter Beard*, pp. 1–23; Alice Hamilton, *Exploring the Dangerous Trades*, Northeastern University Press, Boston, 1985, pp. 240–41. On the formal organizations see Leila J. Rupp, *Worlds of Women: The Making of an International Women's Movement*, Princeton University Press, Princeton, 1997.

46 Sheila Rowbotham, *A New World for Women: Stella Browne – Socialist Feminist*, Pluto, London, 1977, pp. 15–17; Desley Deacon, *Elsie Clews Parsons: Inventing Modern Life*, The University of Chicago Press, Chicago, 1997, fn. 32, p. 434.

47 Jill Liddington and Jill Norris, *One Hand Tied Behind Us: The Rise of the Women's Suffrage Movement*, Virago, London, 1978, pp. 236–7; Thomson, '"Domestic Drudgery will be a Thing of the Past"', p. 115.

48 Fannia Cohn quoted in Orleck, *Common Sense and a Little Fire*, p. 192.

49 Hermia Oliver, *The International Anarchist Movement in Late Victorian London*, Croom Helm, London, 1983, pp. 25–33; Nicolas Walter, 'Charlotte Wilson' in ed. David Goodway, *The Anarchist Past and Other Essays: Nicolas Walter*, Five Leaves, Nottingham, 2007, pp. 220–30.

50 Dora Barrow Montefiore in ed. Elizabeth Crawford, *The Women's Suffrage Movement: A Reference Guide 1866–1928*, UCL Press, London, 1999, pp. 418–23.

51 Deacon, *Elsie Clews Parsons*, pp. 34–53, 121–3.

52 Marie Jenny Howe quoted in Deacon, *Elsie Clews Parsons*, p. 121.

53 Bland, *Beauty and the Beast*, pp. 14–47.

54 Ibid., pp. 250–96; Delap, *The Feminist Avant-Garde*, pp. 49, 122–6; Mathew Thomson, *Psychological Subjects, Identity, Culture and Health in Twentieth-Century Britain*, Oxford University Press, Oxford, 2006, pp. 20–22, 100–101.

55 Mabel Dodge Luhan quoted in Lois Palken Rudnick, *Mabel Dodge Luhan: New Woman, New Worlds*, University of New Mexico Press, Albuquerque, 1984, p. 143.

56 Parsons quoted in Deacon, *Elsie Clews Parsons*, p. 129.

57 Blanche Wiesen Cook, ed., *Crystal Eastman: On Women and Revolution*, Oxford University Press, Oxford, 1978, pp. 46–57.

58 Mrs. Bertrand Russell (Dora Russell), *The Right to Be Happy*, Garden City Publishing, New York, 1927, p. 295.

2 How to Be

1 Dora Montefiore, 'The New Woman', *Singings Through the Dark*, Sampson Low & Co., London, 1898, pp. 62–3.

2 Holmes, 'The "Unwomanly" Woman', p. 13.

3 Emma Heller Schumm, Boston Branch of the Walt Whitman Fellowship, 17 March 1901, Born Papers, The Tamiment Library and Robert F. Wagner Labor Archives.

4 Ibid.

5 Clapperton, *Scientific Meliorism*, p. 140.

6 Teresa Billington-Greig, 1914, quoted in Brian Harrison, *Prudent Revolutionaries: Portraits of British Feminists Between the Wars*, Clarendon Press, Oxford, 1987, p. 63.

7 Mary Simmons, quoted in Martha Vicinus, *Independent Women: Work and Community for Single Women: 1850–1920*, Virago, London, 1985, p. 230.

8 Florence Exten-Hann, quoted in ed. Sheila Rowbotham, *Dreams and Dilemmas: Collected Writings*, Virago, London, 1983, p. 224.

9 Crystal Eastman, quoted in Cook, *Crystal Eastman*, p. 9.

10 Ibid.

11 Elizabeth Cady Stanton, quoted in Crawford, *The Women's Suffrage Movement*, p. 271.

12 Anon., 'Infant Clothing', *The Rational Dress Society's Gazette*, Vol. 2, No. 6, July 1889, p. 76.

13 Quoted in Rita McWilliams, Tullberg, 'Mary Paley Marshall, 1850–1944' in eds Mary Ann Dimand, Robert W. Dimand, Evelyn L. Forget, *Women of Value: Feminist Essays on the History of Women in Economics*, Edward Elgar, Aldershot, 1995, p. 161.

14 Helena Born, 'Whitman and Nature', Mss C. 1890, Born Papers, Tamiment Library and Robert F. Wagner Labor Archives.

15 Gordon and Doughan, *Dictionary of British Women's Organisations*, p. 63.

16 Dennis Hardy, *Community Experiments, 1900–1945*, E. and F. N. Spon, London, 2000, p. 123.

17 Nellie Shaw, *Whiteway: A Colony in the Cotswolds*, C. W. Daniel, London, 1935, p. 109.

18 Gordon and Doughan, *Dictionary of British Women's Organisations*, p. 63.

19 Shari Benstock, *Women of the Left Bank: Paris 1900–1940,* University of Texas, Austin, 1986, p. 302.

20 Charlotte Perkins Gilman, quoted in Lane, *To Herland and Beyond*, p. 285.

21 Christine Stansell, *American Moderns: Bohemian New York and the Creation of a New Century*, Metropolitan Books, New York, 2000, p. 35.

22 Cosmo Gordon Lang quoted in J. G. Lockhart, *Cosmo Gordon Lang*, Hodder and Stoughton, London, 1949, p. 49.

23 Sheila Rowbotham, Interview with Maurice Hann, Mss Notes, 1973.

24 Chew, *Ada Nield Chew*, p. 10.

25 Ibid.

26 Quoted in Harrison, *Prudent Revolutionaries*, p. 189.

27 Milka Sablich, quoted in Ella Reeve Bloor, *We Are Many: An Autobiography,* International Publishers, New York, 1940, pp. 218–19.

28 Quoted in Angela Woollacott, *On Her Their Lives Depend: Munitions Workers in the Great War*, University of California Press, Berkeley, 1994, p. 130.

29 Quoted in Melinda Chateauvert, *Marching Together: Women of the Brotherhood of Sleeping Car Porters*, University of Illinois Press, Urbana, 1998, p. 9.

30 Quoted in Laura Doan, *Fashioning Sapphism: The Origins of a Modern English Lesbian Culture*, Columbia University Press, New York, 2001, p. 120. Doan notes the cultural meanings given to the shift in styles, pp. 96, 120–25.

31 Elsie Clews Parsons, quoted in Deacon, *Elsie Clews Parsons*, p. 129.

32 Max Eastman, quoted in Rudnick, *Mabel Dodge Luhan*, p. 117.

33 Elsie Clews Parsons, quoted in Deacon, *Elsie Clews Parsons*, p. 129.

34 Isabel Leavenworth, 'Virtue for Women', in ed. Freda Kirchwey, *Our Changing Morality: A Symposium*, Albert and Charles Boni, New York, 1924, p. 97.

35 Josephine Baker, quoted in Ann Douglas, *Terrible Honesty: Mongrel Manhattan in the 1920s*, The Noonday Press, Farrar, Strauss & Giroux, New York, 1995, p. 52.

36 Jessie Fauset quoted in Benstock, *Women of the Left Bank*, p. 13.

37 Carby, *Reconstructing Womanhood*, p. 173.

38 Charlotte Perkins Gilman, 'Toward Monogamy' in ed. Kirchwey, *Our Changing Morality*, p. 54.

39 Mabel Dodge Luhan, quoted in Rudnick, *Mabel Dodge Luhan*, p. 62.

40 Sheila Rowbotham, Interview with Margery Corbett Ashby, Mss Notes, 1973.

41 Isabella Ford quoted in June Hannam, *Isabella Ford*, Basil Blackwell, Oxford, 1989, p. 54.

42 *Clarion*, 23 December 1899, quoted in Logie Barrow, *The Socialism of Robert Blatchford and the Clarion Newspaper, 1889–1914*, University of London, PhD Thesis, 1975, p. 273.

43 Julia Dawson, *Clarion*, 30 December 1899, quoted in Barrow, *The Socialism of Robert Blatchford and the Clarion Newspaper*, p. 273.

44 Ada Nield Chew, 'The Economic Freedom of Women', *Freewoman*, 11 July 1912, in ed. Chew, *Ada Nield Chew*, p. 240.

45 Ibid., pp. 20–21.

46 Annie Davison, in eds Jean McCrindle and Sheila Rowbotham, *Dutiful Daughters: Women Talk about Their Lives*, Penguin, London, 1983, p. 64.

47 Dana Frank, *Purchasing Power: Consumer Organizing, Gender, and the Seattle Labor Movement, 1919–1929*, Cambridge University Press, Cambridge, 1994, p. 57.

48 Frank, *Purchasing Power*, p. 57.

49 Children's Rosebud Fountains, quoted in Elsa Barkley Brown, 'Womanist Consciousness: Maggie Lena Walker and the Independent Order of Saint Luke', in eds Ellen Carol DuBois and Vicki L. Ruiz, *Unequal Sisters: A Multicultural Reader in US Women's History*, Routledge, New York, 1990, p. 212.

50 Pauline Newman, quoted in Orleck, *Common Sense and a Little Fire*, p. 35.

51 Mary Heaton Vorse quoted in ed. Dee Garrison, *Rebel Pen: The Writings of Mary Heaton Vorse*, Monthly Review Press, New York, 1985, p. 15.

52 Quoted in Nancy A. Hewitt, *Southern Discomfort: Women's Activism in Tampa, Florida, 1880s–1920s*, University of Illinois Press, Urbana, 2001, p. 115.

53 Emma Goldman, 'The Tragedy of Woman's Emancipation', quoted in June Sochen, *Movers and Shakers: American Women Thinkers and Activists, 1900–1970*, Quadrangle, The New York Times Book Co., New York, 1973, p. 63.

54 Charlotte Perkins Gilman, 'An Anchor to Windward', 1882, quoted in Hill, *Charlotte Perkins Gilman*, p. 93.

55 Charlotte Perkins Gilman to Martha Lane, 20 January 1890, quoted in ibid., p. 160.

56 Kate Courtney and Beatrice (Potter) Webb, quoted in Seymour-Jones, *Beatrice Webb*, p. 209.

57 Beatrice (Potter) Webb, 5 May 1890, in eds MacKenzie, *The Diaries of Beatrice Webb*, p. 139.

58 Elsie Clews Parsons, quoted in Deacon, *Elsie Clews Parsons*, p. 143.

59 Beatrice M. Hinkle, 'Women and the New Morality', in ed. Kirchwey, *Our Changing Morality*, p. 249.

60 Elsie Clews Parsons, quoted in Deacon, *Elsie Clews Parsons*, p. 96.

61 Beatrice Hastings, *New Age*, Vol. XI, No. 11, 11 July 1912, p. 253. On Hastings in Paris see Dan Franck, *The Bohemians: The Birth of Modern Art: Paris, 1900–1930*, Weidenfeld and Nicolson, London, 2001, pp. 187–261.

62 June Sochen, *The New Woman in Greenwich Village, 1910–1920*, Quadrangle, The New York Times Book Co., 1972, pp. 18–23, 34–5. On Susan Glaspell, see Showalter, *A Jury of Her Peers*, pp. 262–3.

63 Elsie Clews Parsons, quoted in Deacon, *Elsie Clews Parsons*, p. 142.

64 Leonora Eyles, 'The Unattached Woman', *Good Housekeeping*, March 1928, in eds Brian Braithwaite, Noëlle Walsh, *Things My Mother Should Have Told Me: The Best of Good Housekeeping 1922–1940*, Ebury Press, London, 1991, p. 74.

65 Leonora Eyles, 'Sex Antagonism', *Lansbury's Labour Weekly*, 28 November 1925, p.13.

66 Elise Johnson McDougald, 'The Double Task: The Struggle of Negro Women for Sex and Race Emancipation', *Survey Graphic*, 1925, in ed. Margaret Busby, *Daughters of Africa: An International Anthology of Words and Writings by Women of African Descent from the Ancient Egyptian to the Present*, Jonathan Cape, London, 1992, p. 184.

67 Garland Smith, 'The Unpardonable Sin', in ed. Elaine Showalter, *These Modern Women: Autobiographical Essays from the Twenties*, The Feminist Press, New York, 1978, p. 120.

68 Ruth Pickering, 'A Deflated Rebel', in ibid., p. 62.

69 Dorothy Dunbar Bromley, quoted in ibid., p. 4.

70 Beatrice M. Hinkle, 'Why Feminism?', in ibid., p. 141.

71 Crystal Eastman, 'Now We Can Begin', 1920, in ed. Cook, *Crystal Eastman*, pp. 53–4.

72 Suzanne La Follette, *Concerning Women*, Arno Press, New York, 1972, p. 303.

73 Emma Goldman to Hutchins Hapgood, 26 October 1927, quoted in Candace Falk, *Love, Anarchy and Emma Goldman: A Biography*, Holt, Rinehart and Winston, New York, 1984, p. 7.

74 Emma Goldman to Alexander Berkman, December 1927, quoted in ibid., p. 10.

3 The Problem of Sex

1 Lillian Harman, 'The Gospel of Self-Respect', *Lucifer*, Vol. I, No. 16, 21 April 1897, p. 125.

2 Sarah Holmes ('Zelm'), 'Love and Ideas, Ideals about Love', *Liberty*, Vol. 5, No. 26, Issue 130, 21 July 1888, p. 7.

3 Sears, *The Sex Radicals*, pp. 252–3.

4 Lillian Harman, *Some Problems of Social Freedom*, (pamphlet), The Adult, London, 1898, p. 4.

5 Holmes, 'Love and Ideas', p. 7.

6 Elmina Slenker, quoted in Blatt, *Free Love and Anarchism*, p. 153.

7 Elmina Slenker, 'Dianaism', *Lucifer*, Vol. I, No. 15, 14 April 1897, p. 117.

8 Ibid.

9 Alice B. Stockham, *Karezza* (1896), quoted in Angus McLaren, *Birth Control in Nineteenth-Century England*, Holmes and Meier, New York, 1978, p. 204.

10 Dora Forster, *The Adult*, October 1897, quoted in Bland, *Banishing the Beast*, p. 172.

11 Amy Linnett, 'Continence and Contraception', *Lucifer*, Vol. I, No. 18, 15 May 1897, p. 39.

12 Elizabeth Johnson, Letter, *Lucifer*, Vol. I, No. 42, 20 October 1897, p. 335.

13 Rosa Graul, *Hilda's Home* (1897), quoted in Kessler, *Daring to Dream*, p. 203.

14 Ibid.

15 Harman, *Some Problems of Social Freedom*, p. 8.

16 Lillie White, *Lucifer*, 19 June 1891, quoted in Sears, *The Sex Radicals*, p. 247.

17 Sarah Holmes ('Zelm'), 'The Problem which the Child Presents', *Liberty*, Vol. 6, No. 2, Issue 132, 1 September 1888, p. 7.

18 Graul, *Hilda's Home*, quoted in Kessler, *Daring to Dream*, p. 203.

19 Kate Austin, 'A Woman's View of It', *Firebrand*, 25 April 1897, quoted in Jessica Moran, 'The Story of Kate Austin: Anarchist Revolutionary Writer', unpublished paper 1999, in Emma Goldman Papers, Berkeley, California.

20 Blaine McKinley, 'Free Love and Domesticity: Lizzie M. Holmes, *Hagar Lyndon* (1893), and the Anarchist-Feminist Imagination', *Journal of American Culture*, Vol. 13, No. 1, Spring 1990, p. 60.

21 Edith Vance, 25 February 1895, quoted in ed. Oswald Dawson, *The Bar Sinister and Illicit Love: The First Biennial Proceedings of the Legitimation League*, W. Reeve, London, 1895, pp. 228–9.

22 Shaw, *Whiteway*, p. 129.

23 Voltairine de Cleyre, 'Those Who Marry Do Ill', *Mother Earth*, Vol. II, No. 11, January 1908, in ed. Peter Glassgold, *Anarchy! An Anthology of Mother Earth*, Counterpoint, Washington, DC, 2001, p. 106.

24 Mona Caird, 'Marriage', *Westminster Review*, Vol. 130, August 1888, quoted in Bland, *Banishing the Beast*, p. 129.

25 Mona Caird, 'Phases of Human Development', quoted in Bland, *Banishing the Beast*, p. 129.

26 Caird, 'Marriage', quoted in Bland, *Banishing the Beast*, p. 129.

27 Margaret McMillan to John Bruce Glaiser, 2 February 1893, quoted in Steedman, *Childhood, Culture and Class in Britain*, p. 123.

28 Meridel LeSueur, 'A Remembrance', in Emma Goldman, *Living My Life: An Autobiography*, A Peregrine Smith Book, Gibbs M. Smith, Salt Lake City, Utah, 1982, p. v.

29 See Bland, *Banishing the Beast*, pp. 95–111.

30 See David J. Pivar, *Purity Crusade: Sexual Morality and Social Control*, Greenwood Press, Westport, Connecticut, 1973, pp. 186, 204, 228–37.

31 Bland, *Banishing the Beast*, p. 115.

32 Pivar, *Purity Crusade*, pp. 261–73.

33 Hamilton, *Exploring the Dangerous Trades*, pp. 92–3.

34 Maimie Pinzer, Letter 27, in eds Ruth Rosen and Sue Davidson, *The Maimie Papers*, The Feminist Press, New York, 1977, p. 81.

35 Quoted in Mary Ritter Beard, *Woman's Work in Municipalities* (1915), Arno Press, New York, 1972, p. 148.

36 Dr. Rosalie Morton, quoted in ibid., p. 129.

37 The Women's Municipal League of Boston, quoted in ibid., p. 125.

38 Angela Heywood, *The Word*, April 1887, quoted in Blatt, *Free Love and Anarchism*, p. 161.

39 Ezra Heywood, *The Word*, July 1884, quoted in ibid.

40 'Ess Tee', 'Wanted: A New Dictionary', *The Adult*, November 1897, quoted in Bland, *Banishing the Beast*, p. 273.

41 Maria Sharpe, 'Conclusion', 5 July 1889, quoted in ibid., pp. 25–6.

42 Lizzie Holmes, Letter, *Lucifer*, 28 August 1891, quoted in Sears, *The Sex Radicals*, p. 269.

43 Dora Marsden, *Freewoman*, 16 May 1912, quoted in Bland, *Banishing the Beast*, p. 273.

44 Dora Marsden, *Freewoman*, 23 November 1911, pp.1–2.

45 Mabel Dodge Luhan, 'Magnetism', 1912, quoted in Rudnick, *Mabel Dodge Luhan*, p. 65.

46 Olive Schreiner to Havelock Ellis, 7 August 1912, in ed. S. C. Cronwright-Schreiner, *The Letters of Olive Schreiner, 1876–1920*, T. Fisher Unwin, London, 1924, p. 312.

47 Kathlyn Oliver, 'Asceticism and Power', *Freewoman*, 15 February 1912, p. 252.

48 New Subscriber, *Freewoman*, 22 February 1912, p. 270; Kathlyn Oliver, *Freewoman*, 29 February 1912, p. 290; New Subscriber, *Freewoman*, 7 March 1912, p. 313; Kathlyn Oliver, *Freewoman*, 14 March 1912, p. 331.

49 Edith Ellis to Edward Carpenter, 5 December 1905, Mss 358/7. Carpenter Collection, Sheffield Archives.

50 F. W. Stella Browne, 'The Sexual Variety and Variability among Women and their Bearing upon Social Reconstruction', 1915, in Rowbotham, *A New World for Women*, p. 104.

51 Ibid., pp. 103–4.

52 Elsie Clews Parsons, 'Wives and Birth Control', 1916, quoted in Deacon, *Elsie Clews Parsons*, p. 159. On the roots of this new sense of self see ibid., p. 125.

53 Stansell, *American Moderns*, p. 307.

54 Neith Boyce to Hutchins Hapgood, 13 April 1899, quoted in Stansell, *American Moderns*, p. 261.

55 Neith Boyce to Hutchins Hapgood, December 1905, quoted in ibid., p. 285.

56 See eds Candace Falk, Barry Pateman, Jessica Moran, *Emma Goldman: A Documentary History of the American Years, Vol. I: Made for America, 1890–1901*, University of California Press, Berkeley, 2003, pp. 13–14.

57 Emma Goldman to Ben Reitman, no date, quoted in Candace Falk, *Love, Anarchy and Emma Goldman: A Biography,* Holt, Rinehart and Winston, New York, 1984, pp. 79-80.

58 Stansell, *American Moderns*, p. 295.

59 Almeda Sperry to Emma Goldman, no date, 1912, quoted in Falk, *Love, Anarchy and Emma Goldman*, p. 173.

60 LeSueur, 'A Remembrance', in Goldman, *Living My Life,* p. xv.

61 Janice R. MacKinnon and Stephen R. MacKinnon, *Agnes Smedley: The Life and Times of an American Radical*, Virago, London, 1988, p. 34.

62 Margaret Llewelyn Davies, draft foreword to Catherine Webb, *The Woman with the Basket*, quoted in Gill Scott, '"Working Out Their Own Salvation": Women's Autonomy and Divorce Law Reform in the Co-operative Movement, 1910–1920', in ed. Yeo, *New Views of Co-operation*, p. 131.

63 Gawthorpe, *Up Hill to Holloway*, p. 151.

64 Ed. Tierl Thompson, *Dear Girl: The Diaries and Letters of Two Working Women 1897–1917*, The Women's Press, London, 1987, pp. 154-5.

65 Ibid., p. 15.

66 Ada Nield Chew, quoted in Chew, *Ada Nield Chew*, p. 61.

67 Mary Archibald, *Seattle Union Record*, 29 April 1918, quoted in Greenwald, 'Working-Class Feminism and the Family Wage Ideal', *Journal of American History*, Vol. 76, No 1, June 1989, p. 136.

68 Rose Schneiderman to Pauline Newman, 11 August 1917, quoted in Orleck, *Common Sense and a Little Fire*, p. 137.

69 Elsie Clews Parsons, 'Changes in Sex Relations', in ed. Kirchwey, *Our Changing Morality*, p. 37.

70 Margaret Leech, quoted in Marion Meade, *Dorothy Parker: What Fresh Hell Is This?*, Heinemann, London, 1988, p. 76.

71 Ann Douglas, *Terrible Honesty: Mongrel Manhattan in the 1920s*, The Noonday Press, Farrar, Strauss & Giroux, New York, 1995, p. 47.

72 Carby, *Reconstructing Womanhood*, pp. 173–4.

73 Mrs Bertrand Russell, *Hypatia or Women and Knowledge*, Kegan Paul, Trench, Trubner and Co., London, 1925, pp. 42–3.

74 Vera Brittain, *Halcyon or the Future of Monogamy*, Kegan Paul, Trench, Trubner and Co., London, 1929, p. 17.

75 Mary Ware Dennett, quoted in Brittain, *Halcyon*, p. 24.

76 Sheila Rowbotham, Interview with Dora Russell, Mss Notes, 1974.

77 Leonora Eyles, *The Woman in the Little House*, Grant Richards, London, 1922, p. 129.

78 Ibid., pp. 133–4.

79 Ibid., p. 136.

80 Annie Williams, in eds McCrindle and Rowbotham, *Dutiful Daughters*, pp. 39–40.

81 Martha, 'Problems of Real Life', *Lansbury's Labour Weekly*, 3 October 1925, p. 2.

82 Leonora Eyles, 'And the Poor Get', *Lansbury's Labour Weekly*, 23 May 1925, p. 14.

83 Leonora Eyles, 'The Husband', *Lansbury's Labour Weekly*, 21 March 1925, p. 14.

84 Leonora Eyles, 'Doing Wrong', *Lansbury's Labour Weekly*, 5 September 1925, p. 17.

85 Andrea Weiss, *Paris Was a Woman: Portraits from the Left Bank*, Pandora, London, 1995, p. 21.

86 Benstock, *Women of the Left Bank*, pp. 184–85.

87 Weiss, *Paris Was a Woman*, pp. 65–6.

88 Doan, *Fashioning Sapphism*, pp. 185–94.

89 Vera Brittain, quoted in Marion Shaw, *The Clear Stream: A Life of Winifred Holtby*, Virago, London, 1999, p. 211.

90 Brittain, *Halcyon*, p. 23.

91 Ibid.

92 Russell, *The Right to Be Happy*, p. 148.

93 Gilman, 'Toward Monogamy', in ed. Kirchwey, *Our Changing Morality*, pp. 57–9.

94 Crystal Eastman, 'Alice Paul's Convention', in ed. Cook, *Crystal Eastman*, pp. 62–3.

95 La Follette, *Concerning Women*, p. 98.

96 Ibid., pp. 99–100.

97 Parsons, 'Changes in Sex Relations', in ed. Kirchwey, *Our Changing Morality*, p. 46.

98 Ibid., p. 47.

4 What Every Girl Should Know

1 Graul, *Hilda's Home*, in ed. Kessler, *Daring to Dream*, pp. 203–4.

2 Lois Waisbrooker, 'Woman's Power', *Lucifer*, Vol. I, No. 16, 21 April 1897, p. 125.

3 Slenker, 'Dianaism', *Lucifer*, Vol. I, No. 15, 14 April 1897, p. 117.

4 Blatt, *Free Love and Anarchism*, p. 164.

5 Linnett, 'Continence and Contraception', *Lucifer*, Vol. I, No. 18, 5 May 1897, p. 39.

6 DuBois, *Harriot Stanton Blatch*, pp. 66–7. On voluntary motherhood see Linda Gordon, *Woman's Body, Woman's Right: A Social History of Birth Control in America*, Viking Press, New York, 1976, pp. 95–115.

7 Annie Besant, 'Preface', *The Law of Population: Its Consequences and Bearing upon Human Conduct and Morals* (1891), Augustus M. Kelley, New York, 1970, p. 4.

8 Clapperton, *Scientific Meliorism*, p. 95.

9 Malthusian League, 'To Working Men and Women: Do Not Have a Large Number of Children', Malthusian League, no date, copy of leaflet in author's possession.

10 Moses Harman, 'The Social Side of Anarchism', *Lucifer*, Vol. V, No. 39, 12 October 1901, p. 7.

11 Beard, *Woman's Work in Municipalities*, p. 68.

12 Jeffrey Weeks, *Sex, Politics and Society: The Regulation of Sexuality Since 1800*, Longman, London, 1981, pp. 128–40.

13 Mark H. Haller, *Eugenics: Hereditarian Attitudes in American Thought*, Rutgers University Press, New Brunswick, 1984, pp. 84, 178; Ewen and Ewen 7, *Typecasting: On the Arts and Sciences of Human Inequality*, Seven Stores Press, New York, 2006, pp. 281–312.

14 Gilman, 'Humanness' (1913), quoted in Lane, *To Herland and Beyond*, p. 283.

15 Blatch, quoted in DuBois, *Harriot Stanton Blatch*, p. 67.

16 Anna Davin, *Growing Up Poor: Home, School and Street in London 1870–1914*, Rivers Oram Press, London, 1996, p. 213.

17 Beard, *Woman's Work in Municipalities*, p. 69.

18 Sears, *The Sex Radicals*, p. 244.

19 Hamilton, *Exploring the Dangerous Trades*, p. 111.

20 McLaren, *Birth Control in Nineteenth Century England*, p. 226.

21 Hannah Mitchell, *The Hard Way Up*, Virago, London, 1977, pp. 88–9.

22 Alice Drysdale Vickery, *A Women's Malthusian League: A Women's League for the Extinction of Poverty and Prostitution through the Rational Regulation of the Birth-Rate*, Pamphlet of The Malthusian League, London, no date, pp. 2–4.

23 Dora Forster, 'America Under Comstock', *New Generation*, January 1927, p. 6.

24 Antoinette Konikow, quoted in Mari Jo Buhle, *Women and American Socialism, 1870–1920*, University of Illinois Press, Urbana, 1983, p. 270. On Konikow's impact see pp. 270–71.

25 Richard Drinnon, *Rebel in Paradise: A Biography of Emma Goldman*, The University of Chicago Press, Chicago, 1961, pp. 166–8.

26 Gordon, *Woman's Body, Woman's Right*, p. 214.

27 David M. Kennedy, *Birth Control in America: The Career of Margaret Sanger*, Yale University Press, New Haven, Connecticut, 1970, p. 23. See also Gordon, *Woman's Body, Woman's Right*, pp. 209–36.

28 Margaret Sanger, 'Comstockery in America', *International Socialist Review*, Vol. XVI, No. 1, July 1915, pp. 46, 48.

29 Stella Browne, Letter, *Freewoman*, 1 August 1912, p. 217.

30 Stella Browne to Margaret Sanger, 7 September 1915, Margaret Sanger Papers Project, New York University.

31 Jane M. Jensen, 'The Evolution of Margaret Sanger's *Family Limitation* (pamphlet), 1914–1921', *Signs*, Vol. 6, No. 3, Spring 1981, pp. 548–55.

32 Margaret Sanger, *The New Motherhood*, Jonathan Cape, London, 1922, p. 225.

33 Agnes Smedley to Margaret Sanger, June 1924, quoted in Mackinnon and Mackinnon, *Agnes Smedley*, pp. 98–9.

34 Robyn L. Rosen, *Reproductive Health, Reproductive Rights: Reformers and the Politics of Maternal Welfare, 1917–1940*, Ohio State University Press, Columbus, 2003, pp. 93–5, 115, 120.

35 Mary Ware Dennett quoted in Chen, *'The Sex Side of Life'*, p. 172.

36 Judge Burrows quoted in ibid., p. 290.

37 Dora Russell, *The Tamarisk Tree: My Quest for Liberty and Love*, Elek/Pemberton, London, 1975, p. 169.

38 Stella Browne, Letter, *New Leader*, 5 January 1923, p. 7; Dora Russell, Letter, *New Leader*, 26 January 1923, p. 13; Evelyn Sharp, Letter, *New Leader*, 9 March 1923, p. 15.

39 Russell, *The Tamarisk Tree*, p. 172.

40 Rowbotham, *A New World for Women*, pp. 54–9. See also Clare Debenham, 'The Origins and Development of the Birth Control Movement in Manchester and Salford, 1917–1935', MA Manchester Metropolitan University, 2006, pp. 107–15.

41 Lesley A. Hall, 'Feminist Reconfigurations of Heterosexuality in the 1920s', in eds Lucy Bland and Laura Doan, *Sexology in Culture: Labelling Bodies and Desires*, Polity Press, Cambridge, 1998, p. 137; Hera Cook, *The Long Sexual Revolution: English Women, Sex, and Contraception 1800–1975*, Oxford University Press, Oxford, 2004, pp. 192–202.

42 Marie Stopes, *A Letter to Working Mothers on How to Have Healthy Children and Avoid Weakening Pregnancies* (pamphlet), Mothers' Clinic for Constructive Birth Control, London, 1926, p. 2.

43 Ibid., p. 16.

44 Marie Stopes quoted in Barbara Evans, *Freedom to Choose: The Life and Work of Dr. Helena Wright – Pioneer of Contraception*, Bodley Head, London, 1984, p. 144.

45 Marie Stopes, *Radiant Motherhood: A Book for Those Who Are Creating the Future*, G. P. Putnam and Sons, London, 1920, p. 176.

46 Margaret Sanger, 'Birth Control and Racial Betterment', 1919, in ed. Esther Katz, *The Selected Papers of Margaret Sanger, Vol. I, The Woman Rebel, 1900–1928*, University of Illinois Press, Urbana, 2003, p. 252.

47 Katz, *The Selected Papers of Margaret Sanger*, p. 274.

48 Margaret Sanger, *Woman and the New Race*, Brentano's, New York, 1920, pp. 45–6.

49 Stella Browne, 'Working Woman Supports Birth Control', in *New Generation*, November 1922, p. 3.

50 Sheila Rowbotham Interview with Dora Russell, Mss Notes, 1974.

51 'SW', 'Birth Control and You', *Woman Worker*, No. 4, July 1926, p. 4.

52 W. E. B. Du Bois, 1921, quoted in Jessie M. Rodrique, 'The Black Community and the Birth Control Movement', in eds Kathy Peiss and Christina Simmons, *Passion and Power: Sexuality in History*, Temple University Press, Philadelphia, 1989, p. 142.

53 Quoted in ibid., p. 145.

54 Suzie Fleming and Gloden Dallas, 'Interview with Jessie Stephen' in ed. Marsha Rowe, *Spare Rib Reader*, Penguin, London, 1982, p. 560.

55 Rowbotham, *A New World for Women*, pp. 23, 56–8.

56 Crystal Eastman, 'Britain's Labor Women', 1925, in ed. Cook, *Crystal Eastman*, p. 142.

57 Mrs E. Williams, Letter, *Lansbury's Labour Weekly*, 11 July 1925, p. 14.

58 Hamilton, *Exploring the Dangerous Trades*, p. 112.

59 Marie Stopes, *Mother England: A Contemporary History*, John Bale and Danielsson, London, 1929, p. 183.

60 Russell, *The Tamarisk Tree*, p. 175.

61 Stella Browne, 'Birth Control in Taff Vale: A Socialist Synthesis', *New Generation*, October 1923, p. 116.

62 Stella Browne, Letter, *The Communist*, 19 August 1922, p. 8.

63 Parsons, 'Changes in Sex Relations', in ed. Kirchwey, *Our Changing Morality*, p. 49.

64 Russell, *The Right to Be Happy*, p. 152.

65 Teresa Billington-Greig, 'Commonsense on the Population Question', 1915, quoted in Harrison, *Prudent Revolutionaries*, p. 63.

66 Dora Marsden, *Freewoman*, 2 May 1912, quoted in Bland, *Banishing the Beast*, p. 272.

67 Helen Winter, *Freewoman*, 7 March 1912, quoted in ibid., p. 234.

68 Crystal Eastman, 'Now We Can Begin', 1920, in ed. Cook, *Crystal Eastman*, p. 52.

5 Motherhood

1 Russell, *The Tamarisk Tree*, p. 171.

2 Richard Evans, *The Feminist Movement in Germany, 1894–1933*, Sage, London, 1976, p. 121; Karen Offen, *European Feminisms, 1700–1950*, Stanford University Press, Stanford, 2000, p. 267; Graves, *Labour Women*, p. 101.

3 Pat Thane, 'Visions of Gender in the making of the British Welfare State: The case of women in the British Labour Party and social policy, 1906–1945', in eds Gisela Bock and Pat Thane, *Maternity and Gender Policies: Women and the Rise of the European Welfare States*, Routledge, London, 1991, p. 102.

4 Andro Linklater, *An Unhusbanded Life: Charlotte Despard, Suffragette, Socialist and Sinn Feiner*, Hutchinson, London, 1980, pp. 97–100.

5 Hollis, *Ladies Elect*, p. 437.

6 Ibid., p. 439.

7 Thane, 'Visions of Gender', p. 102.

8 Liddington, *The Life and Times of a Respectable Rebel*, p. 213.

9 Thane, 'Visions of Gender', p. 101.

10 'The Mothers' Arms', Sylvia Pankhurst Papers, International Institute for Social History, Amsterdam; see also Winslow, Sylvia Pankhurst, pp. 95–6.

11 Thane, 'Visions of Gender', p. 102.

12 Hollis, *Ladies Elect*, p. 438; see also Shena Simon, 'Margaret Ashton and her work', *The Woman Citizen*, (no volume number), No. 281, December 1937, p. 3, Margaret Ashton Papers, Manchester Reference Library.

13 Hollis, *Ladies Elect*, p. 435.

14 Gillian Scott, *Feminism and the Politics of Working Women: The Women's Co-operative Guild 1880s to the Second World War*, UCL Press, London, 1998, pp. 111–16.

15 Ibid., p. 118.

16 Ibid., pp. 118–20; Thane, 'Visions of Gender', pp. 104–7.

17 Pivar, *Purity Crusade*, pp. 204, 228–31; Molly Ladd-Taylor, *Mother-Work, Women, Child Welfare and the State, 1890–1930*, University of Illinois, Urbana, 1994, pp. 46–57.

18 Chicago Afro-American Mothers' Council, 1900, quoted in Anne Meis Knupfer, *Toward a Tenderer Humanity and a Nobler Womanhood: African American Women's Clubs in Turn-of-the-Century Chicago*, New York University Press, New York, 1996, p. 69.

19 Barbara Sicherman, *Alice Hamilton: A Life in Letters*, Harvard University Press, Cambridge, Mass., 1984, p. 316; Beard, *Woman's Work in Municipalities*, pp. 56–65, Ladd-Taylor, *Mother-Work*, pp. 75–81.

20 See Gordon, 'Black and White Visions of Welfare: Women's Welfare Activism, 1890–1945' and Shaw, 'Black Club Women and the Creation of the National Association of Colored Women', in eds Hine, King and Reed, *'We Specialize in the Wholly Impossible'*, pp. 433–85.

21 Clotee Scott quoted in Knupfer, *Toward a Tenderer Humanity*, p. 99.

22 Ladd-Taylor, *Mother-Work*, pp. 81–91, 167–90.

23 Linklater, *An Unhusbanded Life*, p. 99.

24 Hollis, *Ladies Elect*, p. 462; on Margaret McMillan, see Steedman, *Childhood, Culture and Class in Britain*.

25 Mary Chignell, quoted in Steedman, *Childhood, Culture and Class in Britain*, p. 60.

26 On Eleanor Rathbone, see Alberti, *Eleanor Rathbone*.

27 Scott, *Feminism and the Politics of Working Women*, pp. 119–20.

28 Eleanor Rathbone, Letter, *The Times*, 26 August 1918, p. 6.

29 Thane, 'Visions of Gender', p. 110.

30 Russell, *Hypatia*, p. 67.

31 Thane, 'Visions of Gender', p. 111.

32 Report on Family Allowances by a Special Joint Committee, TUC and Labour Party, London, 1930, quoted in ed. Suzie Fleming, *Eleanor Rathbone, The Disinherited Family*, Falling Wall Press, Bristol, 1986, p. 73.

33 Joanne L. Goodwin, *Gender and the Politics of Welfare Reform: Mothers' Pensions in Chicago, 1911–1929*, University of Chicago Press, Chicago, 1997, pp. 4–6, 101–15.

34 Beard, *Woman's Work in Municipalities*, pp. 250–51.

35 Clara Cahill quoted in Beard, *Woman's Work in Municipalities*, pp. 252–3.

36 Ladd-Taylor, *Mother-Work*, pp. 116–17, Rosen, *Reproductive Health, Reproductive Rights*, pp. 46–8.

37 White House Conference on the Care of Dependent Children, quoted in Gwendolyn Mink, 'The Lady and the Tramp: Gender, Race and the Origins of the American Welfare State', in ed. Linda Gordon, *Women, the State and Welfare*, University of Wisconsin Press, Madison, 1990, p. 109.

38 Mink, 'The Lady and the Tramp', p. 110.

39 Linda Gordon, *Pitied but not Entitled: Single Mothers and the History of Welfare, 1890–1935*, The Free Press, New York, 1994, pp. 47–51.

40 Ibid., pp. 287–300.

41 Rathbone, Letter, *The Times*, 26 August 1918, p. 6.

42 Dorothy Jewson, *Socialists and the Family: A Plea for Family Endowment* (pamphlet), ILP Publication, London, no date, p. 5.

43 Dorothy Evans quoted in Graves, *Labour Women*, p. 104.

44 Eastman, 'Now We Can Begin', in Cook, *Crystal Eastman*, p. 54.

45 Ada Nield Chew, 'Mother Interest and Child-Training', *Freewoman*, 22 August 1912, in ed. Chew, *Ada Nield Chew*, pp. 250–51.

46 Benita Locke, 'The Latest Capitalist Trap', *Woman Rebel*, Vol. 1, No. 1, March 1914, p. 4.

47 Stella Browne, 'The Disinherited Family', *New Generation*, February 1925, p. 22.

48 Carrica Le Favre, *Mother's Help and Child's Friend*, Brentano's, New York, 1890, p. 139.

49 Alice B. Stockham, *Tokology*, L. N. Fowler, London, 1918, pp. 130–31.

50 Ibid., p. 333.

51 Charlotte Perkins Gilman, 'Moving the Mountain', 1911, in ed. Carol Farley Kessler, *Charlotte Perkins Gilman: Her Progress Toward Utopia with Selected Writings*, Liverpool University Press, Liverpool, 1995, p. 161.

52 Graul, *Hilda's Home*, in ed. Kessler, *Daring to Dream*, p. 197.

53 Gilman, *Moving the Mountain*, p. 161.

54 Charlotte Perkins Gilman, *Herland*, Pantheon, New York, 1979, p. 69.

55 Mabel Harding, 'Social Motherhood', *Daily Herald*, 19 April 1912.

56 Lillie D. White, quoted in Sears, *The Sex Radicals*, p. 245.

57 Georgia Kotsch, 'The Mother's Future', *International Socialist Review*, Vol. X, No. 12, June 1910, p. 1100.

58 De Cleyre, 'They Who Marry Do Ill', 1908, in ed. Glassgold, *Anarchy!*, p. 109.

59 'A Freewoman's Attitude to Marriage', *Freewoman*, Vol. I, No. 8, 11 January 1912, p. 153.

60 Beatrice Hastings, *New Age*, Vol. XII, No. 10, 9 January 1913, p. 237.

61 DuBois, *Harriot Stanton Blatch*, p. 216.

62 Ada Nield Chew, 'Mother Interest and Child-Training', in ed. Chew, *Ada Nield Chew*, p. 248.

63 Henrietta Rodman quoted in Ladd-Taylor, *Mother-Work*, p. 114.

64 Ibid.

65 Crystal Eastman, 'Marriage under Two Roofs', 1923, in ed. Cook, *Crystal Eastman*, pp. 76–83.

66 Women's Legislative Congress, 1918, quoted in Goodwin, *Gender and the Politics of Welfare Reform*, p. 143.

67 Leonora Eyles, 'Sleep', *Lansbury's Labour Weekly*, 14 April 1925, p. 14.

68 Charlotte Perkins Gilman, *The Home: Its Work and Influence* (1903), University of Illinois, Urbana, 1972, p. 97.

69 Charlotte Perkins Gilman, *Women and Economics* (1898), Harper and Row, New York, 1966, p. 335.

70 Kotsch, 'The Mother's Future', p. 1100.

71 Ibid.

72 Ada Nield Chew, 'Mother-Interest and Child-Training', in ed. Chew, *Ada Nield Chew*, p. 253.

73 A. D. Sanderson Furniss and Marion Phillips, *The Working Woman's House*, Swarthmore Press, London, 1919, pp. 58–9.

74 Agnes Henry, in Augustin Hamon, *Psychologie de l'Anarchiste-Socialiste*, Stock, Paris, 1895, pp. 224–59.

75 Gilman, *Moving the Mountain*, p. 173.

76 Steedman, *Childhood, Culture and Class in Britain*, p. 96.

77 Russell, *The Tamarisk Tree*, p. 199.

78 Gilman, *The Home*, p. 258.

79 Gilman, *Moving the Mountain*, p. 173.

80 Lizzie Holmes, 1892, quoted in Margaret S. Marsh, *Anarchist Women, 1870–1920*, Temple University Press, Philadelphia, 1981, p. 119.

81 De Cleyre, 'Modern Educational Reform', quoted in Paul Alrich, *An American Anarchist: The Life of Voltairine de Cleyre*, Princeton University Press, Princeton, 1978, p. 218.

82 Emma Goldman, 'The Child and Its Enemies', 1909, quoted in Marsh, *Anarchist Women*, p. 119.

83 Annie Davison, in eds McCrindle and Rowbotham, *Dutiful Daughters*, p. 62.

84 Paul Buhle, *The Origins of Left Culture in the US, 1880–1940: An Anthology*, Cultural Correspondence, Boston, 1978, p. 45.

85 Russell, *The Right to Be Happy*, pp. 185–6.

86 Ibid., p. 185.

87 Ibid., p. 149.

6 New Housework: New Homes

1 Gilman, *The Home*, p. 93.

2 Ellen Swallow Richards quoted in Jane Davison and Lesley Davison, *To Make a House for Me: Four Generations of American Women and the Houses They Lived In*, Random House, New York, 1980, p. 102. On Ellen Swallow Richards, see George F. Kunz, 'Tribute to Mrs Ellen Swallow Richards', Association of College Alumnae, no date, The Papers of Ellen Swallow Richards, Box 1, File 2, Sophia Smith Collection, Smith College, Northampton, Massachessets.

3 On Helen Campbell, see Hayden, *The Grand Domestic Revolution*, pp. 185–6; Kessler, *Charlotte Perkins Gilman*, pp. 27–8; Hill, *Charlotte Perkins Gilman*, pp. 238–58.

4 Sarah Leavitt, *From Catharine Beecher to Martha Stewart: A Cultural History of Domestic Advice*, The University of North Carolina Press, Chapel Hill, 2002, pp. 59–61.

5 Helen Campbell quoted in Leavitt, *From Catharine Beecher to Martha Stewart*, p. 51.

6 Hill, *Charlotte Perkins Gilman*, p. 242.

7 Leavitt, *From Catharine Beecher to Martha Stewart*, pp. 51–2.

8 The New York Ladies' Health Protective Association, 1894, quoted in Nancy S. Dye, Introduction, in eds Nora Lee Frankel and Nancy S. Dye, *Gender, Class, Race and Reform in the Progressive Era*, The University Press of Kentucky, Lexington, 1991, p. 3.

9 Beard, *Woman's Work in Municipalities*, pp. 306–7.

10 Ibid., pp. 212–13, 217–18.

11 Rheta Child Dorr, 1910, quoted in Paula Baker, 'The Domestication of Politics', in ed. Gordon, *Women, the State and Welfare*, p. 63.

12 Mabel Kittredge, quoted in Beard, *Woman's Work in Municipalities*, p. 11.

13 Martha Bensley Bruère and Robert W. Bruère, *Increasing Home Efficiency*, The Macmillan Company, New York, 1913, p. 169.

14 Vicinus, *Independent Women*, p. 239.

15 Carol Dyhouse, *Feminism and the Family in England, 1880–1939*, Basil Blackwell, Oxford, 1989, p. 132.

16 'Scotia', 'Our Woman's Corner', *Accrington Labour Journal*, No. 26, July 1914.

17 Mrs Bury quoted in Thomson, '"Domestic Drudgery will be a Thing of the Past"', in Yeo, *New Views of Co-operation*, pp. 110–11.

18 'Scotia', 'Our Woman's Corner'.

19 Thane, 'Vision of Gender', in eds Bock and Thane, *Maternity and Gender Politics*, p. 96.

20 Mitchell, *The Hard Way Up*, p. 99.

21 Ada Nield Chew, 'Men, Women and the Vote', *Accrington Observer*, 9 September 1913, in ed. Chew, *Ada Nield Chew*, p. 220.

22 Mary Macarthur, 'Editorial', *The Woman Worker*, 5 June 1908, p. 1.

23 Margaret G. Bondfield, 'Women as Domestic Workers', 1919, in ed. Ellen Malos, *The Politics of Housework*, Alison and Busby, London, 1980, p. 87.

24 Quoted in Buhle, *Women and American Socialism*, p. 87.

25 Mary Archibald, 1918, quoted in Greenwald, 'Working-Class Feminism and the Family Wage Ideal', *Journal of American History*, Vol. 76, No.1, June 1989, p. 136.

26 Lillie D. White, 'Housekeeping', *Lucifer*, 27 January 1893, quoted in Sears, *The Sex Radicals*, p. 246.

27 White, 'Housekeeping', *Lucifer*, 20 January 1893, quoted in ibid.

28 White, 'Housekeeping', *Lucifer*, 27 February 1893, quoted in ibid.

29 Holmes, 'The "Unwomanly" Woman', *Our New Humanity*, Vol. 1, No.3, March 1896, p. 10.

30 Kate Austin, quoted in Howard S. Miller, 'Kate Austin: A Feminist-Anarchist on the Farmer's Last Frontier', *Nature, Society and Thought*, Vol. 9, No. 2, April 1996, p. 201.

31 Charlotte Perkins Gilman, 'What Diantha Did', quoted in Hayden, *The Grand Domestic Revolution*, p. 196.

32 Kotsch, 'The Mother's Future', *International Socialist Review*, Vol. X, No. 12, June 1910, p. 1101.

33 Gilman, *Women and Economics*, p. 343.

34 Emma Heller Schumm, Speech at Boston Branch of the Walt Whitman Fellowship, 17 March 1901, Helena Born Papers, Tamiment Library and Robert F. Wagner Labor Archives.

35 Chen, *'The Sex Side of Life'*, pp. 20–63; Eileen Boris, *Art and Labor: Ruskin, Morris and the Craftsman Ideal in America*, Temple University Press, Philadelphia, 1986, pp. 32–52.

36 See Laurence C. Gerckens, 'Milestones in American City Planning', *Blueprints*, Vol. X, No. 2, Spring 1992.

37 Kathleen M. Slack, *Henrietta's Dream: A Chronicle of the Hampstead Garden Suburb – Varieties and Virtues*, Hampstead Garden Suburb Archive Trust, London, 1997, p. 11; Hollis, *Ladies Elect*, pp. 450–51.

38 Hollis, *Ladies Elect*, p. 452.

39 Beard, *Woman's Work in Municipalities*, pp. 307–8.

40 Jane Hume Clapperton, *A Vision of the Future – Based on the Application of Ethical Principles*, Swan Sonnenschein, London, 1904, pp. 276–7.

41 Ibid., pp. 276–8.

42 Ibid., p. 334.

43 On Alice Melvin, see Dyhouse, *Feminism and the Family in England*, pp. 118–19.

44 Sochen, *Movers and Shakers*, pp. 36–41.

45 Clementina Black, *A New Way of Housekeeping*, W. Collins and Sons, London, 1918, pp. 6–7, 61–75.

46 Lynn F. Pearson, *The Architectural and Social History of Cooperative Living*, Macmillan, London, 1988, p. 130.

47 Pearson, *The Architectural and Social History of Cooperative Living*, pp. 110–11.

48 Maxine S. Seller, 'Beyond the Stereotype: A New Look at the Immigrant Woman, 1880–1924', in ed. George F. Pozzetta, *Ethnicity and Gender: The Immigrant Woman*, Garland, New York, 1991, p. 66.

49 Crystal Eastman, 'Mother-Worship', in ed. Cook, *Crystal Eastman*, p. 43; Hayden, *The Grand Domestic Revolution*, pp. 268–74.

50 Crystal Eastman, 'Lady Rhondda Contends that Women of Leisure are "Menace"', in ed. Cook, *Crystal Eastman*, p. 105.

51 Clementina Black, 'The Domestic Service Problem', 1919, quoted in Pearson, *The Architectural and Social History of Cooperative Living*, p. 159.

52 Ben Jones, quoted in Thomson ,'"Domestic Drudgery will be a Thing of the Past"', in ed. Yeo, *New Views of Co-operation*, p. 108. During agitation for a nine-hour day in the early 1870s, the broadside ballad 'Nine Hours a Day' had applied the demand to women. Kathy Henderson, *My Song is My Own: 100 Women's Songs*, Pluto, London, 1979, pp. 128–9.

53 Tom Mann, 'Leisure for Workmen's Wives', *Halfpenny Short Cuts*, 28 June 1890, p. 163.

54 Mitchell, *The Hard Way Up*, p. 113.

55 Ibid., p. 109.

56 Elizabeth Gurley Flynn, 'Problems Organizing Women', 1916, in ed. Rosalyn Fraad Baxandall, *Words on Fire: The Life and Writing of Elizabeth Gurley Flynn*, Rutgers University Press, New Brunswick, New Jersey 1987, p. 137.

57 Sylvia Pankhurst, *Delphos*, 1927, quoted in Harrison, *Prudent Revolutionaries*, p. 221.

58 Josephine Conger-Kaneko, 'Does a Woman Support Her Husband's Employer?', 1913, in eds. Rosalyn Baxandall and Lindon Gordon, *America's Working Women: A Documentary History 1600 to Present*, W. W. Norton, New York, 1995, pp. 186–7.

59 Cicely Hamilton, *Marriage as a Trade*, Chapman and Hall, London, 1912, pp. 92–3, 97.

60 Crystal Eastman, 'Now We Can Begin', 1920, in ed. Cook, *Crystal Eastman*, p. 56.

61 Ibid.

62 Mary Alden Hopkins, 'Fifty-Fifty Wives', *Woman Citizen*, 7 April 1923, in Hayden, *The Grand Domestic Revolution*, p. 288.

63 La Follette, *Concerning Women*, p. 194.

64 Bruère and Bruère, *Increasing Home Efficiency*, p. 290.

65 Eunice Freeman, quoted in Knupfer, *Toward a Tenderer Humanity*, p. 17.

66 Lillian M. Gilbreth, *The Home-Maker and Her Job*, D. Appleton and Co., New York, 1927, p. 5.

67 Martha Moore Trescott, 'Lillian Moller Gilbreth and the Founding of Modern Industrial Engineering', in ed. Joan Rothschild, *Machina Ex Dea: Feminist Perspectives on Technology*, Pergamon Press, New York, 1983, p. 23.

68 Christine Frederick, *The New Housekeeping: Efficiency Studies in Home Management*, Doubleday, Page and Company, New York, 1916, p. 3.

69 Ibid., pp. xiii–xiv.

70 Gilbreth, *The Home-Maker and Her Job*, p. 29.

71 Hazel Hunkins, 'Keep a Budget', *Good Housekeeping*, December 1925, in eds Braithwaite and Walsh, *Things My Mother Should Have Told Me*, p. 47.

72 Lillian Gilbreth, quoted in Davison and Davison, *To Make a House a Home*, p. 105.

73 Frederick, *The New Housekeeping*, p. 68.

74 *House Beautiful*, quoted in Davison and Davison, *To Make a House a Home*, p. 76.

75 Christine Collette, *For Labour and for Women: The Women's Labour League, 1906–1918*, Manchester University Press, Manchester, 1989, pp. 161–2.

76 Mabel Tuke Priestman, quoted in Gwendolyn Wright, *Building the American Dream: A Social History of Housing in America*, MIT Press, Cambridge, Mass., 1981, p. 160.

77 Mrs Henry Wade Rodgers, quoted in Davison and Davison, *To Make a House a Home*, p. 75.

78 Frederick, *The New Housekeeping*, pp. xiii–xiv.

79 Leavitt, *From Catharine Beecher to Martha Stewart*, p. 57.

80 Hewitt, *Southern Discomfort*, p. 165.

81 Hayden, *The Grand Domestic Revolution*, p. 274.

82 Gilman, *The Home*, p. 330.

83 Quoted in Hayden, *The Grand Domestic Revolution*, p. 276.

7 Consumer Power

1 Hayden, *The Grand Domestic Revolution*, p. 151.

2 Pearson, *The Architectural and Social History of Cooperative Living*, p. 58; Angela V. John, *Evelyn Sharp: Rebel Woman, 1869–1955*, Manchester University Press, Manchester, 2009, p. 145.

3 Scott, *Feminism and the Politics of Working Women*, pp. 58–9.

4 Dyhouse, *Feminism and the Family in England*, p. 122.

5 Ibid., p. 123.

6 Crawford, *The Women's Suffrage Movement*, p. 112.

7 Ibid., p. 135.

8 Thomson, '"Domestic Drudgery Will be a Thing of the Past"', in ed. Yeo, *New Views of Co-operation*, pp. 119–20.

9 Susan Strasser, *Never Done: A History of American Housework*, Pantheon, New York, 1982, p. 113.

10 Hayden, *The Grand Domestic Revolution*, pp. 267–70.

11 Frank, *Purchasing Power*, pp. 52–60, 71–2.

12 Kathleen Waters Sander, *The Business of Charity: The Women's Exchange Movement 1832–1900*, University of Illinois Press, Urbana, 1998, pp. 86–7.

13 Julia Dawson, *Why Women Want Socialism*, Clarion Pass On Pamphlet, No. 4, Clarion, London, no date, p. 16.

14 Herbert Morrison, *Better Times for the Housewife: Labour's Policy for the Homemaker* (pamphlet), Labour Party, London, 1923, pp. 9–11.

15 Beard, *Woman's Work in Municipalities*, pp. 197–206.

16 Ravetz, *Council Housing and Culture*, p. 28.

17 Hollis, *Ladies Elect*, pp. 452–3; Gillian Darley, *Villages of Vision: A Study of Strange Utopias*, Five Leaves Publications, Nottingham, 2007, p. 203.

18 Hollis, *Ladies Elect*, p. 454; see Mary Higgs and Edward E. Hayward, *Where Shall She Live: The Homelessness of the Woman Worker*, P. S. King and Son, London, 1910.

19 Ravetz, *Council Housing and Culture*, p. 74.

20 Hunter, *To 'Joy My Freedom*, p. 135.

21 Maggie Lena Walker, quoted in Elsa Barkley Brown, 'Womanist Consciousness', in eds DuBois and Ruiz, *Unequal Sisters*, p. 215.

22 Ibid., p. 218.

23 Helen Campbell, *Prisoners of Poverty*, 1887, quoted in Sklar, *Florence Kelley and the Nation's Work*, p. 145.

24 Working Women's Society, quoted in Tax, *The Rising of the Women*, p. 98.

25 Sklar, *Florence Kelley and the Nation's Work*, pp. 308–11.

26 The Label Shop Publicity Committee, 'Women's Trade Union League', *Ladies' Garment Worker*, Vol. II, No. 3, March 1911, p. 5.

27 'Report and Proceedings of Special Convention, May 1st to May 3rd, 1913', *Ladies' Garment Worker*, Vol. IV, No. 6, June 1913, p. 3.

28 Greenwald, 'Working-Class Feminism and the Family Wage Ideal', *Journal of American History*, Vol. 76, No. 1, June 1989, pp. 130–32; Frank, *Purchasing Power*, p. 113.

29 Clementina Black, 'London County Council, Special Committee on Contracts. Inquiry into the condition of the Clothing Trade' in ed. Rodney Mace, *Taking Stock: A Documentary History of the Greater London Council's Supplies Department*, The Greater London Council, London, 1984, p. 29.

30 Advertisement, 'A Remedy for the Sweating System', *The Syndicalist*, Vol. II, Nos 3–4, March–April 1913, p. 6.

31 Teresa Billington-Greig, 'The Consumer in Revolt', c. 1912, in eds Carol McPhee and Ann FitzGerald, *The Non-Violent Militant: Selected Writings of Teresa Billington-Greig*, Routledge and Kegan Paul, London, 1987, p. 284.

32 Margaretta Hicks, quoted in June Hannam and Karen Hunt, *Socialist Women in Britain, 1880s to 1920s*, Routledge, London, 2002, p. 140.

33 Ibid., pp. 141–2.

34 Billington-Greig, 'The Consumer in Revolt', p. 270.

35 Mrs Levy, 1902, quoted in Paula E. Hyman, 'Immigrant Women and Consumer Protest: The New York City Kosher Meat Boycott of 1902', in ed. Pozzetta, *Ethnicity and Gender*, p. 93.

36 Marie Ganz in collaboration with Nat J. Ferber, *Into Anarchy and Out Again*, Dodd, Mead and Co., New York, 1920, p. 251.

37 Ganz, *Into Anarchy and Out Again*, p. 252. On wartime militancy see Elizabeth Ewen, *Immigrant Women in the Land of Dollars: Life and Culture on the Lower East Side, 1890–1925*, Monthly Review Press, New York, 1985, pp. 176–83.

38 Minute Book, Council of the East London Federation of the Suffragettes, 6 August 1914, Sylvia Pankhurst Papers, The International Institute of Social History, Amsterdam.

39 *The Woman's Dreadnought*, 8 March 1914, quoted in Hannam and Hunt, *Socialist Women*, p. 180.

40 On Mary Barbour, Helen Crawford and Agnes Dollan see eds Elizabeth Ewan, Sue Innes, Siân Reynolds, *The Biographical Dictionary of Scottish Women*, Edinburgh University Press, Edinburgh, 2007, pp. 28–9, 84–5, 98.

41 'A Remarkable Demonstration in Glasgow of Women and Children' in Elspeth King, *The Hidden History of Glasgow's Women*, Mainstream Publishing, Edinburgh, 1993, p. 136.

42 Parkhead Shop Stewards, quoted in Hannam and Hunt, *Socialist Women*, p. 146.

43 Sheila Rowbotham, *Friends of Alice Wheeldon*, Pluto Press, London, 1986, pp. 87–92.

44 Martin Pugh, 'Women, Food and Politics, 1880–1930', *History Today*, March 1991, p. 17.

45 Collette, *For Labour and For Women*, p. 163; Noreen Branson, *Poplarism, 1919–1925: George Lansbury and the Councillors' Revolt*, Lawrence and Wishart, London, 1979, pp. 234–7.

46 Hannam and Hunt, *Socialist Women*, p. 144.

47 Winslow, *Sylvia Pankhurst*, pp. 91–2; Barbara Winslow, 'Sylvia Pankhurst and the Great War', in eds Ian Bullock and Richard Pankhurst, *Sylvia Pankhurst: From Artist to Anti-Fascist*, St. Martin's Press, New York, 1992, pp. 102–3.

48 Mary Heaton Vorse, *A Footnote to Folly: Reminiscences*, Arno Press, New York, 1980, p. 170.

49 Margaret Bondfield, 'Women as Domestic Workers', in ed. Malos, *The Politics of Housework*, p. 89.

50 Mitchell, *The Hard Way Up*, p. 208.

51 Pearson, *The Architectural and Social History of Cooperative Living*, p. 144.

52 Pat Thane, 'Women in the British Labour Party and the Construction of State Welfare, 1906–1939', in eds Seth Koven and Sonya Michel, *Mothers of a New World: Maternalist Politics and the Origins of Welfare States*, Routledge, New York, 1993, pp. 365–6.

53 Quoted in Mark Swenarton, *Homes Fit for Heroes: The Politics and Architecture of Early State Housing in Britain*, Heinemann, London, 1981, p. 98.

54 Margaret Allen, "The Women are Worse than the Men": Women's Political Activism in Mining Communities, 1919–1939, MA Dissertation, International Centre for Labour Studies, University of Manchester, 1997, p. 15.

55 Manchester Women's History Group, 'Ideology in Bricks and Mortar: Women's Housing in Manchester between the Wars', *North-West Labour History*, No. 12, 1987, pp. 24–48.

56 'Women's Guild Congress, 1923', *The People's Year Book and Annual of the English and Scottish Wholesale Societies*, The Co-operative Wholesale Society, Manchester, 1924, pp. 33–4.

57 Branson, *George Lansbury and the Councillors' Revolt*, pp. 233–7.

58 Bertha K. Landes, quoted in Sandra Haarsager, *Bertha Knight Landes of Seattle: Big-City Mayor*, University of Oklahoma Press, Norman and London, 1994, p. 134.

59 Ibid., pp. 152–3.

60 Ewen, *Immigrant Women*, p. 127.

61 Quoted in Orleck, *Common Sense and a Little Fire*, p. 222.

62 Ibid., p. 217.

63 Ibid., pp. 225–40.

64 Reproduction of C.W.S. poster. See also eds Lawrence Black and Nicole Robertson, *Consumerism and the Co-operative Movement in Modern British History. Taking Stock*, Manchester University Press, Manchester, 2009; Pugh, 'Women, Food and Politics', *History Today*, March 1991, p. 18.

65 Stuart Ewen, *PR! A Social History of Spin*, Basic Books, New York, 1996, p. 180.

66 Mrs Christine Frederick, *Selling Mrs Consumer*, The Business Bourse, New York, 1928, p. 190; on cinema, glamour and consumption, see Stuart Ewen and Elizabeth Ewen, *Channels of Desire, Mass Images and the Shaping of American Consciousness*, University of Minnesota Press, Minneapolis, 1992, pp. 65–73.

67 Frederick, *Selling Mrs Consumer*, p. 194.
68 Ibid., p. 191.
69 Ibid., p. 264.
70 Hayden, *The Grand Domestic Revolution*, p. 275.
71 Hazel Kyrk, *A Theory of Consumption*, Isaac Pitman and Sons, London, 1923, pp. 46–64.
72 Hannam and Hunt, *Socialist Women*, pp. 153–6.
73 *The Socialist*, 1 December 1918, p. 4.
74 Ethel Puffer Howes, 1923, quoted in Hayden, *The Grand Domestic Revolution*, p. 270.
75 Louise Eberle, 'The Faking of Food', *Collier's*, November 1910, in ed. Harvey Swados, *Years of Conscience, The Muckrakers: An Anthology of Reform Journalism*, Meridian Books, Cleveland, 1962, p. 261.

8 Labour Problems

1 Beatrice Potter to Sidney Webb, 12 (?) September 1891, quoted in Seymour-Jones, *Beatrice Webb*, p. 216.
2 Beatrice Webb, Diary, 1 November 1887, quoted in eds Janice and Norman Mackenzie, *The Diaries of Beatrice Webb*, Virago, London, 2000, p. 94.
3 Sidney Webb, 1891, quoted in Michèle A. Pujol, *Feminism and Anti-Feminism in Early Economic Thought*, Edward Elgar, Aldershot, 1992, p. 55. On the American parallels, see Deutsch, *Women and the City*, pp. 109–12.
4 C. Helen Scott, Letter, *The Oxford University Extension Gazette*, April 1893, p. 95.
5 Clara Collet, Diary, May 1900 (?), quoted in Rosemary O'Day, 'Women and Social Investigation', Clara Collet and Beatrice Potter', in eds David Englander and Rosemary O'Day, *Retrieved Riches, Social Investigation in Britain 1840–1914*, Scolar Press, Aldershot, 1995, p. 177.
6 Harold Goldman, *Emma Paterson*, Lawrence and Wishart, London, 1974, pp. 44–5.
7 Isabella Ford, *Women's Wages* (pamphlet), The Humanitarian League, London, 1893; Isabella Ford, *Women as Factory Inspectors and Certifying Surgeons* (pamphlet), The Women's Co-operative Guild, London, 1898; Isabella Ford, *Industrial Women and How to Help Them* (pamphlet), The Humanitarian League, London, c. 1901.
8 On the match women see Louise Raw, *Striking a Light: The Bryant and May Matchwomen and Their Place in History*, Continuum, London, 2009; on Besant and Dilke, see Hollis, *Ladies Elect*, p. 113; on Black, see ed. Rodney Mace, *Taking Stock: A Documentary History of the Greater London Council's Supplies Department*, Greater London Council, London, 1984, p. 29.
9 Elizabeth Morgan, quoted in Sklar, *Florence Kelley and the Nation's Work*, p. 210.
10 Ibid., pp. 233–8, 246–7.
11 Jenny Morris, *Women and the Sweated Trades: The Origins of Minimum Wage Legislation*, Gower, Aldershot, 1986, p. 142.

12 Eleanor Marx, 'A Women's Trade Union' in eds Hal Draper and Ann G. Lipow, 'Marxist Women Versus Bourgeois Feminism', *Socialist Register*, Merlin Press, London, 1976, pp. 223–4.

13 *Commonweal*, 1 November 1890, p. 351.

14 Quoted in Tax, *The Rising of the Women*, p. 49.

15 Ada Nield Chew, in ed. Chew, *Ada Nield Chew*, p. 75.

16 Ibid., pp. 75–6.

17 Mrs Rigby, Women's Co-operative Guild Conference, *Manchester Guardian*, 19 June 1896, Women's Suffrage Collection, Reel 11, Manchester Central Library.

18 Women's Trade Union League, *Quarterly Report and Review*, April 1891, No. 1, Women's Trade Union League, London, 1892, pp. 9, 13–14.

19 Mary Quaile, 'Margaret Ashton', *Woman Citizen*, (no volume numbers), No. 281, December 1937, p. 5.

20 Nancy Schrom Dye, *As Equals and as Sisters: Feminism, Unionism and the Women's Trade Union League of New York*, University of Missouri Press, Columbia, 1980, pp. 14–16.

21 Cooper, *A View from the South*, p. 254.

22 Maggie Lena Walker quoted in Jacqueline Jones, *American Work: Four Centuries of Black and White Labor*, W. W. Norton, New York, 1998, p. 333.

23 Rosalyn Terborg-Penn, 'Survival Strategies Among African-American Women Workers: A Continuing Process', in ed. Ruth Milkman, *Women, Work and Protest: A Century of US Women's Labor History*, Routledge and Kegan Paul, Boston, 1985, pp. 142–4.

24 Sharon Harley, 'When Your Work is Not Who You Are: The Development of a Working-Class Consciousness Among Afro-American Women', in eds Hine, King, Reed, *'We Specialize in the Wholly Impossible'*, p. 28.

25 Doris Nield Chew, 'The Life', in Chew, *Ada Nield Chew*, pp. 27–8.

26 Avrich, *An American Anarchist*, pp. 70–74.

27 Anzia Yezierska quoted in Alice Kessler-Harris, *Out to Work: A History of Wage-Earning Women in the United States*, Oxford University Press, Oxford, 1982, p. 226. On Anzia Yezierska see Showalter, *A Jury of Her Peers*, pp. 318–21.

28 Charlotte Perkins Gilman, 1933, quoted in Lane, *To Herland and Beyond*, p. 324. On Gilman's distress at being separated from Katharine see Charlotte Perkins Gilman to Emily (Perkins) Hale, 29 May, 1897. Hale Family Papers, Box 108, Sophia Smith Collection, Smith College, Northampton, Mass.

29 Florence Kelley, quoted in Sklar, *Florence Kelley and the Nation's Work*, p. 179.

30 Eileen Boris, *Home to Work: Motherhood and the Politics of Industrial Homework in the United States*, Cambridge University Press, Cambridge, 1994, p. 112.

31 Kessler-Harris, *Out to Work*, p. 230.

32 Alice Kessler-Harris, 'The Paradox of Motherhood: Night Work Restrictions in the United States', in eds Ulla Wikander, Alice Kessler-Harris, and Jane Lewis, *Protecting Women: Labor Legislation in Europe, the*

United States and Australia, 1880–1920, University of Illinois Press, Urbana, 1995, p. 339.

33 Mary Macarthur quoted in Sheila Lewenhak, *Women and Trade Unions: An Outline History of Women in the British Trade Union Movement*, Ernest Benn, London, 1977, p. 126.

34 Gertrude Tuckwell, 'Preface', *Handbook of the Daily News Sweated Industries Exhibition* (pamphlet), Anti-Sweating League, London, 1906, p. 13.

35 Sheila Rowbotham, 'Strategies Against Sweated Work in Britain, 1820–1920', in eds Sheila Rowbotham and Swasti Mitter, *Dignity and Daily Bread: New Forms of Economic Organizing Among Poor Women in the Third World and the First*, Routledge, London, 1994, pp. 179–80.

36 The Black Country Living Museum, *Women Chainmakers: By Anvil or Hammer*, Black Country region of the TUC, Dudley, 2009, p. 13.

37 Sylvia Pankhurst, *Daily Herald*, 29 October 1912, in Winslow, *Sylvia Pankhurst*, p. 30.

38 Sally Alexander, 'The Fabian Women's Group', in ed. Alexander, *Becoming a Woman*, p. 153; Pujol, *Feminism and Anti-Feminism in Early Economic Thought*, pp. 75–93.

39 Rose Safran, quoted in Leon Stein, *The Triangle Fire*, ILR Press, Cornell University Press, Ithaca, 2001, p. 168.

40 Rose Schneiderman, quoted in Orleck, *Common Sense and a Little Fire*, p. 39.

41 Clara Lemlich (Shavelson) quoted in Sarah Eisenstein, *Give Us Bread But Give us Roses: Working Women's Consciousness in the United States, 1890 to the First World War*, Routledge and Kegan Paul, London, 1983, p. 141.

42 Kate Ryrie quoted in ibid., p. 144.

43 Colette A. Hyman, 'Labour Organizing and Female Institution-Building: The Chicago Women's Trade Union League, 1904–1924', in Milkman, *Women, Work and Protest*, pp. 25–9, 34–7; Robin Miller Jacoby, 'The Women's Trade Union League Training School for Women Organizers, 1914–1926', in eds Joyce L. Kornbluh and Mary Frederickson, *Sisterhood and Solidarity*, Temple University Press, Philadelphia, 1984, pp. 10–13; eds Dimand, Dimand, Forget, *Women of Value*, pp. 47–50.

44 Orleck, *Common Sense and a Little Fire*, pp. 67–8.

45 Helen Marot, *American Labor Unions* (1914), Arno and *The New York Times*, New York, 1969, p. 68.

46 Elizabeth Gurley Flynn, 'Address to Workers', *Industrial Worker*, Vol. 1, No. 18, 15 July 1909, p. 3.

47 Elizabeth Gurley Flynn, 'Lawrence', *Industrial Worker*, Vol. 4, No. 10, 25 July 1912, p. 4.

48 Ardis Cameron, 'Bread and Roses Revisited: Women's Culture and Working-Class Activism in the Lawrence Strike of 1912', in Milkman, *Women, Work and Protest*, pp. 55–6.

49 Mary Heaton Vorse, 'The Trouble at Lawrence', *Harper's Weekly*, 1912, in ed. Garrison, *Rebel Pen*, pp. 31, 35.

50 Ardis Cameron, *Radicals of the Worst Sort: Labouring Women in Lawrence, Massachusetts, 1860–1912*, University of Illinois Press, Urbana, 1993, pp. 142–3.

51 Priscilla Long, 'The Women of the Colorado Fuel and Iron Strike, 1913–1914', in Milkman, *Women, Work and Protest*, p. 81.

52 Ernest Barker, 'Equal Pay for Equal Work', *The Times*, 22 August 1918, p. 6.

53 Quoted in Philip S. Foner, *Women and the American Labor Movement: From the First Trade Unions to the Present*, The Free Press, New York, 1982, p. 262.

54 The Standing Joint Committee of Industrial Women's Organizations, 1917, quoted in Barbara Drake, *Women in Trade Unions*, Virago, London, 1984, p. 103.

55 Lewenhak, *Women and Trade Unions*, p. 182.

56 Drake, *Women in Trade Unions*, pp. 68–110.

57 Lewenhak, *Women and Trade Unions*, p. 183.

58 Lily (Webb) Ferguson, 'Some Party History', Typed Mss in author's possession. On the debate about unemployed women see *Out of Work*, Nos 22–37, 1922.

59 Augusta Bratton in eds Baxandall and Gordon, *America's Working Women*, pp. 205–6.

60 Frank, *Purchasing Power*, p. 104.

61 Elise Johnson McDougald, 'The Double Task: The Struggle of Negro Women for Sex and Race Emancipation' (1925), in ed. Busby, *Daughters of Africa*, p. 183.

62 DuBois, *Harriot Stanton Blatch*, pp. 218–24.

63 Pauline Newman quoted in Graves, *Labour Women*, pp. 144–5.

64 Kessler-Harris, *Out to Work*, pp. 207–14.

65 Graves, *Labour Women*, p. 141.

66 Ibid., p. 143.

9 Reworking Work

1 Emma Goldman, 'Intellectual Proletarians', *Mother Earth*, Vol. III, No. 12, February 1914, p. 265.

2 Lily Gair Wilkinson, *Woman's Freedom* (pamphlet), Freedom Press, London, c. 1914, pp. 15–16.

3 Olive Schreiner, *Woman and Labour*, T. Fisher Unwin, London, 1911, p. 196.

4 Ibid., p. 65.

5 Ibid., p. 123.

6 Ibid., p. 201.

7 Ibid., p. 204.

8 Cooper, *A View from the South*, p. 254.

9 Kate Austin, quoted in Miller, 'Kate Austin', *Nature, Society and Thought*, Vol. 9, No. 2, April 1996, p. 201.

10 See Liz Stanley, *Imperialism, Labour and the New Woman: Olive Schreiner's Social Theory*, Sociology Press, Durham, 2002, p. 88.

11 Ada Heather-Bigg, 1894, quoted in Pujol, *Feminism and Anti-Feminism in Early Economic Thought*, p. 61.

12 See Rowbotham, *Edward Carpenter*, p. 214.

13 Alice Clark, Preface, *Working Life of Women in the Seventeenth Century*, Frank Cass and Company, London, 1968, no page numbers for preface.

14 See eds Dimand, Dimand, Forget, *Women of Value*, pp. 44, 47, 51, 53, 55; Maxine Berg, 'The First Women Economic Historians', *Economic History Review*, Vol. 45, No. 2, May 1992, pp. 308–29.

15 Clark, Preface, *Working Life of Women in the Seventeenth Century*, no page numbers for preface.

16 Anthea Callen, *Angel in the Studies: Women in the Arts and Crafts Movement 1870–1914*, Astragal Books, London, 1979, p. 7. See also eds Judy Attfield and Pat Kirkham, *A View from the Interior: Feminism, Women and Design*, The Women's Press, London, 1989.

17 Mary Ware Dennett quoted in Chen, *'The Sex Side of Life'*, pp. 24–7.

18 Boris, *Art and Labor*, p. 132.

19 Jane Addams, quoted in Boris, *Art and Labor*, p. 132.

20 Jane Addams, quoted in ibid.

21 Ibid., p. 133.

22 Ellen Gates Starr, 'Art and Labor', in ed. Jane Addams, *Hull-House Maps and Papers by Residents of Hull-House, A Social Settlement*, Thomas Y. Crowell, New York, 1895, p. 169.

23 Scudder, *Social Ideals in English Letters*, p. 231.

24 Ibid., p. 294. See Vida Scudder, 'Early Days at Denison House', Mss Vida Scudder Papers, Series 1, Box1/1, Sophia Smith Collection, Smith College, Northampton, Mass.

25 Voltairine de Cleyre, 'The Dominant Idea', *Mother Earth*, Vol. V, No. 3, May 1910, p. 134.

26 Emma Goldman, *Anarchism: What It Really Stands For* (pamphlet), Mother Earth Publishing Association, New York, 1911, no page numbers.

27 Emma Goldman, *Anarchism and Other Essays*, Mother Earth Publishing Association, New York, 1910, p. 75.

28 Lily Gair Wilkinson, 'Women in Freedom', *Woman Rebel*, Vol. I, No. 1, March 1914, p. 29.

29 Wilkinson, *Woman's Freedom*, p. 15.

30 Susan Glaspell, quoted in Leslie Fishbain, *Rebels in Bohemia: The Radicals of the Masses 1911–1917*, University of North Carolina Press, Chapel Hill, 1982, p. 66.

31 Susan Lyn Englander, *Rational Womanhood: William M. Gilbreth and the Use of Psychology in Scientific Management, 1914–1935*, PhD, University of California, Los Angeles, 1999, pp. 114–18.

32 Trescott, 'Lillian Moller Gilbreth', in ed. Rothschild, *Machina Ex Dea*, p. 31.

33 Ida M. Tarbell, *All in the Day's Work: An Autobiography*, Macmillan Company, New York, 1939, p. 112.

34 Ibid., p. 114.

35 Ibid., pp. 241–2.

36 June Jerome Camhi, *Women Against Women: American Anti-Suffragism 1880–1920*, Carlson, New York, 1994, pp. 156–7.

37 Tarbell, *All in a Day's Work*, p. 282.

38 Josephine Goldmark, *Fatigue and Efficiency: A Study in Industry*, Charities Publication Committee, New York, 1912, pp. 44, 52.

39 Ibid., pp. 79–80.

40 Ibid., pp. 81–2.

41 Ibid., p. 286.

42 Kathy Peiss, *Cheap Amusements: Working Women and Turn-of-the-Century New York*, Temple University Press, Philadelphia, 1986, p. 40.

43 Elizabeth Hawes, quoted in Bettina Berch, *Radical by Design: The Life and Times of Elizabeth Hawes*, E. P. Dutton, New York, 1988, p. 37.

44 Drake, *Women in Trade Unions*, pp. 196–7.

45 Ed. Pauline Graham, *Mary Parker Follett – Prophet of Management: A Celebration of Writings from the 1920s*, Harvard Business School Press, Boston, Massachusetts, 1995, pp. 14–16; Englander, *Rational Womanhood*, pp. 54–9.

46 Mary Parker Follett, *Creative Experience*, Peter Smith, New York, 1951, p. 200.

47 Mary Parker Follett, *Constructive Conflict*, quoted in Graham, *Mary Parker Follett*, p. 68.

48 Ibid., p. 71.

49 Lewis Mumford, *Sketches from Life: The Early Years*, The Dial Press, New York, 1982, pp. 222–3.

50 Helen Marot, *Creative Impulse in Industry: A Proposition for Educators*, E. P. Dutton, New York, 1918, p. 52.

51 Ibid., p. 7.

52 Ibid., pp. 16–19.

53 Ibid., p. 24.

54 Helen Marot, 'Why Reform is Futile', *The Dial*, 22 March 1919, quoted in Janet Polansky, 'Helen Marot: The Mother of Democratic Technics', in ed. Barbara Drygulski Wright et al., *Women, Work, and Technology: Transformations*, University of Michigan Press, Ann Arbor, 1987, p. 260.

55 Mumford, *Sketches from Life*, pp. 244–7.

56 Kyrk, *A Theory of Consumption*, p. 63.

57 Ibid., p. 57.

58 Eds Dimand, Dimand, Forget, *Women of Value*, pp. 47–8, 60–64.

59 Carby, *Reconstructing Womanhood*, p. 170.

60 Nella Larsen, *Quicksand*, 1928, quoted in Carby, *Reconstructing Womanhood*, p. 170.

10 Democratizing Daily Life

1 Beatrice Webb, 'Introduction to "The Awakening of Women", A Special Supplement to the New Statesman', 1 November 1913, in Lengermann and Niebrugge-Brantley, *The Women Founders*, p. 303.

2 Mitchell, *The Hard Way Up*, pp. 98–9.

3 Cooper, *A View from the South*, p. 61.

4 Frances Ellen Harper, 'Duty to Dependent Races', Transactions of the National Council of Women of the United States, available online: http://womhist.binghamton.edu/aswpl/doc2.htm, p. 4 (accessed 05/06/02).

5 Scott, *Feminism and the Politics of Working Women*, p. 148.

6 Cooper, *A View from the South*, p. 31.

7 Terrell, 'The Progress of Colored Women', available online: http://gos.sbc.edu/t/terrellmary.htm, p. 3.

8 Scott, *Feminism and the Politics of Working Women*, p. 148; see Paula Giddings, *When and Where I Enter: The Impact of Black Women on Race and Sex in America*, Bantam Books, Toronto, 1988, pp. 85–117.

9 Sarah Reddish, 1907, quoted in Hollis, *Ladies Elect*, p. 431.

10 Sarah Reddish, 1894, quoted in Scott, *Feminism and the Politics of Working Women*, p. 77.

11 Enid Stacy, 'A Century of Women's Rights', in ed. Edward Carpenter, *Forecasts of the Coming Century*, The Labour Press, Manchester, 1897, p. 100.

12 Ibid., p. 101.

13 Ibid., p. 97.

14 Mabel Atkinson, *The Economic Foundations of the Women's Movement*, Fabian Tract, No. 175, The Fabian Society, London, 1914, p. 22; see eds Dimand, Dimand, Forget, *Women of Value*, p. 44.

15 Dorothy Jewson, *Socialists and the Family: A Plea for Family Endowment* (pamphlet), ILP Publication, London, no date, p. 6.

16 Ibid., p. 5.

17 Mrs Mabel Harding, 'Social Motherhood', *Daily Herald*, 19 April 1912, p. 11.

18 Hannam and Hunt, *Socialist Women*, p. 145.

19 Hollis, *Ladies Elect*, p. 420.

20 Margaret Ashton, quoted in ibid.

21 Ibid.

22 Margaret Ashton, quoted in ibid.

23 Virginia Woolf, 'Introduction' in ed Llewelyn Davies, *Life As We Have Known It*, p. xv.

24 Florence Farrow, Women's Guild Congress, Report, *Derby Monthly Records*, October 1919, p. 27.

25 Vorse, *A Footnote to Folly*, p. 168.

26 Beatrice M. Hinkle, 'Why Feminism?', in. ed. Showalter, *These Modern Women*, p. 141.

27 Leavenworth, 'Virtue for Women' in ed. Kirchwey, *Our Changing Morality*, p. 86.

28 Crystal Eastman, 'Britain's Labour Women', *The Nation*, 15 July 1925, in ed. Cook, *Crystal Eastman*, p. 142.

29 Crystal Eastman, 'A Matter of Emphasis', *Time and Tide*, 5 June 1925, in ibid., p. 139.

30 Eva Hubback, 1926, quoted in Harrison, *Prudent Revolutionaries*, p. 280.

31 La Follette, *Concerning Women*, p. 53.

32 Ibid., p. 306.

33 Ibid., p. 207.

34 Mary Macarthur, quoted in Drake, *Women in Trade Unions*, p. 45.

35 Drake, *Women in Trade Unions*, p. 31.

36 Ibid., p. 209.

37 Ibid., p. 197.

38 Nelson Lichtenstein, *State of the Union: A Century of American Labor*, Princeton University Press, Princeton, p. 7.

39 Ibid., pp. 8–9.

40 Mumford, *Sketches from Life*, p. 218.

41 Ibid., p. 222.

42 Marot, *American Labor Unions*, p. 9.

43 Marot, *The Creative Impulse in Industry*, p. 63.

44 Mumford, *Sketches from Life*, p. 223.

45 Marot, *The Creative Impulse in Industry*, p. 144.

46 Ibid., p. 144.

47 Mary Parker Follett, *The New State: Group Organization the Solution of Popular Government*, Peter Smith, Gloucester, Massachusetts, 1965, p. 330.

48 Ibid., p. 330.

49 Ibid., p. 238.

50 Ibid., p. 235.

51 Ibid., pp. 233–5.

52 Ibid., p. 222.

53 Ibid.

54 Ibid., p. 241.

55 Ibid., p. 222.

56 Ibid., pp. 234, 240.

57 Showalter, Introduction, in ed. Showalter, *These Modern Women*, pp. 3–29.

58 Ruth Pickering, 'A Deflated Rebel', in ed. Showalter, *These Modern Women*, p. 62.

59 Emma Goldman to Ben Reitman, 13 December 1909, quoted in Falk, *Love, Anarchy and Emma Goldman*, p. 113.

60 Mary Heaton Vorse, quoted in Dee Garrison, *Mary Heaton Vorse: The Life of an American Insurgent*, Temple University Press, Philadelphia, 1989, p. 25.

61 Ibid., p. 189.

62 Leonora Eyles, 'The Unattached Woman', *Good Housekeeping*, March 1928, in eds Braithwaite and Walsh, *Things My Mother Should Have Told Me*, p. 74.

63 Russell, *The Right to Be Happy*, p. 148.

64 Emma Brooke, 1886, quoted in Bland, *Banishing the Beast*, p. 28.

65 Mabel Dodge Luhan, 1914, quoted in Rudnick, *Mabel Dodge Luhan*, p. 73.

66 Holmes, 'The "Unwomanly" Woman', *Our New Humanity*, Vol. 1, No. 3, March 1896, p. 13.

67 Mary Heaton Vorse, quoted in Garrison, *Mary Heaton Vorse*, p. 34.

68 Jane Addams, quoted in Sklar, *Florence Kelley and the Nation's Work*, p. 295.

69 Mary Kingsbury Simkhovitch, quoted in Deacon, *Elsie Clews Parsons*, p. 32.

70 Ibid., p. 38.

71 Isabella Ford, *Women as Factory Inspectors and Certifying Surgeons* (pamphlet), Women's Co-operative Guild, London, 1898, p. 4.

72 Sklar, *Florence Kelley and the Nation's Work*, p. 295. On Britain see Eileen Janes Yeo, *The Contest for Social Science: Relations and Representations of Gender and Class*, Rivers Oram Press, London, 1996, pp. 246–78.

73 Helena Born, *Scrapbooks 1870–1892*, 'Whitman and Nature: Thoreau', Manuscript Lecture Notes, p. 5, Tamiment Institute Library and Robert F. Wagner Labor Archives.

74 Clara Cahill Park, quoted in Beard, *Woman's Work in Municipalities*, p. 252.

75 Cooper, *A View from the South*, p. 186.

76 Ford, *Industrial Women and How to Help Them*, p. 9.

77 On this tension in relation to class see E. P. Thompson, 'Education or Experience', in E. P. Thompson, *The Romantics*, Merlin, London, 1997, pp. 4–32.

78 Gilman, *Women and Economics*, p. 79. See Lane, *To Herland and Beyond*, p. 297.

79 Lane, Introduction to Gilman, *Herland*, pp. xxi–xxii.

80 Lizzie (Swank) Holmes, 'Labor Exchangers' in *Labor Exchange*, 30 April 1887, p. 5.

81 Webb, 'Introduction to "The Awakening of Women"' in Lengermann and Niebrugge-Brantley, *The Women Founders*, p. 303.

82 Mary Parker Follett, quoted in Beard, *Woman's Work in Municipalities*, p. 308.

83 Parsons, 'Changes in Sex Relations' in ed. Kirchwey, *Our Changing Morality*, p. 48.

84 Voltairine de Cleyre, 'Ideas of Anarchism', in *Man: A Journal of the Anarchist Ideal and Movement*, Vol. 3, No. 6, June 1935, p. 5.

85 Ibid.

86 De Cleyre, 'The Dominant Idea', quoted in Avrich, *An American Anarchist*, pp. 169–70.

87 Vida Scudder, quoted in 'Miss Scudder's Criticized Speech', Typescript, p. 2, *The Boston Common*, 9 March 1912, Vida Dutton Scudder Papers, File 3, Articles and Clippings, Sophia Smith Collection, Smith College, Northampton, Mass.

Conclusion

1 Ed. Ray Strachey, *Our Freedom and Its Results*, Hogarth Press, London, 1936, p. 10.

2 Mary Beard to Harriot Stanton Blatch, 15 June 1933, quoted in DuBois, *Harriot Stanton Blatch*, p. 263.

3 Mary E. Van Cleves, quoted in Rosalyn Baxandall and Elizabeth Ewen, *Picture Windows: How the Suburbs Happened*, Basic Books, New York, 2000, p. 71.

4 Darlene Clark Hine, 'The Housewives' League of Detroit: Black Women and Economic Nationalism' in eds Nancy A. Hewitt and Suzanne Lebsock, *Visible Women: New Essays on American Activism*, University of Illinois Press, Urbana, 1993, pp. 223–4.

5 *New Republic*, 8 April 1936, quoted in Orleck, *Common Sense and a Little Fire*, p. 239.

6 Mary Heaton Vorse, *Labor's New Millions*, Arno and The New York Times, New York, 1969, p. 292. On Britain see Henry Srebrnik, 'Class, Ethnicity and Gender Intertwined: Jewish Women and the East London Rent Strikes, 1935–1940', in *Women's History Review*, Vol. 4, No. 3, 1995, pp. 283–99.

7 Kate Weigand, *Red Feminism: American Communism and the Making of Women's Liberation*, Johns Hopkins University Press, 2001, pp. 32–8, 102–13.

8 Dorothy Thompson, 'Occupation: Housewife, Observation of Everyday Life', in ed. Dorothy Thompson, *The Courage to be Happy*, Houghton Mifflin, New York, 1957, p. 203.

9 Stella Browne, Evidence before Interdepartmental Committee on Abortion, Ministry of Health, 1938, National Archives.

10 Naomi Mitchison, *The Home and a Changing Civilisation*, John Lane, The Bodley Head, London, 1934, pp. 49–50, 143–5.

11 Elizabeth Hawes, 'Men Can Take It' (1939) in Bettina Berch, *Radical by Design: The Life and Times of Elizabeth Hawes*, E. P. Dutton, New York, 1988, pp. 81–2.

12 Jean Gaffin and David Thoms, *Caring and Sharing: The Centenary History of the Co-operative Women's Guild*, The Co-operative Union, Manchester, 1983, p. 162.

13 Leon Trotsky, *Problems of Everyday Life* (1924), Pathfinder Press, New York, 1973, p. 65.

14 Michael E. Gardiner, *Critiques of Everyday Life*, Routledge, London, 2000, pp. 34–9.

15 Henri Lefebvre, *Everyday Life in the Modern World*, Allen Lane, Penguin Press, London, 1971, p. 92. In *The Survival of Capitalism*, Allison and Busby, London, 1976, p. 74, Lefebvre comments on how 'the eruption of the female' had enabled the '*body*' to reappear as an element of 'subversion'.

16 Lefebvre, *Everyday Life in the Modern World*, p. 173.

17 See Ruth Lister, *Citizenship: Feminist Perspectives*, Palgrave, Macmillan, New York, 2003; Kathleen Jones, *Compassionate Authority, Democracy and the Representation of Women*, Routledge, New York, 1993; eds Sheila Rowbotham and Stephanie Linkogle, *Women Resist Globalization:Mobilizing for Livelihood and Rights*, Zed Books, London, 2001.

18 Linda Gordon, 'The New Feminist Scholarship on the Welfare State', in ed. Gordon, *Women, the State and Welfare*, p. 28.

19 Lois Waisbrooker, 'A Sex Revolution' (1894) in ed. Kessler, *Daring to Dream*, p. 179. The term 'everyday makers' comes from Denmark, where it is used to describe activist women citizens engaged in local issues around everyday life. Lister, *Citizenship*, p. 151.

Archives Consulted

Angela Tuckett Manuscript on Enid Stacy, Working-Class Movement Library
Charlotte Perkins Gilman Collection, Schlesinger Library, Radcliffe Institute, Harvard University
Eleanor Rathbone Papers, University of Liverpool
Ellen Gates Starr Papers, Sophia Smith Collection, Smith College
Elizabeth Gurley Flynn Papers, Tamiment Library and Robert F. Wagner Labor Archives
Emma Goldman Papers, University of California, Berkeley
Ford Family Papers, Brotherton Library, University of Leeds
Ford Scrapbook, Leeds Archive
Hale Family Papers, Sophia Smith Collection, Smith College
Havelock and Edith Ellis Papers, British Library
Helena Born Papers, Tamiment Library and Robert F. Wagner Labor Archives
Helen Tufts-Bailie Papers, Sophia Smith Collection, Smith College
H. J. Wilson Papers, Sheffield Archives
Jane Addams Papers, Sophia Smith Collection, Smith College
Karl Pearson Collection, University College, London
Margaret Ashton Papers, Manchester Central Reference Library
Margaret Sanger Papers Project, New York University
Marie Stopes Papers, British Library
Mary E. Gawthorpe Papers, Tamiment Library and Robert F. Wagner Labor Archives
Ministry of Health, Interdepartmental Committee on Abortion, National Archive
Richards Papers, Sophia Smith Collection, Smith College
Samuel Bale Collection, Bristol Public Library
Sylvia Pankhurst Papers, International Institute of Social History, Amsterdam
Vida Dutton Scudder Papers, Sophia Smith Collection, Smith College
Wheeldon Papers, National Archives
Women's Rights Papers (Biographies), Sophia Smith Collection, Smith College
Women's Suffrage Collection, Manchester Central Reference Library

Sources of Illustrations

'Fabian Women's Pamphlet' is from the Library of the London School of Economics (Chapter 2); 'Edith Ellis', Carpenter Collection, Sheffield Archives (Chapter 3), Carpenter/8/83; 'Cronwright and Olive Schreiner 1894' (Chapter 9), Carpenter/8/91; 'Bunty Pulls the Strings', National Co-operative Archive (Chapter 7), from *Woman's Outlook*, Vol. 3, No. 28, February 1922; 'The Woman with the Basket' (Chapter 10), from *Woman's Outlook*, Vol. 3, No. 27, January 1922; 'The Tree of Life' (Chapter 10), from *Woman's Outlook*, Vol. 1, No. 5, March 1920.

Every effort has been made to secure all necessary permissions. The author and the publisher will be glad to recognize any holders of copyright who have not been acknowledged in the credits.

Selected Bibliography

Addams, Jane, *Hull-House Maps and Paper by Residents of Hull-House: A Social Settlement*, Thomas Y. Crowell, New York, 1895.

Addams, Jane, *Twenty Years at Hull House*, Macmillan, New York, 1938.

Alberti, Johanna, *Eleanor Rathbone*, Sage Publications, London, 1996.

Allen, Polly Wynn, *Building Domestic Liberty: Charlotte Perkins Gilman's Architectural Feminism*, Pantheon, New York, 1990.

Alexander, Sally, *Becoming a Woman and Other Essays in 19th and 20th Century History*, Virago, London, 1994.

Attfield, Judy and Kirkham, Pat, *A View from the Interior: Feminism, Women and Design*, The Women's Press, London, 1989.

Avrich, Paul, *An American Anarchist: The Life of Voltairine de Cleyre*, Princeton University Press, Princeton, 1978.

Baxandall, Rosalyn Fraad, (ed.), *Words on Fire: The Life and Writing of Elizabeth Gurley Flynn*, Rutgers University Press, New Brunswick, 1987.

Baxandall, Rosalyn and Gordon, Linda (eds), *America's Working Women: A Documentary History 1600 to the Present, Revised and Updated*, W.W. Norton, New York, 1995.

Baxandall, Rosalyn and Ewen, Elizabeth, *Picture Windows: How the Suburbs Happened*, Basic Books, New York, 2000.

Beard, Mary Ritter, *Woman's Work in Municipalities* (1915), Arno Press, New York, 1972.

Benstock, Shari, *Women of the Left Bank: Paris 1900–1940*, University of Texas, Austin, 1986.

Berch, Bettina, *Radical by Design: The Life and Times of Elizabeth Hawes*, E. P. Dutton, New York, 1988.

Besant, Annie, *The Law of Population: Its Consequences and Bearing Upon Human Conduct and Morals* (1891), Augustus M. Kelley, New York, 1970.

Black, Clementina, *A New Way of Housekeeping*, W. Collins and Sons, London, 1918.

Bland, Lucy, *Banishing the Beast: English Feminism and Sexual Morality, 1885–1914*, Penguin Books, London, 1995.

Bland, Lucy and Doan, Laura, *Sexology in Culture: Labelling Bodies and Desires*, Polity Press, Cambridge, 1998.

Blatt, Martin Henry, *Free Love and Anarchism: The Biography of Ezra Heywood*, University of Illinois Press, Urbana, 1989.

Bloor, Ella Reeve, *We Are Many: An Autobiography*, International Publishers, New York, 1940.

Bock, Gisela and Thane, Pat, *Maternity and Gender Policies: Women and the Rise of European Welfare States*, Routledge, London, 1991.

Boris, Eileen, *Art and Labor: Ruskin, Morris and the Craftsman Ideal in America*, Temple University Press, Philadelphia, 1986.

Boris, Eileen, *Home to Work: Motherhood and the Politics of Industrial Homework in the United States*, Cambridge University Press, Cambridge, 1994.

Braithwaite, Brian and Walsh, Noelle (eds) , *Things My Mother Should Have Told Me: The Best of Good Housekeeping 1922–1940*, Ebury Press, London, 1991.

Branson, Noreen, *Poplarism, 1919–1925: George Lansbury and the Councillors' Revolt*, Lawrence and Wishart, London, 1979.

Brittain, Vera, *Halcyon or the Future of Monogamy*, Kegan Paul, Trench, Trubner and Co., London, 1929.

Bruere, Martha Bensley and Bruere, Robert, *Increasing Home Efficiency*, The Macmillan Company, New York, 1913.

Buhle, Marie Jo, *Women and American Socialism 1870–1920*, University of Illinois Press, Urbana, 1983.

Buhle, Paul, *The Origins of Left Culture in the U.S. 1880–1940: An Anthology*, Cultural Correspondence, Boston, 1978.

Bullock, Ian and Pankhurst, Richard, *Sylvia Pankhurst: From Artist to Anti-Fascist*, St Martin's Press, New York, 1992.

Busby, Margaret (ed.), *Daughters of Africa: An International Anthology of Words and Writings by Women of African Descent from the Ancient Egyptian to the Present*, Jonathan Cape, London, 1992.

Callen, Anthea, *Angel in the Studio: Women in the Arts and Crafts Movement 1870–1914*, Astragel Books, London, 1979.

Cameron, Ardis, *Radicals of the Worst Sort: Labouring Women in Lawrence Massachusetts, 1860–1912*, University of Illinois Press, Urbana, 1993.

Camhi, June Jerome, *Women Against Women: American Anti-Suffragism 1880–1920*, Carlson, New York, 1994.

Campbell, Helen, *The Problem of the Poor*, Fords, Howard and Hulbert, New York, 1882.

Carby, Hazel, *Reconstructing Womanhood: The Emergence of the Afro-American Woman Novelist*, Oxford University Press, New York, 1987.

Carpenter, Edward, *Forecasts of the Coming Century*, The Labour Press, Manchester, 1897.

Chambers, John Whiteclay II, *The Tyranny of Change: America in the Progressive Era, 1890–1920*, Rutgers University Press, New Brunswick, 2001. Champney, *The Woman Question*, Comrade Co-operative Company, New York, 1903.

Chateauvert, Melinda, *Marching Together: Women of the Brotherhood of Sleeping Car Porters*, University of Illinois Press, Urbana, 1998.

Chen, Constance M., '"The Sex Side of Life", Mary Ware Dennett's Pioneering Battle for Birth Control and Sex Education', The New Press, New York, 1996.

Chew, Doris (ed.), Ada Nield Chew: The Life and Writings of a Working Woman, Virago, London, 1982.

Clapperton, Jane Hume, Scientific Meliorism and the Evolution of Happiness, Kegan Paul, Trench and Co., London, 1885.

Clapperton, Jane Hume, A Vision of the Future –Based on the Application of Ethical Principles, Swan Sonnenschein, London, 1904.

Clark, Alice, Working Life of Women in the Seventeenth Century, (1919), Frank Cass and Company, 1968.

Collette, Christine, For Labour and For Women: The Women's Labour League, 1906–1918, Manchester University Press, Manchester, 1989.

Cook, Blanche Wiesen (ed.), Crystal Eastman: On Women and Revolution, Oxford University Press, Oxford, 1978.

Cook, Hera, The Long Sexual Revolution:English Women, Sex, and Contraception 1800–1975, Oxford University Press, Oxford, 2004.

Cooper, Anna Julia, A View from the South (1892), Oxford University Press, New York, 1988.

Crawford, Elizabeth, The Women's Suffrage Movement: A Reference Guide, 1866–1928, UCL Press, London, 1999.

Cronwright-Schreiner, S.C. (ed.), The Letters of Olive Schreiner, 1876–1920, T. Fisher Unwin, London, 1924.

Darley, Gillian, Villages of Vision: A Study of Strange Utopias, Five Leaves Publications, Nottingham, 2007.

Davies, Margaret Llewelyn (ed.), Life As We have Known It, Hogarth Press, London, 1931.

Davin, Anna, Growing Up Poor: Home, School and Street in London 1870–1914, Rivers Oram Press, London, 1996.

Davison, Jane and Davison, Lesley, To Make a House for Me: Four Generations of American Women and the Houses They Lived In, Random House, New York, 1980.

Dawson, Oswald, The Bar Sinister and Illicit Love: The First Biennial Proceedings of the Legitimation League, W. Reeve, London, 1895.

Deacon, Desley, Elsie Clews Parsons: Inventing Modern Life, The University of Chicago Press, Chicago, 1997.

Delap, Lucy, The Feminist Avant-Garde: Transatlantic Encounters of the Early Twentieth Century, Cambridge University Press, Cambridge, 2007.

Deutsch, Sarah, Women and the City: Gender, Space, and Power in Boston, 1870–1940, Oxford University Press, Oxford, 2000.

Dimand, Mary Ann, Dimand, Robert W., Forget, Evelyn L. (eds), Women of Value: Feminist Essays on the History of Women in Economics, Edward Elgar, Aldershot, Hants, 1995.

Doan, Laura, Fashioning Sapphism: The Origins of a Modern English Lesbian Culture, Columbia University Press, New York, 2001.

Douglas, Ann, Terrible Honesty: Mongrel Manhattan in the 1920s, The Noonday Press, Farrar, Strauss and Giroux, New York, 1995.

Drake, Barbara, *Women in Trade Unions* (1920), Virago, London, 1984.

Drinnon, Richard, *Rebel in Paradise: A Biography of Emma Goldman*, The University of Chicago Press, Chicago, 1961.

DuBois, Ellen Carol and Ruiz, Vicki L. (eds), *Unequal Sisters: A Multicultural Reader in U.S. Women's History*, Routledge, New York, 1990.

DuBois, Ellen Carol, *Harriot Stanton Blatch and the Winning of Woman Suffrage*, Yale University Press, New Haven, 1997.

Dye, Nancy Schrom, *As Equals and as Sisters: Feminism, Unionism and the Women's Trade Union League of New York*, University of Missouri Press, Columbia, 1980.

Dyhouse, Carol, *Feminism and the Family in England, 1880–1939*, Basil Blackwell, Oxford, 1989.

Dyhouse, Carol, *No Distinction of Sex? Women in British Universities, 1870–1939*, UCL Press, London 1995.

Eisenstein, Sarah, *Give Us Bread But Give Us Roses: Working Women's Consciousness in the United States, 1890 to the First World War*, Routledge and Kegan Paul, London, 1983.

Elshtain, Jean Bethke, *Jane Addams and the Dream of American Democracy*, Basic Books, New York, 2002.

Englander, David and O'Day, Rosemary (eds), *Retrieved Riches: Social Investigation in Britain 1840–1914*, Scolar Press, Aldershot, Hants, 1995.

Evans, Barbara, *Freedom to Choose: The Life and Work of Dr Helena Wright, Pioneer of Contraception*, The Bodley Head, London, 1984.

Ewan, Elizabeth, Innes, Sue, Reynolds, Sian (eds), *The Biographical Dictionary of Scottish Women*, Edinburgh University Press, Edinburgh, 2007.

Ewen, Elizabeth, *Immigrant Women in the Land of Dollars: Life and Culture on the Lower East Side, 1890–1925*, Monthly Review Press, New York, 1985.

Ewen and Ewen 7, *Typecasting: On the Arts and Sciences of Human Inequality*, Seven Stores Press, New York, 2006.

Ewen, Stuart and Ewen, Elizabeth, *Channels of Desire: Mass Images and the Shaping of American Consciousness*, University of Minnesota Press, Minneapolis, 1992.

Ewen, Stuart, *PR! A Social History of Spin,* Basic Books, New York, 1996.

Eyles, Leonora, *The Woman in the Little House*, Grant Richards, London, 1922.

Falk, Candace, *Love, Anarchy and Emma Goldman: A Biography*, Holt, Rinehart and Winston, New York, 1984.

Falk, Candace, Pateman, Barry, Moran, Jessica (eds) *Emma Goldman: A Documentary History of the American Years, Vol. I: Made for America, 1890–1901*, University of California Press, Berkeley, 2003.

Fishbain, Leslie, *Rebels in Bohemia: The Radicals of the Masses 1911–1917*, University of North Carolina Press, Chapel Hill, 1982.

Fleming, Suzie (ed.), *Eleanor Rathbone, The Disinherited Family*, Falling Wall Press, Bristol, 1986.

Follett, Mary Parker, *The New State: Group Organization, The Solution of Popular Government* (1918), Peter Smith, Gloucester, Massachusetts, 1965.

Follett, Mary Parker, *Creative Experience* (1924), Peter Smith, New York, 1951.

Foner, Philip S., *Women and the American Labor Movement: From the First Trade Unions to the Present*, The Free Press, New York, 1982.

Foner, Philip S. and Miller, Sally M., *Kate Richards O'Hare: Selected Writings and Speeches*, Louisiana State University Press, Baton Rouge, 1982.

Frank, Dana, *Purchasing Power: Consumer Organizing: Gender, and the Seattle Labor Movement, 1919–1929*, Cambridge University Press, Cambridge, 1994.

Frankel, Nora Lee and Dye, Nancy S. (eds), *Gender, Class, Race, and Reform in the Progressive Era*, The University Press of Kentucky, Lexington, 1991.

Freeman, Joshua (et al.), *Who Built America? Working People and the Nation's Economy, Politics, Culture and Society*, Pantheon Books, New York, 1992.

Frederick, Christine, *The New Housekeeping: Efficiency Studies in Home Management*, Doubleday, Page and Company, New York, 1916.

Frederick, Mrs Christine, *Selling Mrs Consumer*, The Business Bourse, New York, 1928.

Gaffin, Jean and Thoms, David, *Caring and Sharing: The Centenary History of the Women's Co-operative Guild*, The Co-operative Union, Manchester, 1983.

Ganz, Marie, *Into Anarchy and Out Again*, Dodd, Mead and Co., New York, 1920.

Gardiner, Michael E., *Critiques of Everyday Life*, Routledge, London, 2000.

Garrison, Dee (ed.), *Rebel Pen: The Writings of Mary Heaton Vorse*, Monthly Review Press, New York, 1985.

Garrison, Dee, *Mary Heaton Vorse: The Life of an American Insurgent*, Temple University Press, Philadelphia, 1989.

Gawthorpe, Mary E. *Up Hill to Holloway*, Traversity Press, Penobscot, Maine, 1962.

Giddings, Paula, *When and Where I Enter: The Impact of Black Women on Race and Sex in America*, Bantam Books, Toronto, 1988.

Gilbreth, Lillian M., *The Home Maker and Her Job*, D. Appleton and Co., New York, 1927.

Gilman, Charlotte Perkins, *Women and Economics* (1898), Harper and Row, New York, 1966.

Gilman, Charlotte Perkins, *The Home: Its Work and Influence* (1903), University of Illinois, Urbana, 1972.

Gilman, Charlotte Perkins, *Herland* (1915), Pantheon, New York, 1979.

Glassgold, Peter (ed.), *Anarchy! An Anthology of Emma Goldman's Mother Earth*, Counterpoint, Washington DC, 2001.

Goldman, Emma, *Anarchism and Other Essays*, Mother Earth Publishing Association, New York, 1910.

Goldman, Emma, *Living My Life: An Autobiography* (1931), A Peregrine Smith Book, Gibbs M. Smith, Salt Lake City, 1982.

Goldman, Harold, *Emma Paterson*, Lawrence and Wishart, London, 1974.

Goldmark, Josephine, *Fatique and Efficiency: A Study in Industry*, Charities Publication Committee, New York, 1912.

Goodway, David (ed.), *The Anarchist Past and Other Essays: Nicolas Walter*, Five Leaves, Nottingham, 2007.

Goodwin, Joanne L., *Gender and the Politics of Welfare Reform: Mothers' Pensions in Chicago, 1911–1929*, The University of Chicago Press, Chicago, 1997.

Gordon, Linda, *Woman's Body, Woman's Right: A Social History of Birth Control in America*, Viking Press, New York, 1976.

Gordon, Linda, *Heroes of Their Own Lives: The Politics and History of Family Violence*, Virago, London, 1989.

Gordon, Linda (ed.), *Women, the State and Welfare*, The University of Wisconsin Press, Madison, 1990.

Gordon, Linda, *Pitied but not Entitled: Single Mothers and the History of Welfare, 1890–1935*, The Free Press, New York, 1994.

Gordon, Peter and Doughan, David, *Dictionary of Women's Organisations, 1825–1960*, Woburn Press, London, 2001.

Graham, Pauline, *Mary Parker Follett–Prophet of Management: A Celebration of Writings from the 1920s*, Harvard Business School Press, Boston, Massachusetts, 1995.

Graves, Pamela M., *Labour Women in British Working-Class Politics, 1918–1939*, Cambridge University Press, Cambridge, 1994.

Haarsager, Sandra, *Bertha Knight Landes of Seattle: Big-City Mayor*, University of Oklahoma Press, Norman and London, 1994.

Haller, Mark H., *Eugenics: Hereditarian Attitudes in American Thought*, Rutgers University Press, New Brunswick, 1984.

Hamilton, Alice, *Exploring the Dangerous Trades* (1943), Northeastern University Press, Boston, 1985.

Hamilton, Cicely, *Marriage as a Trade*, Chapman and Hall, London, 1912.

Hamon, Augustin, *Psychologie de L'Anarchiste-Socialist*, Stock, Paris, 1895.

Hannam, June, *Isabella Ford*, Basil Blackwell, Oxford, 1989.

Hardy, Dennis, *Community Experiments, 1900–1945*, E. and F. N. Spon, London, 2000.

Hannam, June and Hunt, Karen, *Socialist Women in Britain, 1880s to 1920s*, Routledge, London, 2002.

Harrison, Brian, *Prudent Revolutionaries: Portraits of British Feminists Between the Wars*, Clarendon Press, Oxford, 1987.

Hayden, Dolores, *The Grand Domestic Revolution: A History of Feminist Designs for American Homes, Neighborhoods and Cities*, The MIT Press, Cambridge, Massachusetts, 1982.

Henderson, Kathy (ed.), *My Song is My Own: 100 Women's Songs*, Pluto, London, 1979.

Hewitt, Nancy A. and Lebsock, Suzanne (eds), *Visible Women: New Essays on American Activism*, University of Illinois Press, Urbana, 1993.

Hewitt, Nancy A., *Southern Discomfort: Women's Activism in Tampa, Florida, 1880s–1920s*, University of Illinois Press, Urbana, 2001.

Higgs, Mary and Hayward, Edward. E, *Where Shall She Live: The Homelessness of the Woman Worker*, P. S. King and Son, London, 1910.

Hill, Mary A., *Charlotte Perkins Gilman: The Making of a Radical Feminist, 1860–1896*, Temple University Press, Philadelphia, 1980.

Hine, Darlene Clark, King, Wilma, Reed, Linda, (eds), *'We Specialize in the Wholly Impossible': A Reader in Black Women's History*, Carlson Publishing, New York, 1995.

Hollis, Patricia, *Ladies Elect: Women in British Working-Class Politics, 1918–1939*, Cambridge University Press, Cambridge, 1994.

Hunt, Karen, *Equivocal Feminists: The Social Democratic Federation and the Woman Question, 1884–1911*, Cambridge University Press, Cambridge, 1996.

Hunter, Tera W., *To 'Joy My Freedom: Southern Black Women's Lives and Labours After the Civil War*, Harvard University Press, Cambridge, Massachusetts, 1997.

Jameson, Storm, *Journey from the North, Vol.1*, Virago, London, 1984.

John, Angela V., *Evelyn Sharp: Rebel Woman, 1869–1955*, Manchester University Press, Manchester, 2009.

Jones, Kathleen, *Compassionate Authority: Democracy and the Representation of Women*, Routledge, New York, 1993.

Jones, Jacqueline, *American Work: Four Centuries of Black and White Labor*, W. W. Norton, New York, 1998.

Katz, Esther, *The Selected Papers of Margaret Sanger, Vol. 1, The Woman Rebel, 1900–1928*, University of Illinois Press, Urbana, 2003.

Kennedy, David M., *Birth Control in America: The Career of Margaret Sanger*, Yale University Press, New Haven, 1970.

Kessler, Carol Farley (ed.), *Daring to Dream: Utopian Stories by United States Women 1836–1919*, Pandora Press, Boston, 1984.

Kessler, Carol Farley, *Charlotte Perkins Gilman: Her Progress Toward Utopia with Selected Writings*, Liverpool University Press, Liverpool, 1995.

Kessler-Harris, Alice, *Out to Work: A History of Wage-Earning Women in the United States*, Oxford University Press, Oxford, 1982.

King, Elspeth, *The Hidden History of Glasgow's Women*, Mainstream Publishing, Edinburgh, 1993.

Kirchwey, Freda, *Our Changing Morality: A Symposium*, Albert and Charles Boni, New York, 1924.

Kirk, Neville, *Labour and Society in Britain and the USA, Vol. 2*, Scolar Press, Aldershot, Hants, 1994.

Knupfer, Anne Meis, *Toward a Tenderer Humanity and a Nobler Womanhood: Afro-American Women's Clubs in Turn-of-the-Century Chicago*, New York University Press, New York, 1996.

Kornbluh, Joyce L. and Frederickson, Mary (eds), *Sisterhood and Solidarity*, Temple University Press, Philadelphia, 1984.

Koven, Seth and Michel, Sonya (eds), *Mothers of a New World: Maternalist Politics and the Origins of Welfare States*, Routledge, New York, 1993.

Kyrk, Hazel, *A Theory of Consumption*, Isaac Pitman and Sons, London, 1923.

Ladd-Taylor, Molly, *Mother-Work, Women and Child Welfare and the State, 1890–1930*, University of Illinois, Urbana, 1994.

La Follette, Suzanne, *Concerning Women* (1926), Arno Press, New York, 1972.

Lane, Ann J. (ed), *Mary Ritter Beard, A Sourcebook*, Schocken Books, New York, 1977.

Lane, Ann J., *To Herland and Beyond: The Life and Work of Charlotte Perkins Gilman*, Pantheon, New York, 1990.

Leavitt, Sarah, *From Catharine Beecher to Martha Stewart: A Cultural History of Domestic Advice*, University of North Carolina Press, Chapel Hill, 2002.

Lefebvre, Henri, *Everyday Life in the Modern World*, Allen Lane, The Penguin Press, London, 1971.

Lefebvre, Henri, *The Survival of Capitalism*, Allison and Busby, London, 1976.

Lengermann, Patricia Madoo and Niebrugge-Brantley, Jill (eds), *The Women Founders:Sociology and Social Theory 1830–1930*, McGraw Hill, Boston, 1998.

Lewenhak, Sheila, *Women and Trade Unions: An Outline History of Women in the British Trade Union Movement*, Ernest Benn, London, 1977.

Lichtenstein, Nelson, *State of the Union: A Century of American Labor*, Princeton University Press, Princeton, 2002.

Liddington, Jill, and Norris, Jill, *One Hand Tied Behind Us: The Rise of the Women's Suffrage Movement*, Virago, London, 1978.

Liddington, Jill, *The Life and Times of a Respectable Rebel: Selina Cooper, 1864–1946*, Virago, London, 1984.

Linklater, Andro, *An Unhusbanded Life: Charlotte Despard, Suffragette, Socialist and Sinn Feiner*, Hutchinson, London, 1980.

Lister, Ruth, *Citizenship: Feminist Perspectives*, Palgrave, Macmillan, 2003.

Lockhart, J. G., *Cosmo Gordon Lang*, Hodder and Stoughton, London, 1949.

MacKenzie, Norman and MacKenzie, Jeanne (eds), *The Diaries of Beatrice Webb*, Virago, London, 2000.

MacKinnon, Janice and MacKinnon, Stephen R., *Agnes Smedley: The Life and Times of an American Radical*, Virago, London, 1988.

McPhee, Carol and FitzGerald, Ann (eds), *The Non-Violent Militant: Selected Writings of Teresa Billington-Greig*, Routledge and Kegan Paul, London, 1987.

Malos, Ellen (ed.), *The Politics of Housework*, Allison and Busby, London, 1980.

Mappen, Ellen, *Helping Women at Work: The Women's Industrial Council 1889–1914*, Hutchinson and Co., London, 1985.

Marot, Helen, *American Labor Unions* (1914), Arno and The New York Times, New York, 1969.

Marot, Helen, *Creative Impulse in Industry: A Proposition for Educators*, E. P. Dutton, New York, 1918.

Marsh, Margaret S., *Anarchist Women, 1870–1920*, Temple University Press, Philadelphia, 1981.

McCrindle, Jean and Rowbotham, Sheila (eds), *Dutiful Daughters: Women Talk About Their Lives*, Penguin, London, 1983.

McDonald, Deborah, *Clara Collet, 1860–1948: An Educated Working Woman*, Woburn Press, London, 2004.

McLaren, Angus, *Birth Control in Nineteenth Century England*, Holmes and Meier, New York, 1978.

Meade, Marion, *Dorothy Parker: What Fresh Hell is This?*, Heinemann, London, 1988.

Milkman, Ruth (ed.), *Women, Work and Protest: A Century of U.S. Women's Labor History*, Routledge and Kegan Paul, Boston, 1985.

Mitchell, Hannah, *The Hard Way Up*, Virago, London, 1977.

Mitchison, Naomi, *The Home and a Changing Civilisation*, John Lane, The Bodley Head, London, 1934.

Montefiore, Dora, *Singings Through the Dark*, Sampson Low & Co., London, 1898.

Morris, Jenny, *Women and the Sweated Trades: The Origins of Minimum Wage Legislation*, Gower, Aldershot, 1986.

Mumford, Lewis, *Sketches from Life: The Early Years*, The Dial Press, New York, 1982.

Oliver, Hermia, *The International Anarchist Movement in Late Victorian London*, Croom Helm, London, 1983.

Orleck, Annelise, *Common Sense and a Little Fire: Women and Working Class Politics in the United States, 1900–1965*, The North Carolina Press, Chapel Hill, 1995.

Pearson, Lynn F., *The Architectural and Social History of Cooperative Living*, Macmillan, London, 1988.

Peiss, Kathy, *Cheap Amusements: Working Women and Turn-of-the-Century New York*, Temple University Press, Philadelphia, 1986.

Peiss, Kathy and Simmons, Christina, *Passion and Power: Sexuality in History*, Temple University Press, Philadelphia, 1989.

Pivar, David J., *Purity Crusade: Sexual Morality and Social Control*, Greenwood Press, Westport, Connecticut, 1973.

Pozzetta, George F., *Ethnicity and Gender: The Immigrant Woman*, Garland, New York, 1991.

Pujol, Michèle A., *Feminism and Anti-Feminism in Early Economic Thought*, Edward Elgar, Aldershot, 1992.

Ravetz, Alison, *Council Housing and Culture: The History of a Social Experiment*, Routledge, London, 2001.

Raw, Louise, *Striking a Light: The Bryant and May Matchwomen and their Place in History*, Continuum, London, 2009.

Richards, Ellen H., *The Chemistry of Cooking and Cleaning: A Manual for Housekeepers*, Home Science Publishing, Boston, 1897.

Richards, Ellen H., *Food Materials and their Adulteration*, Whitcomb and Barrows, Boston, 1906.

Rosen, Robyn L., *Reproductive Health, Reproductive Rights: Reformers and the Politics of Maternal Welfare, 1917–1940*, The Ohio State University Press, Columbus, 2003.

Rosen, Ruth and Davidson, Susan, *The Maimie Papers*, The Feminist Press, New York, 1977.

Rothschild, Joan (ed.), *Machina Ex Dea: Feminist Perspectives on Technology*, Pergamon Press, New York, 1983.

Rowbotham, Sheila, *A New World for Women: Stella Browne, Socialist Feminist*, Pluto, London, 1977.

Rowbotham, Sheila (ed.), *Dreams and Dilemmas: Collected Writings*, Virago, London, 1983.

Rowbotham, Sheila, *Friends of Alice Wheeldon*, Pluto Press, London, 1986.

Rowbotham, Sheila, *Women in Movement: Feminism and Social Action*, Routledge, New York, 1992.

Rowbotham, Sheila and Mitter, Swasti (eds), *Dignity and Daily Bread: New Forms of Economic Organising among Poor Women in the Third World and the First*, Routledge, London, 1994.

Rowbotham, Sheila, *Edward Carpenter: A Life of Liberty and Love*, Verso, London, 2008.

Rowe, Marsha (ed.), *Spare Rib Reader*, Penguin, London, 1982.

Rubinstein, David, *Before the Suffragettes: Women's Emancipation in the 1890s*, The Harvester Press, Brighton, Sussex, 1985.

Rudnick, Lois Palken, *Mabel Dodge Luhan: New Woman, New Worlds*, University of New Mexico Press, Albuquerque, 1984.

Rupp, Leila J., *Worlds of Women: The Making of an International Women's Movement*, Princeton University Press, Princeton, 1997.

Russell, Mrs Bertrand, *Hypatia or Women and Knowledge*, Kegan Paul, Trench, Trubner & Co., 1925.

Russell, Mrs Bertrand, *The Right to Be Happy*, Garden City Publishing, New York, 1927.

Russell, Dora, *The Tamarisk Tree: My Quest for Liberty and Love*, Elek/Pemberton, London, 1975.

Sander, Kathleen Waters, *The Business of Charity: The Woman's Exchange Movement 1832–1900*, University of Illinois Press, Urbana, 1998.

Sanderson Furniss, A. D. and Phillips Marion, *The Working Woman's House*, The Swarthmore Press, London, 1919.

Sanger, Margaret, *Woman and the New Race*, Brentano's, New York, 1920.

Scott, Gillian, *Feminism and the Politics of Working Women: The Women's Co-operative Guild 1880s to the Second World War*, UCL Press, London, 1998.

Scudder, Vida D., *Social Ideals in English Letters*, Houghton, Mifflin and Co., 1898.

Searle, G.R. *A New England? Peace and War, 1886–1918*, Clarendon Press, Oxford, 2004.

Sears, Hal D., *The Sex Radicals: Free Love in High Victorian America*, The Regents Press of Kansas, Lawrence, 1977.

Seymour-Jones, Carole, *Beatrice Webb: Woman of Conflict*, Pandora, London, 1993.

Shaw, Marion, *The Clear Stream: A Life of Winifred Holtby*, Virago, London, 1999.

Shaw, Nellie, *Whiteway: A Colony in the Cotswolds*, C. W. Daniel, London, 1935.

Showalter, Elaine (ed), *These Modern Women: Autobiographical Essays from the Twenties*, The Feminist Press, New York, 1978.

Showalter, Elaine (ed.), *A Jury of her Peers: American Women Writers from Anne Bradstreet to Annie Proulx*, Virago, London, 2009.

Sicherman, Barbara, *Alice Hamilton: A Life in Letters*, Harvard University Press, Cambridge, Massachusettes, 1984.

Sklar, Kathryn Kish, *Florence Kelley and the Nation's Work: The Rise of Women's Political Culture, 1830–1900*, Yale University Press New Haven, 1995.

Slack, Kathleen M., *Henrietta's Dream: A Chronicle of the Hampstead Garden Suburb*, Hampstead Garden Suburb Archive Trust, London, 1997.

Sochen, June, *Movers and Shakers: American Women Thinkers and Activists, 1900–1970*, Quadrangle, The New York Times Book Co., New York, 1973.

Stanley, Liz, *Imperialism, Labour and the New Woman: Olive Schreiner's Social Theory*, Sociology Press, Durham, 2002.

Stansell, Christine, *American Moderns: Bohemian New York and the Creation of a New Century*, Metropolitan Books, Henry Holt and Co., New York, 2000.

Steedman, Carolyn, *Childhood, Culture and Class in Britain, 1860–1921*, Rutgers University Press, New Brunswick, 1990.

Stein, Leon, *The Triangle Fire*, ILR Press, Cornell University Press, Ithaca, 2001.

Sterling, Dorothy, *Black Foremothers: Three Lives*, The Feminist Press, New York, 1987.

Stockham, Alice B., *Tokology*, L. N. Fowler, London, 1918.

Stopes, Marie, *Radiant Motherhood: A Book for Those who are Creating the Future*, G. P. Putnam and Sons, London, 1920.

Strachey, Ray (ed.), *Our Freedom and Its Results*, Hogarth Press, London, 1936.

Strasser, Susan, *Never Done: A History of American Housework*, Pantheon, New York, 1982.

Swados, Harvey, *Years of Conscience, The Muckrakers: An Anthology of Reform Journalism*, Meridian Books, Cleveland, 1962.

Swenarton, Mark, *Homes Fit for Heroes: The Politics and Architecture of Early State Housing in Britain*, Heinemann, London, 1981.

Tarbel, Ida M., *All in the Day's Work: An Autobiography*, Macmillan Company, New York, 1939.

Tax, Meredith, *The Rising of the Women: Feminist Solidarity and Class Conflict, 1880–1917*, Monthly Review Press, New York, 1980.

Thomson, Mathew, *Psychological Subjects: Identity, Culture and Health in Twentieth-Century Britain*, Oxford University Press, Oxford, 2006.

Thompson, Dorothy (ed.), *The Courage to be Happy*, Houghton Mifflin, New York, 1957.

Thompson, E. P., *The Romantics*, Merlin, London, 1997.

Thompson, Tierl (ed.), *Dear Girl: The Diaries and Letters of Two Working Women 1897–1917*, The Women's Press, London, 1987.

Trotsky, Leon, *Problems of Everyday Life* (1924), Pathfinder Press, New York, 1973.

Vicinus, Martha, *Independent Women: Work and Community for Single Women, 1850–1920*, Virago, London, 1985.

Vorse, Mary Heaton, *A Footnote to Folly: Reminiscences* (1935), Arno Press, New York, 1980.

Vorse, Mary Heaton, *Labor's New Millions*, Arno and the New York Times, New York, 1969.

Walter, Nicolas (ed.), *Charlotte Wilson: Anarchist Essays*, Freedom Press, London, 2000.

Weeks, Jeffrey, *Sex, Politics and Society: The Regulation of Sexuality Since 1800*, Longman, London, 1981.

Weigand, Kate, *Red Feminism: American Communism and the Making of Women's Liberation*, The John Hopkins University Press, Baltimore, 2001.

Weiss, Andrea, *Paris Was A Woman: Portraits from the Left Bank*, Pandora, London, 1995.

Wikander, Ulla, Kessler-Harris, Alice, and Lewis, Jane (eds), *Protecting Women: Labor Legislation in Europe, the United States and Australia, 1880–1920*, University of Illinois Press, Urbana, 1995.

Winslow, Barbara, *Sylvia Pankhurst: Sexual Politics and Political Activism*, St. Martin's Press, New York, 1996.

Woollacott, Angela, *On Her Their Lives Depend: Munitions Workers in the Great War*, University of California Press, Berkeley, 1994.

Wright, Barbara Drygulski, et al. (eds), *Women, Work and Technology Transformations*, The University of Michigan Press, Ann Arbor, 1987.

Wright, Gwendolyn, *Building the American Dream: A Social History of Housing in America*, MIT Press, Cambridge, Mass., 1981.

Yeo, Eileen Janes, *The Contest for Social Science: Relations and Representations of Gender and Class*, Rivers Oram Press, London, 1996.

Yeo, Stephen (ed.), *New Views of Co-operation*, Routledge, London, 1988.

Unpublished Theses and Papers

Allen, Margaret, '"The Women are Worse Than the Men": Women's Political Activism in Mining Communities, 1919–1939', MA Dissertation, International Centre for Labour Studies, University of Manchester, 1997.

Barrow, Logie, 'The Socialism of Robert Blatchford and the Clarion Newspaper, 1889–1914', PhD Thesis, University of London, 1975.

Debenham, Clare, 'The Origins and Development of the Birth Control Movement in Manchester and Salford, 1917–1935', MA Dissertation, Manchester Metropolitan University, 2006.

Englander, Susan Lyn, 'Rational Womanhood: Lillian M. Gilbreth and the Uses of Psychology in Scientific Management, 1914–1935', PhD Thesis, University of California, Los Angeles, 1999.

Moran, Jessica, 'The Story of Kate Austin: Anarchist Revolutionary Writer, Unpublished Paper, 1999', in Emma Goldman Archive, Berkeley, California.

Newspapers and Periodicals Consulted

Accrington Labour Journal
The Adult
The Alarm
Clarion
Commonweal
The Communist
Daily Herald
Eugenics Review
Freewoman
Halfpenny Short Cuts
Industrial Worker
International Socialist Review
Ladies' Garment Worker
Lansbury's Labour Weekly
Liberty
Lucifer
Manchester Guardian
Mother Earth
New Age
New Generation
New Leader
The Nineteenth Century
Out of Work
Oxford University Extension Gazette
The Social Democrat
The Syndicalist
The Times
Woman Citizen
Woman's Dreadnought/Workers' Dreadnought
Woman Rebel
Woman Worker
Women Workers: Quarterly Magazine of the Birmingham Ladies' Union

Index